The Metaphysical Blueprint to Decoding Hollywood's Evil Genius

TC Carrier

Published by, Not-So Common Scents.

Code Cracka presents...
The Metaphysical Blueprint to Decoding Hollywood's Evil
Genius

Copyright © 2017 by TC Carrier

Editor: Petra Tuttle

ISBN: 13: 978-0983446200

To contact TC Carrier for lectures, appearances, consultations and
workshops:

Website: www.TCCarrier.com

email: frequeofnature@gmail.com

Facebook: Freque of Nature

Instagram: Freque of Nature

Table of Contents

INTRODUCTION

I have always been fascinated by the whole, "going to the movies" experience. At a young age, I was drawn to the theaters and looked upon the experience as a major event in my childhood. Even today, I still cannot attend a movie without a large bucket of popcorn with extra butter and a half-gallon size soft drink, which consists of my own concoction of half fruit punch, preferably Hawaiian Punch and half 7-Up, Sprite or Sierra Mist. On those special occasions I would add the five pound box of Junior Mints, Kit Kat bar or the 8 pack size of Reese's Peanut Butter Cups. Even though I know these items will eventually kill me, I am still drawn to them like Pavlov's dog, each time I smell that freshly popped popcorn when I first arrive in the movie theater lobby.

This is the exact moment where the brainwashing begins. As soon as one steps inside one of these mega, multiplex movie monstrosities, the moviegoer falls prey to its traps and pitfalls. This is where Hollywood holds its audience hostage in the palm of its hands without them even knowing it. This is where the concept of the "captive audience" originated from. First, Hollywood sets you up in a comfortable, sometimes leather, plush, reclining chair with a cup holder. Then they make sure the theater is nice and cold so that you will pay close attention to the screen and not get too comfortable where they lose your focus and undivided attention. The theater lights are then dimmed so that you will only have the capacity to concentrate on what's on the screen and not be distracted by your immediate surroundings. This forces your undivided attention on the screen in front of you. Next, they pump in surround sound, stereo, THX, HD sound system that has you turning your head every which way, trying to figure out where a particular noise came from. It is very disturbing and embarrassing to look sharply to your right because you thought you heard a baby crying in the seat next to you, only to see a man staring back at you looking for the same source from which the crying sound was coming from. For final measure, they prop this giant 50 foot screen in front of you that acts as a portal to transport the audience from their current reality to an illusion of a reality they force upon their unsuspecting and vulnerable captive audience minds. This is a very powerful tool in mind control. The ability to have an audience see, believe and hear things

1

that do not exist! Do you understand this statement I just made? Hollywood has the capacity and ability to create YOUR reality! Hollywood has the power to control how one perceives not only their environment but how one defines THEMSELVES as well. Hollywood is the master illusionist that uses it audiences as puppets by controlling them with invisible strings.

I continued my passion for cinema, when I furthered my education in college. I remember selecting my first elective course, which was entitled Film 101. This course gave me a whole new perspective on how to watch movies and also to study film as an art form. I went from "watching movies" to analyzing the intricacies of the art form called, film. I remember the instructor teaching us the underlining themes and images of Orson Wells' classic, cinematic masterpiece, "Citizen Kane." This is where I recognized the story within the story. From that moment on, I looked at all films from a different perspective and maintained a deep passion and appreciation for the message behind the story. From here on out my goal was to not only decipher the plot and theme of a film, but to dissect the spaces in between the plot and theme of the film. I relate this practice similar to observing the raw film on its reel. All film really is is a series of images put together and run through a projector at a certain speed to give the illusion of motion, depth, light and substance. I was more focused on the spaces between the images and not the images themselves. It is in theses "spaces" where the secrets and science of Hollywood were revealed to me. Instead of "reading between the lines" of a book, I was "reading the spaces between the images of a film." This procedure opened up a new and unique vantage point and gave me the foundation from which to interpret and decipher movies from here on out.

Besides my passion for cinema, I also carry a passion for Afrikan centered thought, philosophy and culture. This concept also includes traditional, Afrikan spirituality which was the basis for the highest and most advanced civilization known to man. This civilization was known as Kemet, which is located in modern day Egypt. Through my studies of this Afrikan culture, I soon realized the concept of Afrikan spirituality was the foundation for what is known as Metaphysics today. Metaphysics can be broken into two words, Meta and Physics. Meta means after, beyond or adjacent. Physics means the science of matter and energy or the study of nature. So Metaphysics is the science of nature beyond or adjacent to matter and energy. It can be described by the following statement. Less than five percent of reality (seen energy) can be deciphered through our five senses of touch, taste, smell, sight or hearing. Ninety-five percent of our reality (unseen energy) cannot be measured or deciphered through these five senses. Metaphysics is the study and recognition of unseen energy through other means besides our five senses. For example, we can see colors, taste foods, hear music, smell fragrances and touch water. These things can be labeled as seen energy. Metaphysics is unseen energy labeled as, invisible energy waves, unseen energy rays, telepathy, "being in the zone," intuition, dreams, spirits, ghosts, angels, spirituality and love. In other words, Metaphysics deciphers the characteristics and properties of unseen energy and how they affect us as living beings. All energy must be accounted for or acknowledged and their distinctive personalities must be taken into consideration when defining one's reality according to the seen or unseen energies that surround us on a daily basis

My unique view on Hollywood and the film industry may be in direct contrast with the dominant perception today. In my delving into the Afro centric or metaphysical world, I discovered many aspects of science and consciousness that helped me develop a blueprint or key to deciphering Hollywood symbols and images. Hollywood realizes, the best place to hide information from its audiences, is to put it right in front of their faces. Hollywood has made this tactic an elegant art form. I will unveil all my findings to help bring clarity to this unique, sinister and esoteric industry that hypnotizes its victims and makes no apologies for it. Be conscious to the reality or world that has been given to you without you having a say so, in its definition. Consciousness can simply be defined as what an individual pays closest attention to. It is that which we invest our time and energy in focusing on or paying attention to. Consciousness is our unique focal point and interpretation of reality. For example, I may be conscious of the cars zooming by when I am trying to cross a busy street. But I may be unconscious of the tiny creatures, puddle of water and the secret world that dwells under my feet, on the side of the road. So consciousness has different degrees and levels of participation according to the initiation of the individual. We are all conscious of one thing or another. It is for us to define and interpret for ourselves. Nobody has the right to take that right from us. It is the coercion and invasion of the greatest gift God has given us. The gift of free will or the power to decide and choose for ourselves how we define ourselves and the world we live in. We are all conscious of one thing or another. The trick is to decipher what was forced fed on us and what is innately our personal conclusion in self-actualization. So I ask you, the reader, to be conscious of the concepts, philosophy and images that will be revealed in this book. Don't be afraid to put old paradigms aside so you can see things from a different perspective. Cross the threshold into a whole new and different world or reality. Let the cars go by for a second when crossing that same street you have crossed a thousand times before and focus on the world I am about to reveal to you that was right under your feet this whole time. Be like a child whose mind is open to discovering a reality they never knew existed. I hope it will be as fascinating for you as it was for me. Discover the secret and occult world of Hollywood exposed and the hidden agenda behind their programming.

The Occult History of Holly-Wood

Occult researcher and leading authority on esoteric symbolism, Jordan Maxwell describes the making of Hollywood as such and I paraphrase. "The name Hollywood comes from the ancient mythology of Merlin the Wizard. Merlin used a wand made out of Holly wood from the Holly tree. Legend has it that this wood contained magical powers that could be used to cast spells on its unsuspecting victims. This wand would be used by Merlin to manipulate behavior and control anyone who it was used upon." The film industry in "Holly-wood" uses its power, influence and resources to manipulate and control its unsuspecting audiences. "Holly-wood" is used as the primary tool of this elite, secret and select class to keep the masses asleep, disorientated, confused and oblivious to the fact that they are nothing more than sheep that are being led to slaughter by the institutions that enslave them without them even knowing they are slaves. Jordan Maxwell points out other myths of this mysterious Holly wood that was derived by European mythology throughout their history:

- *The Celts of the British Isles & Gaul believed the Holly King ruled over death. The Holly King was a warlike giant who bore a great wooden club made of a thick holly branch.*

- *Japanese legend, Prince Yamato, one of the greatest of the doomed heroes of history & myth, was said to have done battle with a spear the handle of which was made of holly wood, a symbol of divine authority.*

- *The Yule tree, the Holy Tree ("Holly Tree") (recognized in modern times as the "Christmas tree") is an ancient symbol of life, fertility and vitality.*

- *Holly is one of the trees said to be the tree of Christ's cross. Legend tells us that the trees of the forests refused the defilement of the cross, splintering into tiny fragments at the touch of the ax. Only the holly behaved like an ordinary tree, allowing itself to be cut and formed into a cross. It is as a Passion symbol that holly is found in pictures of various saints. Its presence indicates that the*

5

saint is either reflecting upon Christ's Passion or foretelling it.

- In Germany, holly is called Christdorn in memory of Christ's crown of thorns. According to legend, the holly's branches were woven into a painful crown and placed on Christ's head while the soldiers mocked him saying, "Hail, King of the Jews."

- While many other plants and often weeds (such as Mistletoe) have been deliberately or ignorantly raised up as having ancient significance to our ancestors, no other plant or more universally sacred, more universally mysterious than the Holy Tree, the "Holly".

The Wizard with the magic wand used to cast magical spells on his unsuspecting victims. Notice the modern version of the same Magician using the same hat and "magic" wand made out of the mystical holly wood to perform his "Magic.".

The orchestra conductor also manipulates and controls the musicians playing their instruments by using his wand or holly wood.

According to Jordan Maxwell's research on the mythology of the Holly tree, it has been represented as such;

a) A superior warlike weapon, having divine authority.

b) Represents vitality & fertility.

c) Higher consciousness & knowledge.

d) Used to ridicule or mock.

e) Used to crucify or condemn.

f) Maintains mysterious powers.

These attributes undeniably describe the essence of the film industry. Hollywood is being used as the tool (the wand). This wand is implemented by these elite, secret and occult societies (the wizards). The wizards rule the world in an effort to control ("cast a spell") on the unsuspecting masses in order to further their agenda. All this is being done while the masses stay deaf, dumb and blind to their enslavement.

Furthermore, the actors who portray the characters in Hollywood productions are called the "Cast." They are the ones being used to "cast the spell" on the audiences. The word cast can be defined as; *To cause to fall upon something or in a certain direction; send forth:* Hollywood also controls television "Broad-Cast." Broad means to cover a wide scope and area. So broadcast is to cast a spell over a wide area. These broadcasts are called television programs. According to Webster's Online Dictionary the word Program means: *1) a brief usually printed outline of the order to be followed, of the features to be presented, and the persons participating (as in a public performance).*

2) a plan or system under which action may be taken toward a goal.

3) a plan for the programming of a mechanism (as a computer) b: a sequence of coded instructions that can be inserted into a mechanism (as a computer) c: a sequence of coded instructions (as genes or behavioral responses) that is part of an organism

This definition sheds light on the secret and hidden agenda of Hollywood. According to these formal definitions we are being brainwashed and manipulated by Hollywood programming, broadcasts and movies. Make no mistake about it. There is a hidden agenda behind every media outlet in America, as well as the world. This book will reveal the concentrated and coordinated effort of the secret power elite behind Hollywood's hidden agenda and programming. This book will expose this hidden, diabolical plot to enslave the masses through esoteric manipulation and control coordinated by a secret society

In Kemet or what is referred to today as modern day Egypt, our Afrikan ancestors used images and symbols in the form of Metu Neter or what is called hieroglyphics today to communicate with each other and their subconscious minds. There was no written word. Metu Neter when translated literally means God's word. Our ancestors were so advanced that they knew the best form of communication was on the subconscious level. The subconscious level is responsible for controlling over 90% of human behavior. Symbols and images, ie. Hollywood films, speak directly to a person's subconscious mind. This is where we get the saying, "A picture is worth a thousand words." Symbols and images are more powerful than any words that can be spoken. Hollywood uses the power of images and symbols in its film to speak directly to our subconscious in an effort to control and manipulate our behavior, without us ever even knowing it. Remember, all film is a series of images spliced together and run through a projector at a high rate of speed to make it look like the images are animated and alive. This is a very valuable weapon and this science has been deliberately kept from the masses because of its power, influence and diabolical agenda to enslave the masses.

"The idea that flashing words and images can seep into the _subconscious mind_ and persuade an observer to do something without their awareness came into the public eye in the 1950s. That's when a marketing experiment flashed the message "Drink Coca-Cola" onto a New Jersey movie screen and correlated this to increased Coke sales in that area. The idea behind the crafty technique: by flickering visuals at a speed greater than your eyes and brain can process or speaking at a slightly lower volume than your ears can hear allows messages to sneak past your conscious _mind_ and into your subconscious. The word subliminal derives

itself from the Latin word "sub" meaning *below* and "limen" meaning *threshold*--below a person's threshold of awareness." -- Do Subliminal Messages Really Work?

- By Michelle Bryner

18 March 2010 8:45 AM ET

This is further evidence of Hollywood's secret agenda to program its audience in an elegant method of mind control and brainwashing the masses. Hollywood was founded by wealthy European Jews but they do not control Hollywood. We are just led to believe that they are in control. *They were the first to establish the film industry by usurping Thomas Edison of his patent on the movie projector.* Later, they were coerced and strong armed into promoting the agenda of the" Illuminati" or secret ruling class that runs the world in the shadows. *These Jewish founders such as Louis B. Mayer, Adolph Zukor, Carl Laemmle, Samuel Goldwyn, William Fox and the Warner brothers were willing to do anything they had to do to keep their lucrative, Hollywood film studios and industries.* The hidden power of elites that also control world governments, unleashed the witch hunt of "McCarthyism" into the film industry in regards to the "so-called" infiltration of Communist in Hollywood. This Communist conspiracy or perceived threat shook the foundation of Hollywood. The Jewish heads of these studios immediately took heed that all that they had built could come tumbling down by means of character assassination and propaganda directly pointed at them, as America's perceived public enemy number one, the Communist. Remember the Jews had the immediate history of persecution by the Nazis so they were very fearful and vulnerable to the process of being singled out and ostracized.

In October 1947, a number of persons working in the Hollywood film industry were summoned to appear before the House Committee on Un-American Activities, which had declared its intention to investigate whether Communist agents and sympathizers had been surreptitiously planting propaganda in U.S. films. -- Schwartz, Richard A. (1999) "How the Film and Television Blacklists Worked". Florida International University. **Retrieved 2010-03-03**.

10

The Motion Picture Alliance for the Preservation of American Ideals (MPA), a political action group cofounded by Walt Disney, issued a pamphlet advising producers on the avoidance of "subtle communistic touches" in their films. Its counsel revolved around a list of ideological prohibitions, such as "Don't smear the free-enterprise system ... Don't smear industrialists ... Don't smear wealth ... Don't smear the profit motive ... Don't deify the 'common man' ... Don't glorify the collective". --Cohen (2004), pp. 169–70. Forbidden Animation: Censored Cartoons and Blacklisted Animators in America. Jefferson, N.C.: McFarland.

The HUAC (House of Un-American Activities Committee) hearings had failed to turn up any evidence that Hollywood was secretly disseminating Communist propaganda, but the industry was nonetheless transformed. The fallout from the inquiry was a factor in the decision by <u>Floyd Odlum</u>, the primary owner of <u>RKO Pictures</u>, to get out of the business. As a result, the studio would pass into the hands of <u>Howard Hughes</u>. Within weeks of taking over in May 1948, Hughes fired most of RKO's employees and virtually shut the studio down for half a year as he had the political sympathies of the rest investigated. Then, just as RKO swung back into production, <u>Hughes made the decision to settle</u> a long-standing <u>federal antitrust suit</u> against the industry's <u>Big Five studios</u>. This would be one of the crucial steps in the collapse of the <u>studio system</u> that had governed Hollywood, and ruled much of world cinema, for a quarter-century. - Lasky, Betty (1989). RKO: The Biggest Little Major of Them All. Santa Monica, California: Roundtable.

These Jewish, Hollywood moguls were all but willing to do whatever they had to do in an effort to blend in with the American culture to be accepted and at the same time, keep their lucrative, Hollywood empire. With the ruling class secretly pulling the strings and with the support of the U.S. government, these Jewish puppets were more than eager to serve the agenda of their secret and powerful masters. As a consolation prize for serving their masters, these Jews became very wealthy in the process and were allowed to use a percentage of films to promote their Zionist agenda and propaganda as well. There are only six Hollywood film production studios that control which films are made and which ones are not. In order for any film to be made, one must go through one of these studios in order to put out and distribute a film. If they agree to let your film be made, they will be in charge of the overall production of the film. They will have complete control and autonomy of the film. This is why we seem to have the same themes in movies being played over and over again. Hollywood has its own agenda they want to promote. It has nothing to do with the integrity or artistic value of the art of film.

"Hollywood's a place where they'll pay you a thousand dollars for a kiss, and fifty cents for your soul. I know because I turned down the first offer often enough and held out for the fifty cents."
- **Marilyn Monroe**

Movies are an integral part of the fabric of our society. Movies have historically done well for themselves, especially in times of financial hardship or turmoil. During the depression and times of recession, movie profits and attendance always seem to be at their highest. One can relate this phenomenon to the fact that the general population wants to "escape" their own dreary or mundane reality by attending a movie that is going to always have the hero overcome the villain. They relate to the disenfranchised overcoming their hardships. They want to see the good guys always win. They need a hero where one person can defeat all the odds and overcome adversity to achieve their dreams. These images and scenarios are what keep the masses from rebelling. Just like playing the lottery, we all believe we can beat the odds and strike it rich. Sometimes all a person really needs is hope. It's what keeps us getting out of bed every day to go to work at a job that we hate and can't ever seem to get ahead. Hollywood represents the carrot (hope) held in front of the horse (the people) that keeps the cart (the diabolical system) moving forward. We internalize that we are Cinderella. We are Rocky Balboa. We are Bambi. We are Clark Kent. We are Peter Parker. We are Snow White. We are the Lil' Engine That Could. But in reality we are all gullible fools! For every one of us that lives the so-called American Dream, hundreds of thousands are the victims of the American nightmare. We can't all hit the lottery at the same time. There must be millions of losers for the system to function and reward the one winner. But the system only shows us the winner and not the millions of losers who sacrificed everything for a chance to strike it rich. This is how the system flourishes. The illusion that the American Dream can be achieved by "all," is the cruelest and biggest scam America has ever played on the rest of the world and Hollywood serves it up for us to consume on a silver platter.

Tinsel- *Something sparkling or showy but basically valueless. Attracting attention to in a vulgar manner. To give a false sparkle to. Superficial. A sham. Shameful or Indecent.*

Tinsel Town- *A flashy, vulgar tone or atmosphere believed to be characteristic of the American film industry.*

"Whoever controls the image and information of the past will determine what and how future generations will think; and, whoever controls the information and images of the present, will also determine how these same people will view the past."
— George Orwell, author of the book

So let's recap.

- The Zionist Jews usurped the motion picture projector invented by Thomas Edison in attempt to control the newly found motion picture industry.

- They moved to Southern California and set up their elaborate movie studios in what used to be an area exclusively for Orange grove trees and farms. It was later named Hollywood by the Illuminati.

- In order to strong arm the Jewish movie industry and studio owners, the Illuminati through politics and more particularly Congress, set up special hearings targeting these Jews for being communist. Being labeled a "Communist" at this time was like being labeled a "Terrorist" today and had devastating implications.

- This Jewish witch hunt was labeled, "McCarthyism." In order to keep their movie empire and riches, the Jewish, movie studio owners did whatever the Illuminati wanted them to do. They were given an ultimatum, either go along with the Illuminati and give them full control over the subliminal messages and brainwashing in their movies and keep their studios and all their riches or don't go along with them, be labeled a Communist, lose everything and be thrown in jail and be disgraced for the rest of their lives.

- Of course the Zionist Jews agreed and the Illuminati took control over the Hollywood movie industry. Their first major project was the release of "The Wizard of Oz" in 1939.

Let us break down this historic movie which set the tone for how Hollywood will be used as a major tool to suppress, influence and manipulate the masses without them even knowing it.

- "The Wizard of Oz" takes place in middle America in the state of Kansas. Kansas represents the middle of America or the heart in America's "Heartland." It also is shaped as a square whose sides total 360 degrees of knowledge in the Occult. So the Illuminati wants to hit the "Heart" of America to instill its science and knowledge to manipulate and control the masses.

- The movie starts off in black and white. "The Wizard of Oz" was the first movie to be used in color! The beginning of the movie in black and white signifies that Dorothy has no knowledge of herself or the world she lives in. She is a slave and doesn't even know it. Thus, her worldview is limited to the two basic colors of black and white with no "gray areas" or knowledge in between.

- When Dorothy is transported to the Land of Oz she immediately sees things in vibrant colors and illumination! This symbolizes Dorothy's initiation into higher consciousness. She is now waking up to the knowledge of self and her environment and is discovering that the world she used to live in was really her dream and this new world was her reality!

- Dorothy's only companion through this shift in consciousness was her fateful, Black dog named Toto. Toto represents the ancient Egyptian god named, Anpu. Anpu represents our intuition that dwells in our higher self. He guides us in the spiritual realm. The world we can't, see, touch, taste, hear or smell.. For us to utilize our intuitive, higher state we must raise our consciousness and follow our hearts and not be fooled by what seems logical in the physical realm.

- This is why Dorothy must "follow the yellow brick road" in order to find her true self and get back "home" or her higher self. The road made of gold bricks is Dorothy overcoming her fears and lower self in an effort to stay on the path her heart has laid out for her.

- The road is treacherous at times and very scary but Dorothy stays steadfast, overcomes her fears and stays the course. This is what every individual must do in an effort to meet their "true" or higher, spiritual self.

- The first character Dorothy meets on her journey to find her higher self is the Scare Crow. In legal terms, on all legal documents your name is in all capital letters. This is called your Straw Man. It is on your driver's license, mortgage, court and legal documents and credit cards. Your "Straw Man" represents you as a volunteer slave to a system that thinks of you in terms of your earning power and potential to make money off of you over your lifetime. You are bonded to a lifetime of slavery and don't even know it. From the time they issue you a Birth Certificate until the day they issue you a Death Certificate you are considered nothing but chattel to your secret slave owners. This is why Dorothy meets "her" Straw Man first! This is why the Scare Crow is searching for a brain because he has no knowledge of the legal system that enslaves him. He is ignorant and dumb to the fact that he is far from free and has been a slave all his life!

- The next character Dorothy meets on the way to following her heart in search of meeting her higher self is the Tin Man. The Tin Man is cold and made of metal. The Tin Man has no feelings and chops down living trees not knowing the damage to the world he inflicts. He does not know his lifestyle is predicated on the death and destruction of the world that is kept from him. He is logical, cold and calculating. He only sees the world in terms of his lower self, the world where you only recognize and acknowledge that which you can only see, touch, taste hear or smell. He is a paid employee whose only goal is to pay rent, feed his family, obtain shelter, transportation and clothing. He is motivated by self-survival, which is the lowest level of consciousness one can descend to. This is why the Tin Man is in search of a heart. He has never really acknowledged it let alone listened to it or followed it. He has always been concerned and preoccupied with greed and his own self-survival. Following your heart means giving up those things that make us feel "safe" and stepping out on faith and overcoming our fears. The Heart Chakra is the first level of higher consciousness.

- The next character Dorothy meets on her way to discover her higher self and be free is the "Cowardly Lion." The Cowardly Lion doesn't know his own strength. He doesn't believe in his self. He doesn't step out of his comfort zone when he is confronted with adversity. He is a coward through and through even when other people can see the strength within him. The Cowardly Lion represents Dorothy's fragile psyche. She has been conditioned to live and be motivated by fear as a means of control and manipulation by the Powers That Be. Since she doesnt know her own strength, her higher self, she doesn't question authority and will always fall in line with the status quo presented to her as her reality. She will never rise up and fight for a freedom she doesn't know she never had in the first place. In Dorothy's journey to following her heart she is going to need the courage and bravery housed in her higher self that she never knew she had in the first place. This is why the all mighty Lion has been reduced to a shell of himself, his lower self, and is looking for the courage he never knew he already had.

- Ultimately, Dorothy makes it to Oz, her higher self, and is met with a stern, all-powerful and menacing figure named the "Wizard of Oz." It is her dog Toto or the god Anpu that literally pulls the curtain back to reveal the all-knowing, all-powerful Wizard is just a feeble, old white man using smoke and mirrors to perpetuate the myth of his strength and power. The system that enslaved her was really only a façade of illusions that really had no power. The only power the system had was duping Dorothy into believing she needed it in the first place. Dorothy finally realizes that she had everything she needed within herself and voluntarily gave her power to a system that always meant to enslave her and keep her from her higher self.

- It is finally revealed to Dorothy that she had to ability to "go home" any time she wanted to. This reveals that Dorothy finally transcended into her higher self which was kept from her by a system that had enslaved her since birth. Reaching your "higher" spiritual self is the key to freedom and the only way to achieve that is overcoming your ego, fears and insecurities and follow your heart.

The Esoteric Symbolism of Hollywood Movie Studios

The lamp represents the Illuminati or the "Enlightened Ones." The lamp proceeds to stomp out the letter "I" and replaces it. The letter "I" represents the individual or Revolutionary that goes against the masses which are led to slaughter like sheep. This logo basically communicates subliminally that the Illuminati seeks to destroy all individuals who think for themselves and don't go along with their programming.

The Paramount Studios logo features the masculine principle represented by the mountain. It is the erection of the male. The 22 stars represent man at his highest self. The number 22 translates to the number 4 in Biblical numerology. Four is the number of creation. The circle of stars represents the feminine principle or the womb. So the mountain penetrating the circle creates life represented by the stars. It's always about sex on a metaphysical level.

Same holds true for the Disney logo. The castle represents the male phallic symbol and the circular pattern of the shooting star represents the female womb. Again, this union produces a star or a human at its highest level of consciousness. Notice the water in the forefront representing when a woman's water breaks while giving birth.

The Dream Works logo is a little more elaborate. The Moon is the esoteric symbol of the sacred feminine or the woman. The fishing pole represents the phallic symbol or masculine principle. The fact that the boy has his left foot down symbolizes that he is acting in accordance with his higher self. The term "fishing in the dark" is appropriate. It stems from using your intuitive, spiritual or higher level of consciousness to interpret yourself and your reality. He does not rely on his lower self or what he can decipher with his sight, smell, taste, hear or touch to determine his reality. Thus, all of his dreams can be created and manifested.

Keys to the Metaphysical Blueprint of Hollywood

KEY NUMBER ONE:

The Ancient Kemetic Mystery Systems.

This is the first and most important key to understanding the occult and esoteric secrets behind the film industry. Superior knowledge, science and consciousness can be traced back to Afrika in a country called Kemet, thousands of years ago. This country, known as Egypt today, maintained a highly advanced and metaphysical society that was founded and established by Afrikan people. Make no mistake about it these people were Black! This is part of the secret that has been kept by the masses and Black people in general, in an effort to keep them asleep and subservient to Europeans or white people throughout the world. Mind you, people who define themselves as white are also victims of this perpetual lie that has been injected in the world history books and the media. You see Hollywood needs to subliminally support white supremacy in order for Caucasians to maintain a mindset of superiority. It is in the promotion of this racist mindset that the elite's agenda and system flourishes throughout the world. The white supremacy system that the elites have established and nurtured is predicated on the inferiority complex of the darker people of the world. Darker people of the world must look up to and depend upon the people who classify themselves as white, otherwise their resources as well as the masses of people of color, could not be exploited. In this sense, white people are also victims to this dysfunctional belief system that has them in a constant state of fear and superiority, when it comes to defining their relationships with people of color throughout the world.

The science or what is known as the mystery systems in Kemet were established for man to achieve his higher self or what is called, "god consciousness." There were a set of rules, practices and rituals that helped man attain and define himself and his environment through his higher, spiritual consciousness. Once this procedure was mastered, man was considered a god, here on Earth. Man's objective was to master his lower self, which included his physical body and thoughts by discipline and selflessness which led to an outstanding moral and ethical life. The main objective of this ancient society as a whole was to overcome lower thoughts and deeds in an effort for the population to experience heaven here on Earth.

The secret societies, the elite and ruling class now use this secret knowledge but in reverse. Instead of using these ancient mystery systems and rituals to uplift the masses in search of higher knowledge, spiritual awakening and self-actualization, they now secretly implement it in reverse to keep the population in a lower state of consciousness. Their goal is to keep the general population, ignorant, docile and impressionable to their will. The ancient Kemetic sciences have been reversed engineered. This ancient, Afrikan knowledge has been perverted and is now the driving force behind the people that rule the world in secrecy today. We are now being bombarded and force fed lower level energy that promotes and nurtures the worst in us. We are in an "ego driven" society that preys on our insecurities and fears by means of perpetuating materialism, sexism, racism, classism jealousy, greed, desires, false pride, passions, individuality and immaturity. This is what is going on in advertising, education, nutrition & health, entertainment, the economy, law, sports, politics, religion and any other facet in our lives. We are being trained to define ourselves and our environment by the lowest of our consciousness and not the very best in us. We are being brainwashed into embracing our lower, animalistic consciousness and deny our higher, spiritual consciousness.

Once you understand the ancient, Kemetic science of symbols, mythology, God consciousness and man's life purpose, one will unlock the mysteries of not only Hollywood secrets but life in general. We will refer to different Kemetic mystery systems as they pertain to concepts and ideas exploited in the film, for there are far too many concepts to cover in a general context. Out of all the keys in deciphering the hidden messages in Hollywood films, this is the most important one to know. Understand that we are being programmed and conditioned without our consent to define ourselves and our reality through the worst in us, so that we will never recognize or transcend to that which is best in our potentials as spirits having a human experience.

20

Hollywood uses as its foundation, one basic story that comes from Kemet, pertaining to their culture, worldview and cosmology. This story can be seen in a majority of Hollywood movies in one form or another. The basic theme seems to be retold, reinterpreted and repeated many times over.

Let us break down one of the most important stories our ancestors wrote on the walls of their temples. Our ancestors wrote in symbols, known as Metu Neter or what people call hieroglyphs today, because that is the best form of communication when speaking to the subconscious of the individual. They knew that they must bypass the conscious state of Black people in order for real change in behavior to incur. The story goes as follows; In the beginning there was a god named Ausar and his goddess wife named Auset. They were happily married. Ausar had a jealous brother named Set. Set was jealous because he did not have a beautiful wife of his own. Set's jealousy became uncontrollable to the point where he plotted to kill his brother so that he can have Auset for himself. Set secretly took Ausar's measurements and built an elaborate sarcophagus with gold and precious stones according to his brother's exact measurements. Set then held a party and invited his brother to come celebrate with him. At the party, Set showcased the beautiful sarcophagus he had built. Set announced that anyone who can fit in the coffin, could have the sarcophagus for themselves. Of course, Ausar climbed into the coffin and it was a perfect match. Just then, Set slammed and nailed the sarcophagus shut, trapping Ausar inside as he whisked him away. Set murdered his brother and then proceeded to chop his brother's body into fourteen pieces and scattered them far and wide throughout the land of Kemet. Set then approached Auset to force her hand in marriage. Auset adamantly refused his wishes and set out on a long journey to try to find the fourteen pieces of her late husband's body, that was scattered far and wide. Auset never gave up her quest of finding all the pieces of her late husband's body. She searched high and low and would go to great lengths to secure and gather all the pieces to her man. She was relentless and never gave up hope in putting him back together, piece by piece. Auset had found thirteen pieces of Ausar's body and was down to looking for the one last piece. Coincidently, that last piece was probably the most important out of all the pieces she had already collected, his penis. While searching in the depths of the Nile River, Auset finally found Ausar's last piece. Just as she was getting ready to retrieve it, a catfish came out of nowhere and swallowed it. This did not detour Auset's mission of putting her man back together. She reassembled the thirteen pieces she had found on a slab or table. She missed and wanted her husband with such passion, she climbed on top of his reassembled body, in an effort to be with him one last time. In an instant, she turned into a hawk as she straddled her husband and vigorously started to flap her wings. Because of her dedication, faith, determination, will and perseverance, Ausar miraculously was resurrected! Auset also conceived a male child and named him Heru. This was the original Immaculate Conception that other religions copied or stole from. When Heru was of age, he went after his uncle Set, to avenge his father's murder. Heru eventually overcame Set and was proclaimed the victor of their long battles. Heru had to overcome his fears when everything seems to go against him. Heru displayed bravery, courage, strength and undying loyalty in his battles to restore his father's honor.

So here is how Hollywood reinterprets the basic themes of this Kemetic story. Father, who represents everything good, loses his life by betrayal of someone close to him, who represents evil or bad. Mother mourns the death of her husband but never lets go of his memory. Son grows up to avenge father's death by overcoming his fears and displaying courage, commitment and intestinal fortitude. Son takes fathers place and dedicates his life to uphold his father's memory. Mother is exalted by son.

In fact, the very word Hero comes from the Kemetic god, Heru. Here are a few pictures whose themes are based on this ancient, Kemetic story; All the Rocky Movies, all the Jason Bourne movies, all the James Bond movies, Harry Potter movies, Avatar, Brave heart, Passion of the Christ, Titanic, Batman, Superman, Spiderman, Iron Man, Terminator movies, Lord of the Rings movies, Transformer movies, Bambi, Lion King and any other Disney movie, anything with Sylvester Stallone, Bruce Willis, Arnold Schwarzenegger, Clint Eastwood, John Wayne, Charles Bronson, Jason Statman, Mel Gibson, Paul Newman, Tom Cruise, Brad Pitt, Matt Damon, Leonardo DiCaprio, Russell Crowe, Johnny Depp, Sean Connery, Nicholas Cage and any other white man that saves the world!

I believe Hollywood reinterprets this story as a means to keep the masses from rising up and righting what is wrong in today's society. Nature and human beings are always in a perpetual state of trying to correct that which is not balanced in them. It is a drive or instinct in man that cannot be ignored or eliminated from his being. Because of this, the elite, secret societies that rule and enslave the masses, must neutralize this trait in man in order to keep them oppressed and asleep. They retell this ancient Kemetic story, which was originally interpreted to uplift man into a higher state of consciousness, but now use it to pacify that nature in man they want to keep dormant in him. Remember, Hollywood films are designed to communicate with the subconscious level in a person's brain. The subconscious is manipulated and duped into thinking that the actions that it interprets while watching a movie is a real life experience. The subconscious mind cannot decipher what is real from what is fantasy. Because of this, the subconscious level in man is satisfied that the person watching the film, is actually participating and playing out the story that the movie is displaying. This appeases or satisfies that part in man that wants to correct that which is not balanced in real life. Because of this, the masses will not try to better themselves and will continue to be a part of a system that does not have their best interests at heart. Hollywood is playing a cruel trick on the subconscious mind in order for man to remain docile and asleep to his true nature.

In Kemet, the people were misclassified as worshipping many gods. This is far from the truth. They were the first people to introduce monotheism or the worship of one god. What they did was break down God's personality or characteristics according to anthropomorphic ideals. This was seen by representing different gods with different animal heads with the body of men and women. These animal heads represented the multiple characteristics the one God would possess according to a specific ideology or personality trait man must display to reach higher consciousness. For example, the Kemetic god Tehuti, was the god of knowledge and wisdom. He was shown as a bird having a long beak. The long beak represented the writing instrument from which the sacred knowledge was written on scrolls. So one would pray to one of god's personalities named, Tehuti, when they needed higher knowledge, intelligence or wisdom. They didn't worship Tehuti, but they paid homage and acknowledged the characteristic of the one god that he represented. Tehuti, also being a bird, could see nature from a higher perspective in the sky. Thus, his "higher" consciousness allowed him a heighten perspective of nature and man. In Hollywood films, one will see these different animals. Different animals are placed in these movies because they represent a secret principle that was stolen from the ancient, Kemetic gods. We will go further into this concept in the movie when it presents itself.

The Afrikan land of Kemet held many systems and sciences that helped to uplift man into higher consciousness. The Europeans who invaded this land, called them "Mystery Systems, because they did not understand them. Hollywood now uses these sciences and systems to control and manipulate man. Out of all the keys I will mention, understanding the culture, mindset and worldview of these ancient Afrikan people is the most important one of all. I encourage everyone to dedicate their time and energy into further study of the ancient, Afrikan civilization called Kemet or "Land of the Black."

Marvel Comics also uses the science of Ancient Kemet. The god Heru represented by the colors Red and White. Hero comes from the word Heru. He symbolizes the "Hero" in all of us fighting our evil, lower self with courage, bravery, honor and relentlessly!

KEY NUMBER TWO:

Biblical Numerology

The Bible is coded with hidden knowledge and esoteric signs and symbols that have their roots in Kemet. We are oblivious to this knowledge because we are operating at such a low frequency and mundane level of consciousness. The Bible was never to be taken literally. Literal translation of scripture is the lowest level to understanding higher consciousness, universal law and cosmology held within the Bible. Literal translation is like pre-school in the school of life or higher consciousness. One must graduate or raise their consciousness to have access to the Bible's hidden, higher knowledge and understanding of life. The Bible is coded with ancient Kemetic concepts and ideologies. These mystery systems are hidden in parables, characters and the history or dates within the Bible itself. If you understand the deeper meaning of the concept of numbers, one will have the capacity to unlock the blue print to deeper knowledge and wisdom in all aspects of life. Look at numbers according to this key and you will be able to see life more clearly. Use numbers as a blueprint or key to the map of life. One will find, once you are conscious of the numbers around you, one will be able to see the pattern of the reality that one choose to accept. Numbers don't lie.

Numbers also play a very integral part in deciphering concepts and hidden messages in movies. We will refer back to this key when the appropriate time presents itself in deciphering a scene in a film. Please take the time to learn this system of Biblical Numerology as it pertains to all aspects in life, not just in movies. Life, as well as the universe is a mathematical equation.

ONE (1): Symbol of unity of the one life force that permeates all things. It is the state of being first and foremost. It represents the beginning. This number is associated with the concept of Atum. Atum represents the one, hidden life force that flows through all things. It is the hidden energy that always was and always will be. This number represents the recognition of the one life force that makes up all things.

TWO (2): The number of division or separation. It is the first number that can be divided unto itself. Man has two natures, human & divine. There are 2 testaments, Old & New. This number represents separation or division of the mind, body or spirit. There is male and female. It represents the Yin and the Yang. This number accounts for the space between ideals. It is the opposite ends of the same thing; Man & woman, Hot & cold, Higher & lower or Good & evil.

THREE (3): Divine perfection represented by the trinity. It is the father, the mother (Holy Spirit) & the Son. The necessary three dimensions for the physical rule of law. It represents the mind, body & soul. It is the past, present & the future. It represents time, space & matter. It is the three qualities of the universe, represented by solid liquid & gas. It is length, width & depth. It is the third dimensional plane. To exist all 3 are required. This number promotes the idea that everything is made up of three parts when you dissect it down to its basic core. Jesus rose on the third day. Resurrection or new life needs to incorporate the three in order to manifest.

FOUR (4): The number of creation in the physical dimension. It is the North, South, East & West. It is represented by the 4 seasons. The fourth 4th commandment refers to the Earth or creation in the physical dimension. The 4th clause of Lord 's Prayer, "One Earth as it is in heaven." It is a new beginning of creation. There are 4 Gospels. There are the 4 winds. It represents the Base, Balance, Order and Harmony.

FIVE (5): The number of god's grace. It represents redemption. It is Creation, (4) plus a new beginning (1). David picked 5 stones to slew Goliath to symbolize that God was on his side. God is pleased with your undertaking. Jesus wore 5 garments. Man has 5 fingers, five toes and five senses. A five pointed star represents man's highest nature. Man's temperature is 98.6= 9+8+6= 23 or 2+3=5. God is pleased in his creation of man.

SIX (6): The number of imperfection. The number of lower man or the beast in man. Creation (4) plus division (2) equals 6. It represents man's fall or separation from God. Man was created on the 6th day. Thou shalt not kill is the 6th Commandment. Mark of the beast is the number 666, which represents man's lowest physical, mental and spiritual consciousness. The symbol for the number 6, looks like the pregnant mother or the number 1 that is pregnant. It represents God giving birth or life to the physical dimension. Elemental chart number 6 is Carbon. Carbon is the oldest element we know on Earth. There are six pall bearers, 6 sided coffin buried 6ft. under ground. KKK= 11+11+11= 33= 3+3=6.

SEVEN (7): Divine completion. The term Seventh Heaven represents divine bliss. It is the number of spiritual perfection. God rested on 7th day. There are 52 or 5+2=7 weeks in the completion of one year. There are 7 colors in a spectrum. Seven of Ten Commandments begin with the word "Not." Jesus made 7 statements on the cross. Man has 7 layers of skin, 7 chakras, 7 key notes, 7 orifices, 7 seas, 7 continents, 7parts of brain and heart. There are 7 deadly sins & virtues. The human body replaces its entire cells every 7 years. Seven is the Creator's personality expressed in the physical realm.

EIGHT (8): The number of infinity or eternity. The symbol for the number eight has no beginning & no ending. Eight is the symbol for infinity laid on its side in mathematics. There were eight people on Noah's ark representing God's eternal love for man. God made 8 covenants with Abraham. God's word is forever.

NINE (9): Symbol of judgment. Nine is the womb upside down or the number 6 turned on its head. It represents man's test before he can move on. The numbers repeat themselves after the number nine. Man must pass the lessons of 9 in order to move on to higher numbers. It is the 5 senses overcoming 4 elements = 9. The Sphinx or Harmaket riddle. What walks on four legs in the morning, two legs at noon, and three legs in the evening? Oedipus solved the riddle, answering that man crawls on all fours in infancy, walks upright on two legs in adulthood, and uses a cane as a third leg in old age. 4 +3 + 2 = 9. There are 360 degrees of knowledge or 3+6+0= 9. There are 18 breaths per minute or 1+8=9. There are 72 pulses per minute in the human body or 7+2=9. Nine represents the struggle one must endure and overcome to reach a higher place. Nine is man's test to be graded on.

TEN (10): Symbol of perfection. It is the number one standing next to 360 degrees of knowledge or the number zero. It represents the mastery of the Ten Commandments. It is the completion of order.

ELEVEN (11): A MASTER NUMBER. The number of duality. The reflection of the one or yourself. It has two meanings according to the level of consciousness of the individual. A person in lower consciousness, the number eleven means a flawed addition to the perfect order. One more than ten. If you representing the "One" looking at your reflection and don't like what you see, you are flawed and didn't learn an important life lesson that got you to this point. It represents, "Too much of a good thing will reflect the worst in you." Or one who cannot handle their success. However, you representing the "One" looking at your reflection, are pleased at what you see, then you will reflect your higher self to others. You have reached a level of consciousness where you have mastered your lower self. Very important in Kabala mysticism.

TWELVE (12): **Symbol of divine completion or accomplishment.** God rules over creation. There were 12 apostles, 12 tribes of Israel. 12 months in a year and 12 jurors. 144,000 will be saved in the book of Revelations or 12x12 = 144. The first account of the boy Jesus in the Bible was at 12 years of age. It is the completion of cycle or initiation into higher consciousness.

THIRTEEN (13): **Number of resurrection and new beginning in higher consciousness.** The 13th month is considered a new year. There were 13 colonies in the New World. There are 12 jurors & 1 judge. There are 13 stars & stripes on original flag. Society has demonized the number 13 for fear of the Black man's resurrection from the dead. You have superstitions like Friday the 13th & no 13th floors in high rise buildings. It is the transformation represented by the New Testament that has 13 books. One the $1.00 bill the level of bricks on the pyramid equals 13 steps. The eagle is holding 13 olive branches with thirteen olives on them. In the other claw he is holding 13 arrows. The number thirteen is very powerful in the upliftment of man into higher consciousness.

FORTY (40): **Number of triumph over final trial or test.** Jesus was tested in the desert for 40 days and 40 nights. The children of Israel wandered in the desert for 40 years. The flood lasted for 40 days & 40 nights. Moses went to the mountain top of 40 days. Age 40 one is considered "Over the hill." Ancient Kemet, masters went to school until they reached 40 years old. Forty is the number of triumph over a hard fought lesson one needed to reach higher consciousness.

The first key in numerology is to understand these 14 basics numbers above, as well as their meanings. Every other number, besides the master numbers, will add up to these basic numbers. For example, the number 541 can be broken down as such; 5+4+1. This number equals 10. The number 10 stands on its own so you don't have to break it down any further. Look up the meaning of the number ten to reveal the hidden message being revealed in that scene. Another example would be the number 14. You break it down to 1+4. This number equals 5. This number stands on its own as well.

Another concept is assigning numbers to letters. Learn the following key:

A-1	J-10	S-19
B-2	K-11	T-20
C-3	L-12	U-21
D-4	M-13	V-22
E-5	N-14	W-23
F-6	O-15	X-24
G-7	P-16	Y-25
H-8	Q-17	Z-26
I-9	R-18	

You might see a license plate or address with a mixture of letters and numbers such as #304B. This is broken down to 3+0+4+2. This number equals 9. The number 9 stands on its own. You would then look up the meaning of the number nine to understand the hidden message that is being revealed.

Look at numbers according to this key and you will be able to see life more clearly, not just in the movie theater. Use numbers as a blueprint or key to the map of life. One will find, once they are conscious of the numbers around them, they will be able to see the pattern of the reality that they choose to accept. Numbers will layout a street map as th where your life is headed according to the decisions and choices on makes in their life. Numbers can predict the outcome as well as warn a person of an upcoming event.

Numbers are used in movies to communicate with the audience's subconscious mind. Once one deciphers the language of math, one will be able to unveil a level of consciousness or reality that they never knew existed. Hollywood uses the science of numerology to communicate with other elite initiates to communicate certain worldly events that will arise in the future. In this way, the initiates will be given a "heads up" and plan accordingly to capitalize on the upcoming, orchestrated, epic, world event or crisis. Numbers don't lie but Hollywood does.

KEY NUMBER THREE:

The Chakra System

I want the moviegoer to understand the concept of different energy levels within one's body which display certain aspects of their consciousness. We have seven energy levels in the body that we potentially have access to. Each level has a unique color, characteristic and personality unto itself. We have all heard the phrases; "Green with envy." "Seeing red in anger." or "Feeling blue." In movies, pay attention to the color of clothing, lighting, cars, signs and other tall tale signs that demonstrate the state of consciousness being revealed in the scene. Movies are very particular with their props and images they place in scenes. Colors are used to display a character's level of consciousness. Colors act as clues as to what energy, personality or level of consciousness the characters are exhibiting. Be very aware of colors in movie scenes. Colors of the props used in movies are not picked at random. They are chosen to represent an underlining energy or mystical theme that lies under the surface of the scene. We will refer back to this key when colors are prominently displayed in movie scenes.

The first energy level or Chakra is called the, "Root Chakra." It is located at the base of the spine or tail bone. This is the lowest Chakra which symbolizes are connection to this world as an animal. This Chakra is red in color and symbolizes all our survival instincts. One who embraces this Chakra is only interested in pleasing and sustaining himself. He is ruled by his carnal urges his motivation is survival of the fittest. The Root Chakra being the first, is where all humans start out at. It is up to our freewill as to whether we raise our consciousness or live life like animals, intent on just surviving and satisfying our carnal urges.

First: Red Chakra

Location: Base of the spine

Element: Earth

Principal: Gravity

Characteristic: Survival; Man defined as an animal.

Purpose: "To Have."

In Hollywood they have the ritual of "walking on the red carpet" before its elaborate award ceremonies. This ritual has very dark, hidden meanings and purpose. The red carpet stands for man represented at its lowest level of consciousness. It is man as a beast or animal. It's the worst level man can descend or fall to. It represents the beast, devil or the lowest evil man can embrace. So walking on the red carpet can be interpreted as its participants sacrificing all that is good from within them to be used and promoted as "stars" Hollywood. They are making a pledge, oath or pact to the "Hollywood gods" to do whatever is necessary with them in exchange for riches, fame and power. The red carpet represents the devil or Satan's tongue. The doorway they walk through to enter the event represents the devil's mouth. So the exclusive "stars" that walk on the red carpet to enter through the venues doors are metaphysically sacrificing themselves to the devil to be consumed by him in exchange for fame, fortune and wealth. There is one thing the devil doesn't tell you. There is no reneging or going back on your contract with him. Once you sign your name in blood it is for eternity.

The second Chakra is located in the abdominal region. It also entails the sexual organs. This Chakra is orange. Characteristics of this Chakra are emotions and sexuality. The purpose of this Chakra is pleasure and not disrupting the rhythm. Its only principle is attraction to the opposite sex. People who dwell in this Chakra make all their decisions based on their emotions and sexual urges. These people let their emotions control them instead of vice-versa. These people also define their reality by superficial things that actually get in the way of their best interests. They are easily angered, distracted and let foolish pride control their lives. They define struggle or a challenge as an obstacle that needs to be avoided at all costs. Sex is used as a pacifier. The statement. "No pain, no gain," does not make sense to the people who embrace this level of consciousness.

Second: Orange

Location: Abdomen; Hips

Element: Water

Characteristic: Sexuality, Lust, Addiction & Emotions

Purpose: Pleasure, Rhythm

Principal: Attraction of Opposites

The third Chakra is located at the Solar Plexus area of the body. It is represented by the color yellow. This Chakra is responsible for holding all your fire, passion and desires. Its element is fire, thus the "Solar" Plexus location. Characteristics of this Chakra are desire, will and passion. The purpose of this Chakra is to act and its characteristics are combustion and will power. People who operate at this level are very passionate people. They have dreams and desires that nobody can convince them that they cannot have them. They are very passionate about anything they partake in and will not make excuses for being so. These people need to learn to balance their passions and desires with the other Chakras in the body.

This level is driven by man's desires and passions. It operates on the basis of raw emotions. It is fueled by man's deepest and rawest form of emotions. It dwells in the place where a man's tears and perspiration are born. It exposes a man's hidden strengths, as well as his weaknesses at the same time. It does not discriminate. It cannot hide or deceive. It finds strength in its vulnerabilities. It is an uncontrollable fire that cannot be extinguished. This is what motivates a man to pursue his deepest dreams, thoughts and desires. It is the spark or catalyst to his physical existence. It is his only reason for living when he cannot find anything else to live for.

Third: Yellow

Location: Solar Plexus

Element: Fire

Characteristic: Desire, Passion & Will

Purpose: To Act

Principal: Combustion

The fourth Chakra is located in a person's heart. It is represented by Love. This Chakra is green in color. Its characteristics are acceptance and compassion. The principle of this Chakra is equilibrium. The object to obtain is to think with your heart and feel with your mind. In other words, this ideology is the exact opposite of the motto, "Its just business, don't take it personal." This Chakra expresses that everything you do is personal. One cannot separate what one does from who one is no matter what their intentions are. This Chakra doesn't change hats according to the task at hand. This Chakra only wears one hat, humility.

To achieve this level, man has to overcome all his fears, face all his insecurities, embrace humiliation and shame and sacrifice himself for a cause greater than himself. A piece of cake right? This may seem like a daunting task, but don't fret. Simply put, man must overcome and "kill his ego." Man's ego, has switched places with his true self. It has tricked and confused the individual to define themselves and their reality, based on the ego's perception, which manipulates and controls our true self through fear. We voluntarily give up our true selves, in favor of this imposter, who wants to keep us functioning at a lower level for its survival at the expense of our demise. How can we, "keep it real." If one has no knowledge of their "real" selves? Man must learn to love "true" self first, before he can love anybody else. Man needs to be reintroduced to his real self. The greatest of these is love.

Fourth: Green

Location: Heart

Element: Air

Characteristic: Acceptance, Compassion

Purpose: To Love

Principal: Equilibrium

The "Green Room" in Hollywood.

The Green room refers to a room usually located backstage of Hollywood film studios where "the Cast" lounge when they are not on stage performing. It is a place for them to relax before they are called to the set or on stage to play their role. Mind you when the "cast" goes on stage they play the role their master's

have for them. They are nothing more than pawns or puppets used to promote propaganda and their master's agenda as a means of controlling the audience. Green representing the heart or first level of higher consciousness, is the only place the Cast can relax and be their higher selves. All other times when they are called to perform they must be slaves to their master's will and motivated to please him and him alone. They let their master's demons possess them in the role they are called to play oblivious to the purity and sacredness of their own pure hearts. Thus, the "Green Room" is the only sacred place on the studio the cast members can find peace of mind.

The fifth Chakra we will discuss is located in the throat region. It is represented by the color blue. Its element is sound and its characteristic is communication. The purpose of this Chakra is to communicate. Mind you the simplest form of communication is to speak. We communicate with each other on so many different levels that we do ourselves a disservice when we talk too much. On the other hand, be careful of the words you use to speak because words are very powerful. Remember the Bible teaches us that God created the Universe by speaking it into existence. When we express ourselves through words we are creating "spells" to whoever we are communicating with. Choose your spells wisely. The principle of this Chakra is sympathetic vibrations and the acknowledgement of all frequencies. All vibrations and frequencies are forms of consciousness communicating with us.

Fifth: Blue

Location: Throat

Element: Sound

Characteristic: Communication

Purpose: To Speak

Principal: Sympathetic; Vibrations

The sixth Chakra is located on the forehead between the eyes. This Chakra is represented by the color Indigo. This Chakra is known as the "First Eye." It acknowledges the activation of one's Pineal Gland, which produces Melanin. It is represented by the element light and its characteristic is intuition. This Chakra's purpose is to see and its principles are perception and projection. Sometimes we have to close our eyes in order to really see the truth. Remember we only decipher 10% of energy we call reality through our five senses. There is 90% of reality that we cannot decipher by seeing, touching, smelling, tasting or hearing. So this tells me, that the real truth is something our senses cannot tell us. One must rely on their intuition and projection to fully understand what is so-called real. One must raise his consciousness in order to decipher what is considered real.

Sixth: Indigo

Location: Forehead, First-eye

Element: Light

Characteristic: Intuition

Purpose: To See

Principal: Perception &Projection

The last Chakra in the body is located on the top of the head. It is also known as the Crown Chakra. The seventh crown chakra. It is represented by the color purple. That is why royalty wore crowns and were only allowed to wear purple. This Chakra's element is thought. Its characteristic is the concept of understanding and its purpose is to know. The Crown Chakra's principle is consciousness. Once one has reached this level, one is able to have an out of body experience. Although this Chakra is located on the top of the head, it shoots up straight above the body. Mastering the other Chakras is the only path to obtain access to the Crown Chakra.

Seventh : Purple

Location: Top of the Head

(Crown)

Element: Thought

Characteristic: Understanding

Purpose: To Know

Principal: Consciousness

Chakra Color Key:

RED – The animal in man or the lower self. This attribute belongs to the character that displays the lowest behavior man could achieve. It is the characters worst attributes in himself. This character is motivated by the ego and self-survival.

ORANGE – This color has sexual connotations. The character is driven by sexual desires, needs and wants. Motivated by pleasure avoids pain or discomfort at all costs.

YELLOW – This color represents passion. It is raw emotion that drives a character's behavior. It is what motivates a character in the film. Passion and desires are expressed without prejudice of morality.

GREEN – This color represents love and one who is grounded or close to nature. Green is all heart. It has no ulterior motives but unconditional love. To put one person's needs and wants ahead of your own. The ability to sacrifice yourself for a cause greater than yourself.

BLUE – This color represents communication. It holds an ideology or specific point that must be made. This does not necessarily mean it is verbal. More times than not the communication is implied. Hearing is a more powerful tool to communicate than speaking.

INDIGO – This color represents intuition or a sixth sense. It is the state of knowing and acting on faith when all others have doubts. It is believing in yourself when everything around you does not support you. It is the level of consciousness where miracles are manifested.

PURPLE – This color was reserved for royalty. It is the state of higher consciousness . This color must be respected, listened to and obeyed. It is a sign of physical, mental and spiritual enlightenment. It is the level of the Shaman or holy enlightened beings. They are the masters of self able to transcend into higher spiritual dimensions.

The majority of fast food restaurants use the colors of specific chakra energy levels to manipulate its customers into purchasing their food. The color red resonates to your animalistic characteristics, such as hunger and the color yellow communicates with your desires and passions. Using these two colors in conjunction with each other manipulates man into acting according to his animalistic hunger, desires and immediate self-gratification.

KEY NUMBER FOUR:

Secret Societies & the Occult

We need to understand that there are secret groups of people and organizations that control and manipulate all facets of life, in order to control the masses' definition of reality. The best slaves are the people who do not even recognize that they are slaves. These secret organizations have infiltrated governments, banking systems, multinational corporations, religions, the food industry, medical field, sports, politics, educational systems as well as the entertainment industry. There direct agenda is to exploit the masses so that the elite few can dominate and rule the world for the betterment of their select group members and inner circle. World domination and power is there only goal, at the expense of oppressing the world's population. These esoteric groups have been running the world in the shadows for a long period of time throughout world history

One of the most powerful and influential secret society is called the Illuminati. The name literally means, "The Illuminated Ones." This means that these select few have "shed light" on the system and are conscious of what is taking place while the rest of us are living in the dark. Their goal is to establish a New World Order or system to govern and control the people and resources of the world under one leadership, direction and goal. The Illuminati have infiltrated another secret society called, the Free Masons. The Illuminati willingly and secretly hide under the umbrella of the Free Masonry organization , but they are by all means a separate entity. Within Free Masonry there are levels that even Free Masons are oblivious to. It is in the secret confines of these levels, that the Illuminate hide in plain sight and without detection. This select group controls Hollywood for its own diabolical purposes. In order for an inspiring actor, director or writer to receive work and be successful in the industry, they must me initiated into the secret society. They will have to take an oath of allegiance to only perpetuate the will of the secret society even if it comes at the expense of hurting the masses. The general population is expendable to them. They are looked upon as cattle. So the aspiring actor, director or writer must uphold this oath for if it is broken, they will be destroyed and never be able to pursue their art or craft in the entertainment industry. Have you ever wondered why so many people in the entertainment industry suffer from catastrophes that don't seem to make sense? They are either being warned, blackmailed or punished for an act that goes against the oath of allegiance they took to get the fame and wealth that they have acquired in their field. This holds true in the music industry, sports field and the entertainment industry as a whole.

These secret societies have many secret signs, symbols and gestures as well. The majority of these symbols have their foundations in ancient Kemet. These are the same group of elites who have usurped this knowledge in order to manipulate and control the masses instead of using this knowledge for what it was designed for and that was to uplift the human race.

A common symbol in the film industry is the Free Mason god named Mendes or Baphomet. Baphomet is shown with the head of a goat, the body of a male & female and the legs of an animal. [*see illustration below*] The goat head represents the person being privy to the hidden knowledge that keeps the masses enslaved. The masses are represented as sheep because they live in the valley, which is "lower" ground. The sheep do not think for themselves, they just blindly follow the lead sheep. Sheep are very gullible, simple and docile creatures. They are easily led to slaughter by manipulation and control. Goats are the opposite. Goats live "above" the sheep and see the valley or "system" for what it truly is. Goats are sure footed and do not go along without a fight. A goat will stand up and defend himself if provoked or coerced to do something he does not want to do. Goats have horns to protect themselves. Goats are stubborn. In Kemet, the pharaoh braided goat's hair and wore it on their chin to signify that they were enlightened and wise beings.

The reason for the body of the Baphomet displaying both male and female characteristics signifies the oneness or omnipotence of god. God has the ability to create within him or herself. God does not have to look outside of itself to manifest or create that which it wills. These are the characteristics worshippers of the Baphomet want to possess.

The left hand of the Baphomet is pointing down towards the ground and the dark crescent moon. The right hand of the Baphomet is pointing up towards the sky towards an illuminated crescent moon. The left hand represents man's higher consciousness because it is controlled by the right hemisphere of the brain. This side of the brain is responsible for man's higher, spiritual consciousness. The pointing down of the left hand symbolizes the suppression of man's higher, spiritual consciousness that leaves him in the dark represented by the dark moon. The moon also represents the feminine principle of energy which contains man's higher consciousness. So in order for the world's elite to stay in power they most promote and feed man's lower self.

The right hand of Baphomet is raised up and pointing towards the sky. The right hand is controlled by the left hemisphere of the brain. This side of the brain is responsible for man's lower or animalistic consciousness. So this symbol represents the promotion and nurturing of man's lower consciousness so that he can be easily manipulated and controlled.

The wings on the Baphomet figure represent man's ability to attain higher consciousness. Since man defines himself through his lower consciousness, he does not realize that he has "wings" or the capacity to raise his consciousness and see the system that oppresses him in his lower state.

The star on the forehead of the Baphomet that has a flame shooting out represents the activation of the Pineal gland. The Pineal gland was known as the "first eye" in Kemet. This gland produced a chemical called Melanin that was need to "see" the spiritual world in higher consciousness. The flame represents the knowledge or enlightenment of the initiate.

The Baphomet is sitting on a sphere which represents his domination of the world's resources and the enslavement of its people. This sphere also represents his mastery of 360 of knowledge, which he uses to promote his own agenda and oppress the masses.

The pole in the lap of the figure has two serpents wrapped around it from the bottom to the top. The pole represents man's spinal cord. The two snakes represents the kundalini energy one possesses that defines their level of consciousness according to their position on the pole or spinal cord. This is represented by the chakras or concentrated energy centers located along the spine. Kundalini energy is always represented by two snakes. All energy travels in spirals or waves like the snake. Energy is always displayed in pairs, both positive or masculine and negative or feminine.

41

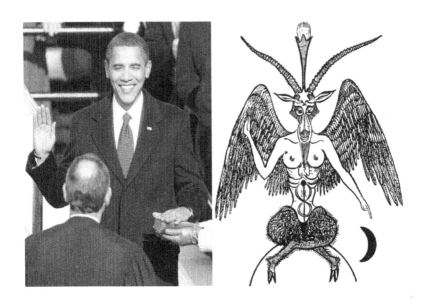

The picture of President Obama, on the left, taking the "oath" to become the President of the United States. Notice the Freemason god Baphomet, in the picture on the right, is giving the same pose or stance. The right hand pointing up signifies the promotion of lower consciousness housed in the left hemisphere of the brain, and the left arm pointing down symbolizes the suppression of higher consciousness housed in the right hemisphere of the brain. This is the conspiracy that secret societies implement in order to control and manipulate the masses into embracing their lower consciousness, while at the same time, never letting them acknowledge their higher selves. Anyone that holds a position of power or influence over the masses must pledge their allegiance to these secret societies first and foremost. They will only stay in power if they serve their hidden masters and not the common people.

In the picture above, George Bush reads a book entitled, The Pet Goat in front of second graders while the planes collide into the World Trade Center buildings on September 11^(th). This was a direct and intentional sign given to all the elite and secret society members as to their plan being put into action. Notice the president is holding the book upside down as he pretends to follow along.

"Masonry, like all religions, all Mysteries, Hermeticism and Alchemy, conceals its secrets from all except the adepts and sages, or the elect, and uses false explanations and misinterpretations of its symbols to mislead those who deserve to be mislead; and conceal the truth, which it calls Light, from them, and to draw them away from it. The teachers, even of Christianity, are in general, the most ignorant of the true meaning of that which they teach. There is no book of which so little is known as the Bible.... Masonry jealously conceals its secrets and intentionally leads conceited interpreters astray.

ALBERT PIKE

(Morals & Dogmas, 1871)

We will refer back to this key and shed more light on these secret groups that manipulate the masses as a puppet master pulls the strings attached to his puppet. As the film reveals these secret symbols and signs, we will address them accordingly. There are many of these secret societies that go by different names. Although they are all vying for world domination, they understand that they must work together in their effort to slice and divide the world's resources to satisfy their own personal power and greed. These organizations do exist and they use the entertainment industry to reveal their secret agenda. I will provide the reader the blueprint into deciphering these hidden signs and symbols.

KEY NUMBER FIVE:

Right & Left Brain Functions

Our brains our divided into two sections the right hemisphere & the left hemisphere of the brain. One can only activate one side of the brain at any given time. The left side of your body is controlled by the right side of your brain & the right side of your body is controlled by the left side of your brain. Each side of your brain serves different functions of your perceptions of reality.

LEFT BRAIN	RIGHT BRAIN
-uses logic	-uses feelings
-details	-abstract "big picture."
-facts	-imagination rules
-words, language	-symbols, images
-present, past	-present, future
-math, science	-philosophy,
-order, patterns	-faith, believes
-perception	-appreciates, possibilities
-names	-spatial, risks
-safe	-not detailed
-reality, defined	-fantasy
-rationality	-intuition
- formal intelligence	-spirituality
-positive (Post or sit)	-negative (no gates)

44

The Left Brain is the defined sense of your personal or physical self. This hemisphere of the brain must adhere to the laws of the physical dimension. It represents man's lower self, which is the physical form.

The Right Brain is the oneness of infinite creative energy. This hemisphere of the brain does not abide by the laws of the physical dimension. It represents man's higher self, which is the spiritual realm of infinite possibilities. This is where miracles are conceived.

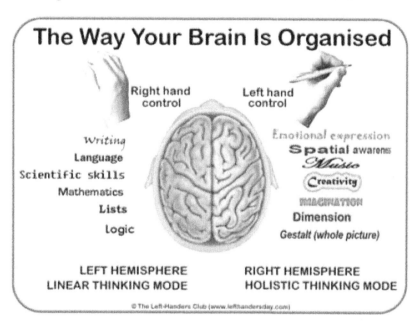

Society rewards left brain functioning people. Our school system is designed to produce left brain dominated thinking, as it suppresses right brain functions. As a result, society rewards those who can get in line and do what they are told & taught to do. Our school system trains us to be good sheep. Always raise your hand & get permission to speak. Wait in line to get what you want. Dress, talk, behave & think like we want you to. Be able to regurgitate the information we uploaded to your brain. No thinking outside the box. Left hand people are dominated by their right brain. This is why they used to demonize them in the past. Right brain dominated people do not make good sheep. They even burned them at the stake and called them demons or witches.

Our right brains are designed to decipher unseen energy or what we call the spiritual realm. Unseen energy comprises of over 90% of our reality that goes unrecognized. Seen energy can be deciphered with our five senses of touch, taste, smell, hear or sight. We have been coerced into believing that this 10% of seen energy makes up 100% of our perceived reality. This is another game that is being played on us. With this knowledge, faith takes on a whole new meaning. Faith is our ability to acknowledge unseen forces that can be manipulated in order to change our reality according to our thoughts and will.

We all have the ability to define ourselves through our lower selves or higher selves. We all have a twin. The lower self is defined by our egos. The higher self is defined by our ability to give our lives unselfishly for a person or cause greater than ourselves. This is further exemplified in movies and television by the good angel on the left shoulder and the devil on the right shoulder of a character. This happens when a character is going through a moral dilemma as to which self he should listen to. The angel on the left represents the right brain function. It represents man's higher or spiritual self. The devil on the right shoulder represents the left brain function. This is ruled by man's ego in the material world. It is his lower self. Also remember, the left side of the body is controlled by the right brain and the right side of the body is controlled by the left brain. That is why the angel or higher self is on the left and the devil or lower self is on the right shoulder. This illustration represents man's perpetual, internal struggle of right brain vs. left brain functioning, otherwise known as higher consciousness versus man's lower consciousness. Man was given free will from which to decide how he will interpret and define himself and his reality. We will refer back to this key when characters are introduced in the movie to further break down their hidden meanings.

The angel on the left shoulder represents higher or spiritual consciousness represented by the right hemisphere of the brain. The devil on the right shoulder represents lower or animalistic consciousness represented by the left hemisphere of the brain. Man has the free will to decide how he will interpret himself and his reality.

KEY NUMBER SIX:

Etymology & the Meaning of Names.

1) the history of a linguistic form (as a word) shown by tracing its development since its earliest recorded occurrence in the language where it is found, by tracing its transmission from one language to another, by analyzing it into its component parts, by identifying its cognates in other languages, or by tracing it and its cognates to a common ancestral form in an ancestral language - http://www.merriam-webster.com/dictionary/etymology

The names of characters in Holly-wood movies must be studied for their meanings in order to get the hidden messages that are contained in their definitions. For example, there may be a character named Thomas whose brother has died in the movie. The name Thomas actually means twin. So the hidden message in this character's name may be that his brother actually represented his lower self. The death of his brother actually represented Thomas' triumph of overcoming his lower self and is now able to portray the attributes of a hero, by defining himself through his higher self. All men have the freewill to define themselves by their higher or lower selves. Coincidently, all men have a twin.

I came to hear about etymology and what it entails by my studies of Malcolm X. It was in reading his autobiography that I first was introduced to this science. Malcolm used etymology to further understand and articulate the oppression Black people continued to be subjected to during his lifetime. I hope to use the same science of to further his struggle and commitment to free our people from the system that oppresses us without us even knowing it. We will refer back to this key when the appropriate characters are introduced in the storyline of the movie.

KEY NUMBER SEVEN:

Melanin: Miracles & Manifestation

There is a chemical called, Melanin, which is in abundance in darker skinned people or people of Afrikan descent. It is manufactured in the Pineal gland which is located in the center of your brain. Another name for it is called the third or first eye, because it allows you to see in the spiritual world. I labeled Melanin, "the fruit of the gods." Without this chemical functioning properly in the body, one cannot transcend into the spiritual world. In other words, people who are classified as European, because of their lack of Melanin, cannot experience the same quality of spiritual or higher consciousness experiences that people of color can. Europeans, generally have a calcified Pineal gland. Because of this, they cannot produce Melanin or the Melanin they can produce is of a weakened state or quality. Melanin allows the person to have access to experiences in the spiritual realm that are timeless and have no boundaries. In the book, "The Secret," they gave hints to this principle. But because it came from a European perspective, it sadly missed its mark. Basically, with Melanin, one can manifest like thoughts and energies and make them appear in the physical realm. This is a powerful tool one has access to. It is a sad state of affairs that people of color have never been exposed to this knowledge or have it explained to them. For good reason, the powers that be want the darker peoples of the world to keep focusing and giving life to their own agenda and not on the dreams of their own. Melanin is the key to accessing the spiritual realm. The soul is the driver of the body. With access to this knowledge, the physical realm is unlocked. Melanin has divine properties that allow the darker peoples of the world to manifest their thoughts and dreams into becoming reality in the physical dimension. For one to truly see, in the unseen world, the eyes need to be eliminated from the physical dimension. In other words, true sight comes from the Pineal gland or what's called the "first eye." This is how we are able to visualize dreams without the aid of our eyes. This is where true consciousness or sight dwells. For us to truly "see" on a spiritual level, our eyes have to be eliminated from the equation. If one can master this technique, one would be able to manifest whatever they desire from the spiritual realm to the physical realm. Also, mysteries of questions you had can be solved in this state of mind. Healing ailments of the body, in this state are also possible. Depending on the level of consciousness of the man, will dictate the limitless boundaries a couple could manifest during this state of consciousness.

There was an expression in ancient Kemet which said, "He who does not have a boat, cannot cross the river." That boat is the Pineal gland and the river is the Melanin it produces. People of European descent or classify themselves a white, because of their lack of Melanin cannot obtain a level of consciousness or humanity that the darker people of the world can obtain.

Melanin is what miracles are made of. In movies, you will see this concept played out over and over again. They won't call it by its name. They will use names such as, "The Force" in Star Wars, "The Spice Menage" in the movie "Dune" or the element "Unobtainium" in the movie "The Core" and "Avatar," Morpheus in the Matrix Trilogy movies, Sam the dog in the movie, "I Am Legend," The substance that turns Spider-Man black in, Spider-Man 3," Klatu's medicine in the movie, "The Day the Earth Stood Still," "Liquid Luck" in the movie "Harry Potter/Half-Blood Prince." Vibratium in the Marvel comic movies. We will refer back to this key when the movie presents this concept.

These are the seven keys to deciphering the hidden messages in movies. They may seem complicated or confusing at first glance, but I promise, if the reader takes their time in understanding these principles, the mysteries of Hollywood and its hidden agenda will be as clear as day. Devote yourself to looking at the symbols and science that I have laid before you and you will open yourself up to a whole new world of discovery. Empower yourself with this knowledge and the forces Hollywood tries to manipulate you with will be to no avail. Pass this knowledge to your friends and you both will be able to see things in movies that one of you might have missed. I have just scratched the surface to this science. The reader will be able to decipher symbols and images this author has missed in this book. This I guarantee. Hollywood is the unequivocal masters of this science. Once you have gotten familiar with this art form, one can appreciate the complexity and how sinister this knowledge can be if used for the wrong principles. When deciphering movies in the future, one will be able to witness the brilliance of Hollywood's evil genius. I have armed you with the keys you need. Let us put these keys to the test and dissect Hollywood's evil genius used to manipulate and control our behavior!

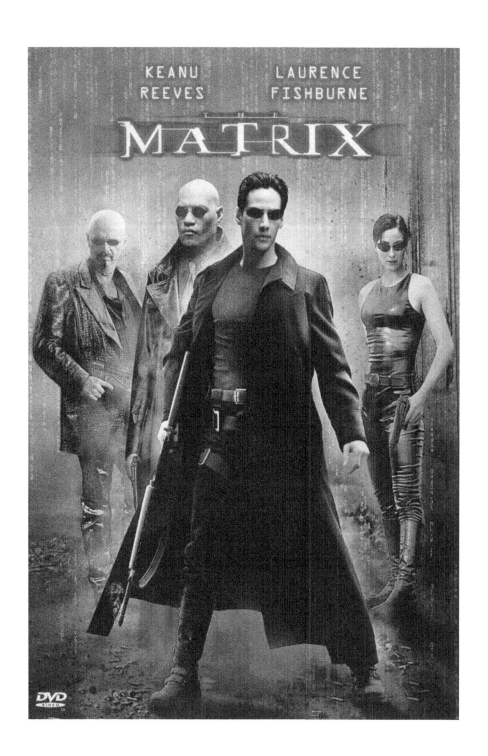

Contents

Character Assassinations & Breakdowns

Just by understanding the meaning of character's names, one can decipher the plot and theme of the movie before it has even started. Remember, everything in Hollywood is calculated and deliberate. There is no prop, symbol, name or image left to chance. Whatever name, prop, symbol or image that is in a film, is there because it serves a specific purpose. Hollywood is calculating and cunning. Its practices and methods are methodical and precise. They are masters and geniuses at the science they implement into the film industry. They create the illusion of chance to keep this knowledge hidden. There are no coincidences in Hollywood. We will break down the meanings behind the main character's names in the movie. Embrace and internalize their meanings when one views the DVD and one will be enlightened to a deeper understanding of what is being played out.

I suggest you use this book as a guide or blueprint when watching this particular DVD. Depending on how deep you want to get into dissecting the film, one can use the pause and rewind button on their remote control every time the book highlights a scene in the movie that is showing an occult sign or metaphysical message. In this way, the viewer will train their eyes to be able to decipher the esoteric codes when they view the movie a second time in its entirety. I highly suggest that you use the book when watching the movie instead of reading it without referencing the film. Although, reading the book without watching the DVD would give the reader ample satisfaction, reading the book while watching the DVD is a much more fulfilling and rewarding experience! Be patient during your first movie, as it can get monotonous, because of all the starting and stopping of the movie. Once you have memorized the seven keys, one will be able to decipher any movie they watch without the book. This book does not reveal all of the hidden messages in this particular movie. The viewer may find other hidden symbols and images the author has missed or left out intentionally. This book only gives its readers the foundation and blueprint for cracking the code in the Hollywood film industry. I hope the reader will find a rejuvenated passion that I have in deciphering the hidden meanings behind the symbols and images of Hollywood. Keep in mind, your friends and loved ones may consider you a little crazy at first, because of all the intricacies that you will point out to them that they have never paid attention to. Be patient with them and walk them through it and then you will all be able to enjoy movies from a different and much more fulfilling perspective.

Neo- This character represents the higher self of man. Man's higher self represents a man who views and defines himself and his reality through his spiritual self. This is a man who has mastered his lower self. Man's lower self is defined by his physical desires and urges. If a man acts like an animal, responding to and being enslaved by his lower nature, he cannot reach is higher, spiritual nature. Man's higher self is not limited to the rules and physics of the physical dimension. This is how Neo can circumvent the laws and physics of our seen reality. He is operating at his highest consciousness which is not mandated to follow the rules of the lower, physical dimension. Neo is allowed to make up his own rules and his own reality as he sees fit.

Man has been given free will to define himself and his reality as he pleases. Neo, meaning "new," defines the resurrection of man's higher self by the death or triumph over his lower, physical self. Thus, he is considered "born again" or has a "new "life. This is a "new" beginning by seeing life and defining reality for the first time, through the lenses of higher, spiritual consciousness.

Thomas Anderson- Thomas means "twin." Neo's real name is Thomas because every man has a twin. Every man has a higher self as well as a lower self. Man has the free will to define himself by his higher or lower selves. Thus, man has a dual nature from which to define himself. Thomas represents Neo's lower self and the name Neo represents his higher self.

Andrew means "from or of a man." This name represents Neo's lower self which is defined by his physical body. Neo's higher self is defined by his spiritual body. Also, Andrew was the first apostle to follow Jesus. Jesus can be represented as higher consciousness in the occult world. Thus, Neo was the first to transcend into his higher, spiritual consciousness.

It was also said that Andrew was crucified on a cross in the shape of an "X." The "X" in the occult world represents resurrection.

55

Resurrection can be defined as the putting to death of one's lower self and the rebirth of one's higher self. This is the only way to achieve higher consciousness.

Morpheus- meaning "shape." It refers to the shapes seen in dreams. In Greek mythology, Morpheus was the god of dreams. A deeper understanding of this character is that he represents the chemical Melanin. Melanin is secreted by the Pineal Gland at night when we fall asleep. Melanin is needed in order to reach higher consciousness or the spiritual dimension. Thus, in order for Neo to reach his higher self, he must activate his melanin. This is why this character is vital towards Neo's transformation. Melanin is the key to transcending into higher consciousness. Without it, one cannot attain this level of consciousness. This is why Morpheus is the one that shows Neo the matrix as well as believes unequivocally that he is the One, when the physical dimension has its doubts and uncertainties. Understand, with the activation of one's Melanin, one can create miracles and break the prison and the rules of the physical dimension.

Trinity- Gives homage to the ancient Kemetic belief of the three principles of life. They are, Masculine energy represented by the father or the god Ausar, the feminine principle of energy, represented by the mother or goddess Auset and the result of the union between the two energies, represented by the son or god Heru. These three deities represent the building blocks of not only life but the universe as a whole. They represent God's perfection in the physical dimension. Without these three principles, life could not happen. These three laws must be acknowledged and be present in order to manifest life from the spiritual dimension to the physical world.

The knowledge and mastery of these three principles of universal law is mandatory in order for Neo, who represents man, to transcend to higher consciousness. Thus, Neo needs "Trinity" in order to transcend into his higher self or consciousness. Without the knowledge of the "Trinity," Neo could have not succeeded in his undertaking. The Trinity or God's law of perfection must be mastered and implemented as a blueprint to raise one's consciousness.

The Oracle- This character represents God's insight, intuition and knowledge. The first concept of god in Afrika, which spread around the world, was god as a Black woman. This is why the Oracle is represented by a Black woman. She is the epitome of higher spiritual consciousness and awareness. The Black woman represents the quintessential knowledge of God. She is the one closest to the Creator so it makes sense that she has the best form of communication in the spiritual realm.

Switch- The name of this character represents the anomaly of homosexuality. Although this character is a woman, she displays characteristics of a man. This character has "switched" genders. In ancient Kemet, homosexuality went against universal law. Masculine or positive energy "gives out" energy. Feminine or negative energy "receives" energy. This is why opposites attract and likes repel. All substances in the universe must adhere to this law, from the largest galaxy, to the smallest sub-atomic particle. To go against this universal law was to go against nature. In Kemet, nature and God meant the same thing.

Switch is the only one that wears white clothing. She wears different sunglasses from the rest. She is the only one with blonde hair. These attributes led me to believe that the character Switch represents the Caucasian. Like homosexuality, the Caucasian goes against the laws of nature. Switch represents this character trait. She does not fit in, thus she disrupts the natural order of things. Same can be said of the Caucasian when they have come in contact with the darker peoples of the world. Check your history books.

Dozer- I believe this character is in reference to the Kemetic, Black pharaoh named Djoser. In Kemet, the pharaoh was considered to be a god in human form. Djoser was also known as Netjerikhet, meaning body of the gods. This is a clue into the insight of the true knowledge of god being contained in the body of the Black man. Djoser commissioned the first multiple genius named Imhotep, to build him the first step pyramid.

Agent Smith- From the English surname meaning Blacksmith. To smite or to hit. The definition of this character states it all. This character is Neo's arch nemesis. For true transformation to occur, one must be faced with adversity and struggle. One must challenge themselves physically, mentally and spiritually in order to achieve higher consciousness. Agent Smith provides this adversity for Neo. In that sense, this character enhances Neo's ability to transcend. Without him, Neo would never fully understand and appreciate his higher self. Agent Smith provides the litmus test or threshold Neo must master in order to achieve higher consciousness.

Cypher- Short for Lucifer. This is another name for Satan or the devil. In the occult world, man has the ability to define himself through God consciousness, symbolized by heaven or man's lower self, symbolized by the devil and hell. Heaven and Hell represent man's state of consciousness or state of mind and not a geographical location.

This character represents the lower self in man. He is driven by greed, selfishness, fame, wealth, material things and notoriety. He is motivated by and defines his reality through his ego. All these character traits represent man's lower consciousness. He defines his reality by his physical self and the physical dimension. This character represents the potential all men have to fall into a lower state of consciousness. Cypher represents the worst in all of us.

Apoc- Apocalyptic eschatology is marked by the conviction that God will intervene decisively in the present evil age and vindicate his suffering elect over their oppressors, raising the dead, consigning the wicked to eternal destruction, and establishing a new creation. - **http://encyclopedia2.thefreedictionary.com/Apocalypsis**

This definition states the theme to the whole movie. It is all about the righteous who are suffering now, will be vindicated in the future despite what it seems at the present moment. Never accept a reality based on the falseness of the majority. Always stand up for what is right and correct. You will be rewarded for your persecution even when it seems you are in dire straits.

Mouse- This represents the European's contribution to the universal knowledge of humanity throughout history. This character is puny in size and needs to be looked out for. He is like a child. He looks sickly. His two claims of fame in the movie are creating a food concoction that is a synthetic version of the original and also designing a computer program that taps into man's lower consciousness.

So Mouse, not being the "original" or Black man, represents the white value system and contribution to the world. His culture goes against nature or tries to conquer it. He is represented by his synthetic materials that pollute the Earth. The European also, designed a culture or society that appeals to man's lower self, instead of trying to raise man's consciousness. The European has mastered and built an "ego driven" society and uses man's lower consciousness as a means of control and manipulation. When compared to the Afrikan who, claimed himself a god on earth and had the greatest civilization known to man, the white man's contribution looks more like a mouse than a man.

Nebuchadnezzar- This is the name of Morpheus' ship. In the Bible, Nebuchadnezzar was a king who tried to force three captives into worshiping his religion and forgetting their own. When the three refused to worship the king's idol, they were thrown into a fiery furnace to be burned alive. The three men were protected by their god while in the furnace and escaped unharmed.

This story is directly related to the mindset one has to have in order to achieve higher consciousness. An individual has to "walk out on faith," in the midst of a hostile environment in order to manifest miracles. One must not be detoured by self doubt, fear, pain or ridicule if one wants to achieve higher consciousness. The fact that Morpheus and his crew, all took the red pill to reach higher consciousness, signifies they all took that "leap of faith" and overcame their fears for what they believed in. In the end, their faith was rewarded. This is the only way one can achieve higher consciousness. One must overcome their fears, ego and persecution for what they know is right. There is no other way to achieve higher consciousness.

Tank- This character represents the potential and under appreciation of the Black man. The name Tank can be referred to as a military weapon with strong armor. We know the physical prowess of the Black man to be the most elite athlete amongst all the races. He is a physical specimen that has no equal. For all the abuse he has taken throughout history, no other race would have been able to function let alone survive. This is irrefutable.

Also, tank can be defined as a vessel from which to carry pertinent or valuable cargo, information or substance, such as a water tank. In the Black man's body, mind and soul is the key to higher consciousness. He has yet to discover his true potential.

This character is the one who saves Neo from Cypher when he is about to unplug him. He is also responsible for finding the way out for all the Matrix characters when they are in the matrix. Tank is also the main pilot for the Nebuchadnezzar. He is its navigator as well as its mechanic. Tank is the underappreciated character in the movie who holds everything together. Just like the Black man in today's society. Without him, everything falls apart.

Sunglasses- The sunglasses the characters wear in the Matrix symbolize the activation of the Pineal gland, which produces the chemical Melanin. In Kemet, the activation of the Pineal gland was called the "First Eye." Melanin is also known for its black pigment, thus we have "black sunglasses" representing the higher consciousness or the activation of the Pineal gland of the characters that where them in the Matrix.

Telephone- One will notice that all the telephones are black in the movie. This is because the phone represents the intuition or internal voice inside the character that is activated by the black chemical called Melanin. Melanin is needed for one to reach higher consciousness. This is the only way the characters can exit or escape the Matrix, which represents lower consciousness. The characters usually hold it up to their left ear which symbolizes the activation of the right hemisphere of the brain which represents higher consciousness. So the telephone is actually the individual listening and trusting their inner voice or intuition. This is what guides and leads them into higher consciousness.

Chapter One: Trinity in a Jam

Summary:

Before the film begins we see the production company of the film. It is called Village Roadshow Pictures. Its logo is represented by 6 letter "V's" stacked on top of one another. There is a green tint to the start of the movie.

Metaphysical Breakdown

In the occult world, the letter "V" represents the feminine principle of energy. This is represented by the upside down triangle. This principle states that feminine energy is labeled as negative or has "no gates" or boundaries. Electrons, which are negatively charged, have no boundaries when they revolve around the positively charged proton. Negative energy receives energy and then manifests a new energy from the initial energy it accepted. Feminine energy "receives" energy. Since it receives energy, it is represented as a vessel or cup from which to hold the energy it receives, thus the "V" or cup shape.

In order to manifest or give birth to life, ideas or thoughts one must use feminine energy to do so. This is why the occult forefathers of this country distinctively placed the capital city of Washington D.C., which begins with the letter "W" which is represented by two "V's" coming together, in the middle of the states of Virginia, (the virgin) and Maryland (the name used to define the mother of God.) They wanted this location to give "birth" to the "New World" or the United States.

The fact that there are six "V's" that are stacked on top of each other also represents the concept of bringing art, concepts or film to life. In numerology, the number six represents the lower physical dimension. The number 6 looks like the number 1 which has gotten pregnant. The number one represents God in the spiritual realm. So the number six represents God's fall or manifestation into the physical realm by allowing itself to give birth in this lower dimension. The number one or God has given birth into the physical dimension. So this production company uses this occult science to communicate these concepts in its films. So right from the beginning the conscious viewer will know that films made by this production company will contain secret and occult symbols and esoteric and metaphysical science. We will discuss the use of the color green later on in the book.

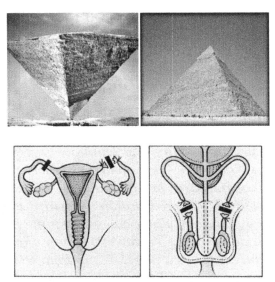

"The upside down triangle resembling the womb of the woman on and thus representing feminine principle of energy, on the left and the pyramid or triangle on the right, representing the erection of the man or the masculine principle of energy."

"The Kemetic symbol Sephedet. It represents the coming together of male and female energy to manifest the spiritual realm into the physical dimension. It was stolen by the so-called Jews that renamed it the Star of David or the Seal of Solomon."

Summary:

In the opening of the scene we see the title of the movie spelled out on the screen. All the letters eventually fade away. The last letter remaining is the letter "M."

Metaphysical Breakdown

The letter "M" is the thirteenth letter in the alphabet. The number thirteen in ancient Kemetic science, represents resurrection. (see Numerology.) Right away, we know that this film will be about raising oneself from a lower level of consciousness, to a higher level of consciousness. That is what resurrection truly means, nothing more nothing less. It represents the putting "to death" of lower level consciousness, so that one can be reborn into a higher level of consciousness.

Summary:

Next scene we see a computer screen that says: "Call trans opt: received. 2-19-98 13:24:18 REC: log>"

Metaphysical Breakdown

In numerology, these numbers add up to the number 13. As previously stated, this number is the symbol for resurrection. The putting to "death" of lower consciousness so that on can be reborn into a higher level of consciousness.

Summary:

Next, there is a series of numbers that randomly appear on the top of the screen. They are; 3, 5, 2, 5, 5, 6 & 9.

Metaphysical Breakdown

These series of numbers, in numerology add up to the number 8. This number signifies the state of the system or the Matrix we live in. If one does not change their consciousness and how they define and perceive their reality, the system will go on for an eternity. The number eight represents this concept of infinity.

This is why they say the concept of Hell is eternal. It is all about one's consciousness and how they define and perceive their reality. If a person is content with living in a state of lower consciousness, they will never change their reality or existence, thus they are condemned to live their lives in "Hell" for eternity. Hell is a state of consciousness, not a geographical location.

Summary:

Now we see three numbers on the screen. They are, 5 0 6. The camera focuses in on the number zero as if it goes through the middle of it.

Metaphysical Breakdown

Man is represented by the number "0." Man is an empty vessel from which to define his reality through experiences and thoughts that he chooses to internalize. The number 5 on the left side of the number zero, represents God's grace or favor in our undertaking. The left side represents our higher, spiritual consciousness because it activates the right hemisphere of the brain. This side of the brain houses our higher consciousness.

The number "6" being on the right side of the zero, represents our lower self or consciousness. It is located on the right side because the right side of the body is controlled by the left hemisphere of the brain. This hemisphere of the brain is responsible for our lower consciousness.

So the concept of this scene is pretty simple. Man has the free will to define himself through his higher consciousness on the left or his lower consciousness on the right.

Summary:

Now we see a police officer holding his weapon and a flashlight up to a hotel room door where Trinity is trapped in. The number on the door is 303.

Metaphysical Breakdown

In numerology, these numbers add up to the number 6. This number represents man as a beast or lower level consciousness. We can presume that there will be fighting, killing and animalistic behavior being displayed in this room. Look at the signs and one will be able to predict behavior of characters in films at a particular time.

Summary:

Trinity is seen seated inside the hotel room. Her back is to the officers. They tell her to put her hands on top of her head. You can see four lights from the flashlights of the officers behind her as she raises both hands displaying all ten of her fingers.

Metaphysical Breakdown

When you count Trinity's ten fingers with the four lights, one gets the number 14. In numerology, this number is broken down to the number 5. Five represents that God is on the side of the character that is being seen. God sees favor in Trinity's undertaking to escape and get out of the Matrix, even though she must display lower level behavior or consciousness.

Summary:

We then see the outside of the building. It is a hotel called the "Heart O' the City."

Metaphysical Breakdown

In ancient, Kemetic mythology, the goddess Maat must weigh an individual's heart in the afterlife for them to move on to heaven.

If the heart is not balanced or is "too heavy," the individual must go back to live another life until they learn their life lesson.

In this scene, the director is displaying this ideology. All moral and ethical battles a person has must be fought and measured in the "Heart" of the individual. The heart is ground zero.

Summary:

The agents show up in a car with the license plate number 70858.

Metaphysical Breakdown

These series of numbers add up to the number 10 in numerology. This number represents perfection. In this scene it refers to the building of the Matrix and the agents who keep it functioning. In the machines eyes, they have built a perfect system from which to enslave, oppress and imprison the humans of the earth.

Summary:

The police lieutenant tells Agent Smith, "I sent two units. They are bringing her down now." Agent Smith responds, "No lieutenant, your men are already dead."

Metaphysical Breakdown

The number 2 in numerology represents division or separation. In this scene this concept refers to Trinity's ability to escape from her would-be captives.

Summary:

The police have badges with the six pointed star on their chests and hats.

Metaphysical Breakdown

The symbol of the six pointed star originated in Kemet. It was called Sephedet. It represented the coming together of the masculine principle and the feminine principle to produce a manifested thought or being into the physical dimension. It is the coming together of two triangles to produce a hexagon in the middle of the symbols. One triangle is upside down representing the feminine principle and one right side up, representing the masculine principle. This hexagon is the "gateway" from the spiritual realm into the physical dimension.

The fact that they have it on their chests, represents the significance of the heart in the ability for an individual to use this knowledge. If the heart is not right, then one cannot use this science. Also, the star being in the middle of their hats represents the location of the pineal gland. If one does not have the melanin produced by the pineal gland than one cannot use this science as well.

Although, this symbol was adopted by the "so called" Jews in their flag and also the law enforcement field, they do not understand what it represents. But the makers of this film obviously understand these concepts and arrogantly display them in front of their ignorant audiences.

Summary:

As the police move to handcuff Trinity, the camera focuses in on the right side of her face, mainly her eye.

Metaphysical Breakdown

The right eye represents a person's lower or animalistic consciousness because it is controlled by the left hemisphere of the brain. The focusing in on this eye tells the viewer that Trinity is about to partake in lower level, animalistic behavior. In this case she breaks the bones and slaughters the policemen trying to apprehend her.

Chapter Two: Impossible Pursuit (3:30)

Summary:

Morpheus informs Trinity that the lines have been cut and that she has to find a new line. The new location is at Wells and Lake.

Metaphysical Breakdown

Trinity's character represents man's spirituality. In order for her to escape the Matrix, which represents lower consciousness, she must be born again or baptized into higher consciousness. Her escape from the Matrix is located at Wells and Lake. Both of these names suggests bodies of water. This is where Trinity will be "baptized" in order to be reborn into higher consciousness and escape the Matrix.

Summary:

Trinity is now on the run to escape the agents. Her first move is to follow an exit sign that tells her to make a left.

Metaphysical Breakdown

The answer or solution to Trinity's escape is signified by the exit sign that tells her to make a left to get out. It refers to her activating the right hemisphere of her brain which is responsible for her higher, spiritual consciousness. In ancient Kemet, they would signify the activation of higher consciousness by activating the left side of the body. The left side of the body, i.e. The foot, leg, arm, hand or eye, are all controlled by the right hemisphere of the brain. So for man to activate their higher, spiritual consciousness, he must move the left side of their body first.

Summary:

She heads for the roof tops. Her next move is to jump from one building to another with her left foot forward.

Metaphysical Breakdown

If you pay close attention, Trinity is able to defy the laws of physics by jumping from building to building. She does this by jumping out with her left foot forward. The left foot moving first activates the right hemisphere of the brain which is responsible for her higher, spiritual consciousness. When one activates their higher consciousness, laws and rules in the physical dimension can be manipulated, broken or tossed out altogether. Higher or spiritual consciousness does not adhere to the law of physics or any other laws in the physical dimension. The spiritual world or higher consciousness super cedes the laws of the lower, physical dimension.

Summary:

She is then seen running up and down roof tops that have triangular shapes to them.

Metaphysical Breakdown

This scene pays homage to the ancient Kemetic, mystery systems that secret societies and the occult world abuse and manipulate to control and oppress the masses. Trinity is running over the top of the pyramids. Their builders hold the secret knowledge that the secret societies use as the foundation to subjugate the masses under their rule.

Summary:

After she gets off these triangular roof tops, she makes another left to escape the agent's pursuit.

Metaphysical Breakdown

This is another occult symbol. The initial movement of the left side of the body activates the right side of the brain which contains man's higher, spiritual consciousness. For Trinity to escape the prison of the Matrix, she must activate her higher, spiritual consciousness.

Summary:

Trinity then makes a spectacular jump from one building to the next. She also jumps this building with her left foot first.

Metaphysical Breakdown

As we alluded to earlier, this is the ancient Kemetic symbol for higher spiritual consciousness. The initial movement of the left side of the body, activates the right hemisphere of the brain. This is where man's higher, spiritual consciousness dwells. Higher consciousness is not limited to the laws of physics in the physical dimension. This allows Trinity to do super human feats. It is all about the activation of man's higher, spiritual consciousness. This is the only way man can escape the Matrix, which represents the perversion of lower consciousness.

Summary:

An agent is seen landing on the building Trinity just leaped from. He lands with his right foot forward, in a kneeling position.

Metaphysical Breakdown

The agent is displaying the opposite of Trinity. He is initially moving his right foot first. The right side of the body is controlled by the left hemisphere of the brain. This side of the brain is responsible for man's lower level or animalistic consciousness. The agent wants to kill or enslave Trinity. He wants to keep her locked into lower level consciousness. This is the procedure of the elite, secret societies to control the masses. If one can keep the people operating at a lower level, they can be controlled, manipulated and enslaved. As soon as they recognize their potential to reach their higher selves, is the day they start to become free.

Summary:

In the far distance, Trinity sees a pane glass window in the shape of a cross. She runs to it and jumps through it to escape the agent. She breaks through the glass and lands safely. While lying on the ground, she is frozen in disbelief that she made the jump. She has to tell herself to get up and keep going.

Metaphysical Breakdown

The pane (pain) or cross in the window represents the religious institution, more specifically, Christianity. For Trinity to reach higher consciousness, she must break through the brainwashing of religious institutions and dogma. Religions are manipulated by the elite secret societies to keep the masses at a lower level of consciousness. Religion has been used to take God or higher consciousness out of man itself and place it in a mystical place in the sky, away from man's grasp. Once a person can break this reality and look within for the concept of God, they will be closer to attaining higher, spiritual consciousness. This is the way for man to free himself from the Matrix.

Because of the strong ties and beliefs that religion has ingrained in us, it is very difficult to break this level of consciousness. Trinity, displays this by freezing after she breaks the window pane cross. We are taught that we will go to Hell if we defy our religious beliefs. It takes Trinity a moment before she gathers herself and moves on. She realizes that nothing happened to her and that she will be okay. She continues on with her escape from the Matrix, or lower consciousness.

Summary:

Her right eye is noticeably covered by her hair. Her left eye is not covered. The broken window pane now resembles the letter "L" or a right angle.

Metaphysical Breakdown

The covering of Trinity's right eye is a symbol that she is operating at a higher level of spiritual consciousness. The covering of the eye represents the covering of lower consciousness behavior. The right eye is controlled by the left hemisphere of the brain. The left side of the brain is responsible for man's lower level, animalistic consciousness.

The "L" seen in the broken window, represents the number 12. In numerology, twelve represents the concept of completion. Trinity completed her "leap of faith" into higher consciousness, by breaking the grasp that religion had on her.

Summary:

Trinity reaches the phone booth. It also has cross symbols on its glass walls. The grill of the garbage truck also has this same cross pattern.

Metaphysical Breakdown

These are symbols of the religious institution that keeps man at a lower level of consciousness. Notice, the grill of the truck tries to run over and destroy Trinity. It is used to keep her from attaining higher consciousness represented by the phone.

Trinity also breaks a second cross inside the phone booth in order for her to reach higher consciousness through the phone line.

Summary:

The phone begins to ring inside the phone booth. The truck smashes the phone booth as Trinity puts out her left hand. Trinity has blood over her left eye. She escapes in the nick of time.

Metaphysical Breakdown

The black phone represents the properties of Melanin. For man to reach higher consciousness, they must activate the chemical melanin produced in the Pineal gland. It is through the phone line, which represents melanin that Trinity is allowed to reach her higher consciousness. It is the melanin or phone line that helps her escape the Matrix, which keeps her imprisoned by promoting and feeding her lower level, animalistic consciousness.

The fact that Trinity puts out her left hand and has blood over her left eye, before she escapes, is further proof of the activation of the right hemisphere of the brain which is responsible for man's higher, spiritual consciousness. These two actions call attention to this character trait or state of mind.

Summary:

As the three agents get out to inspect the wreckage, one of them replies, "She got out." The other agent is covering the left headlight with his body of the garbage truck so only the right headlight is visible.

Metaphysical Breakdown

The significance of the three agents represents Trinity's ability to transcend to her higher consciousness. The number three in numerology represents God's perfection in the physical realm. This is why there were three kings that followed the star to the place of birth of the Christ child. It is also why it took three days for Christ to resurrect himself after he was crucified. So the three agents represent Trinity's resurrection into higher, spiritual consciousness in the phone booth. In fact, Trinity's name signifies this concept

The covering of the left headlight of the truck so that only the right headlight is visible, is a symbol of lower consciousness housed by the agents in the Matrix. The headlights represent the "eyes" of the truck. The right headlight symbolizes the right eye and the covering of the left headlight represents the covering of the left eye. The right headlight being exposed represents the activation of the left hemisphere of the brain, which houses mans lower level or animalistic consciousness. The fact that the left headlight is covered represents the suppression or lack of higher, spiritual consciousness.

Chapter Three: Follow Instructions (6:36)

Summary:

This scene begins with the camera seemingly going through the letter "a" on the computer screen from the word "searching." The screen later says, "Manhunt underway."

Metaphysical Breakdown

The letter "a" is the first letter in the alphabet. In numerology, the letter "A" represents the number one. It relates to Neo being the "One." Morpheus is "searching" for the "One," which is Neo.

Summary:

Neo is seen sleeping on the right side of his face in front of his computer.

Metaphysical Breakdown

This is an ancient Afrikan, initiation ritual. The laying on the right side of the individual's body, suppresses the left hemisphere of the brain. This is where man's lower level or animalistic conscious dwells. The fact that the left side of the body is on top of the right and can move freely, suggests the superiority of the right hemisphere of the brain which contains the individual's higher, spiritual consciousness. Neo is ready to receive messages from his higher, spiritual consciousness.

Summary:

A message from Morpheus appears on Neo's computer screen. It says, "Wake up, Neo........." Suddenly Neo wakes up to view the message.

Metaphysical Breakdown

[The message that Neo receives is really from the activation of his melanin. When one seeks higher consciousness, they must

75

start to listen to their melanin or voice within for the answers to their reality. This is why Neo recognizes the message on the screen before he awakens. He is listening to his inner voice or higher consciousness for the first time.]

Summary:

The next message Morpheus leaves on Neo's computer says, "The Matrix has you." Neo responds by saying, "What the hell?"

Metaphysical Breakdown

[This scene relates to another Kemetic philosophy. Man has a higher self, represented by God, heaven or the spirit. Man also has a lower self, represented by Hell, the physical dimension or man defined as an animal. Man has the free will from which to choose how he will define himself and his environment.

Morpheus, who represents the activation of Neo's melanin, tells him he is in a lower level of consciousness environment called the Matrix. Neo confirms this statement by referring to this environment as Hell.]

Summary:

Neo then presses the Control key and then the "X" key on his keyboard.

Metaphysical Breakdown

[In ancient Kemet the symbol or letter "X" represented the god Ausar. Ausar was the first god that had the ability to resurrect himself. So the symbol or letter "X" in the occult world symbolizes resurrection. Resurrection can be defined as putting "to death" lower level consciousness, behavior and thinking and transcending into a higher level of spiritual consciousness, behavior and thought. The pushing of the "X" key on the keyboard symbolizes Neo's resurrection into higher, spiritual consciousness.

Neo's pushing of the control key on the key board symbolizes Neo taking "control" of his reality and consciousness.]

Summary:

Morpheus' next message tells Neo to, "Follow the white rabbit." Neo then presses the Escape key on his keyboard.

Metaphysical Breakdown

The symbol of the white rabbit pays homage to the "Alice in Wonderland" story where she follows the white rabbit into another reality or dimension.

Neo pushes the "Escape" key on the keyboard to symbolize his escape from lower level consciousness represented by the Matrix, into higher consciousness represented by listening to his melanin or Morpheus the voice or intuition inside of him.

Summary:

Suddenly, there is a knock at Neo's door. Neo asks, "Who is it? " The man on the other side of the door tells him his name is Choi.

Metaphysical Breakdown

Choi means one who governs the high mountains in Korean. The character Choi represents Neo's climb or ascent into his higher consciousness. Throughout history the idea of enlightened or spiritual men has been represented by climbing and isolating themselves on mountain tops to achieve their level of higher consciousness.

Summary:

Neo's apartment number is 101. He informs Choi that he is 2 hours late. Choi tells Neo that he has two grand. Neo takes the money and closes the door.

Metaphysical Breakdown

We see the number two being represented on three different occasions; 101, 2 hours and 2 grand. In numerology, the number two represents division or separation. This is Neo's introduction into higher consciousness by listening to his melanin represented by Morpheus. He is separating or dividing himself from lower consciousness into higher consciousness.

These three numbers also add up to the number six. In numerology, the number 6 represents man at his lowest level of consciousness. The fact that they are exchanging money for stolen programs attests to this level of lower consciousness motivated by material wealth.

Summary:

Neo retrieves a book entitled, "Simulacra & Stimulation." He takes out a computer disc and puts the money inside the hollowed out book.

Metaphysical Breakdown

This book sheds light on people's perception and reality which are based on illusions and paradigms that they define as truth for the simple reason that they have never questioned or sought truth outside of what has been forced fed on them. This book is a synopsis into the overall theme of the Matrix film, that theme being "Question Reality and Authority."

Summary:

The chapter Neo opens the book to is called On Nihilism.

Metaphysical Breakdown

The term nihilism is sometimes used in association with anomie to explain the general mood of despair at a perceived pointlessness of existence that one may develop upon realizing there are no necessary norms, rules, or laws.[2] ^ Bazarov, the protagonist in the classic work *Fathers and Sons* written in the early 1860s by Ivan Turgenev, is quoted as saying nihilism is "just cursing", cited in *Encyclopedia of Philosophy* (Macmillan, 1967) Vol. 5, "Nihilism", 514

The fact that Neo stores his programs and money in this chapter is very significant. It suggests that life is more than the working, buying and selling of material objects. People dedicate and work all their lives to acquire material things and their lives are still unfulfilled. This term generally describes the feeling when an individual comes to this tragic realization, usually after 35 years of service and loyalty to a company that could care less about you.

Summary:

Neo gives Choi the disc. Choi says, "Hallelujah. You're my savior man. My own personal Jesus Christ."

Metaphysical Breakdown

Choi responds to Neo in Christian terms. The concept of Christ can be found in ancient, Kemetic philosophy. They used the term Kerast to describe a person who transcended into higher consciousness. This person mastered their lower selves to achieve this level of Kerast or higher consciousness. This is why the character of Jesus was known as the Christ or Kerast. He mastered his lower, physical self to achieve this level of higher, spiritual consciousness.

So in the movie, Choi basically refers to Neo as his Christ or Kerast, which symbolizes Neo's journey into higher consciousness.

Summary:

Neo warns Choi if you get caught using that…. Choi interrupts and tells Neo, "I know this never happened. You don't exist."

Metaphysical Breakdown

Choi gives evidence that the whole mythical story of the Biblical Jesus Christ was really a take from the ancient Kemetic philosophy of spiritual awakening. By eluding that this concept or story never happened or took place and that the character of

Jesus in the Bible never existed. The ruling elite will periodically give hints or clues about the true nature or myth of Christianity.

Listen to Choi's line without taking into account Neo's dialogue. It spells it out as plain as day. Just listen to Choi's dialogue directed at Neo.

Summary:

Choi tells Neo, "Something wrong, man? You look a little whiter than usual."

Metaphysical Breakdown

The comment Choi gives Neo gives credence that the philosophy of the Jesus Christ myth comes from the ancient Afrikan civilization of Kemet. Being that these people were Black, Choi's character establishes that this was an Afrikan philosophy before Europeans stole it and called it their own. That's why he comments that Neo, who represents the ancient Kemetic, Kerast, looks a little "whiter" than usual. Neo is really a Black man acting out Afrocentric ideologies.

Summary:

Neo tells Choi, "Have you ever had that feeling if weren't sure if you were awake or still dreaming?" Choi responds, "All the time, its called mescaline. It's the only way to fly." Choi is a red head with green eyes.

Metaphysical Breakdown

Neo is referring to the properties of melanin that Black people naturally have that is secreted from the Pineal gland at night. Choi, representing the Caucasian, must use artificial means to give them the same effects. People with red hair and green eyes have the lowest doses or amounts of melanin inside their system. Mescaline sounds very similar to Melanin.

Summary:

Choi and his girl, Du Jour coerces Neo into going out with them. Neo sees the white rabbit on Du jour's left shoulder and decides to go with them. Neo's left side of his face is illuminated and the right side is in a shadow.

Metaphysical Breakdown

The illumination of Neo's left side of his face corresponds to the activation of the right hemisphere of his brain which contains his higher, spiritual consciousness. The shadowing of his right side of his face represents the suppression of the left hemisphere of the brain which houses his lower level or animalistic consciousness. The meaning of Choi's girlfriend's name, "of the day" or temporary. Which relates to Neo's lower consciousness status being raised to a higher consciousness.

Chapter Four: The Question (9:44)

Summary:

At the club. Choi and DuJour are seen sitting together. Behind them on the wall is a piece of art that resembles the Sun.

Metaphysical Breakdown

The Sun in ancient Kemet as well as the occult world, symbolizes consciousness, wisdom and overall awareness. Choi and DuJour brought Neo to this location for him to experience these attributes.

Summary:

Trinity introduces herself to Neo. Neo says, "The Trinity that cracked the IRS D-base?"

Metaphysical Breakdown

In numerology, these letters and numbers, IRS D-base, add up to the number five. Five represents God seeing favor in your undertaking. It represents God's grace. In ancient Kemet, the first concept of God was a woman. This is who Trinity represents to Neo. It is Trinity that ushers Neo into higher consciousness. It is Trinity who Neo cannot do without. Trinity represents Neo's spirituality that he must embrace in order to achieve higher consciousness.

Summary:

Neo in disbelief says, "Jesus." Trinity answers by saying, "What?"

Metaphysical Breakdown

We just explained that the first concept of God in Afrika, was a woman. Neo saying Jesus, who represents God in Christianity, is answered by Trinity as if Neo was calling to her.

Summary:

Neo responds by saying, "I just thought you were a guy." Trinity answers, "Most guys do."

Metaphysical Breakdown

Again, in western society, especially religion, there is a sexist attitude that permeates all facets of life. The concept of God is not excluded. Male chauvinistic culture produces male dominated ideologies, thus the concept of God became a white man.

Summary:

Trinity explains to Neo that he is being watched and is in danger. She steps to his left ear and tells him, "I know why you are here Neo. I know what you have been doing. You're looking for him."

Metaphysical Breakdown

The fact the Trinity chooses to whisper in Neo's left ear denotes that he is operating at a higher level of consciousness. The left ear is receiving the message from "God." This activates the right hemisphere of the brain which is responsible for man's higher, spiritual consciousness.

Summary:

Trinity further explains, "When he found me…he told me I really wasn't looking for him. I was looking for an answer. It's the question that drives us Neo. It's the question that brought you here."

Metaphysical Breakdown

The left hemisphere of the brain is responsible for logic and is very analytical. It defines reality through our five senses. If our five senses cannot detect it, this part of the brain tells us that it doesn't exist, no questions asked, problem solved.

The right hemisphere of the brain operates through intuition, creativity and imagination. It does not have the boundaries the left hemisphere of the brain has. So it has the capacity to question all reality no matter what it sees in the physical dimension. So for one to have higher consciousness, they must operate from the right hemisphere of the brain. The clear sign somebody is operating from the right hemisphere of the brain, is the questions and curiosity they ask and seek to know.

Summary:

Trinity says, "You know the question as much as I did." Neo answers, "What is the Matrix?" Trinity continues, "The answer is out there Neo. It's looking for you. And it will find you, if you want it to."

Metaphysical Breakdown

As we covered the concept above, it applies to this concept as well. Activating the right hemisphere of the brain which contains our higher, spiritual consciousness, allows our reality to be fully known if we actively try to seek it. But before that can happen, one has to be open to the many forms of truth. If we humble ourselves and are willing to master our lower selves, i.e. ego, we can unlock the mysteries of the universe. The answers are waiting for us to raise our consciousness so that they can be revealed from within.

Chapter Five: They're Coming For You (11:59)

Summary:

This chapter opens up with Neo's alarm clock going off while he is in bed asleep. The time on the clock is 9:18. Neo is laying on his right side.

Metaphysical Breakdown

In numerology, these set of numbers add up to be the number nine. This number represents man's judgment or test he must pass to move on to higher consciousness. If the number six represents man being born from the womb into lower consciousness, then the number nine represents turning the womb or the number 6 upside down. This is man's test when his world is upside down. This is a test of a man's true character, when he is put into an uncomfortable situation or forced to face adversity.

So right away the viewer knows that Neo will have to make a tough decision in order to move on to higher consciousness. Neo will be tested or his whole world will be turned upside down.

Summary:

The next scene shows the building where Neo works. It resembles a spinal column with thirteen floors if you count the tan areas of the building. The name of the company is called, "Metacortex."

Metaphysical Breakdown

This building represents Neo's spinal column. There is an ancient Afrikan system to measure consciousness that the Indians use to show levels of consciousness. This energy is called Kundalini. It travels up and down the spinal column according the level of consciousness of the individual.

The fact that there are thirteen floors is very significant. In numerology, the number thirteen represents the resurrection of man. Man's ability to go from lower consciousness and transcend to higher consciousness. This is why we see thirteen floors to the building where Neo works that represents his spinal column.

The name of the company on the building is called Metacortex." *When we split this name up we get Meta. Meta means to go beyond or transcend. The second part of the word is Cortex. Cortex is the outer, gray matter of the brain. So the hidden meaning of this name is for Neo to transcend and define himself and his environment above the outer layer of his brain and search deeper enlightenment, if he wants to attain higher consciousness or freedom.*

Summary:

Men are seen outside Neo's bosses' office. They are washing the windows.

Metaphysical Breakdown

This scene displays a simple concept in regards to what is happening to Neo's consciousness. Neo is being aware of the system of the Matrix and is "seeing" it for what it really is. The lenses to his eyes are being cleaned so that he can now see clearly. The washing of the windows is a metaphor for what is taking place within Neo's consciousness.

Summary:

Neo's boss tells him, "You believe that you are special, that rules do not apply to you."

Metaphysical Breakdown

Neo is finally believing in himself and listening to his inner voice to guide him. This is a very dangerous trait to have for those who wish to enslave the masses. Neo is breaking the chains of lower consciousness.

Summary:

Neo's boss continues, "The time has come for you to make a choice Mr. Anderson. Either you choose to be at your desk on time from this day forth or you choose to find another job."

Metaphysical Breakdown

This is Neo's judgment in the form of his bosses' ultimatum. Neo must choose to stay in his lower conscious state or transcend into higher consciousness.

Summary:

Neo responds by saying, "Yes Mr. Rhineheart. Perfectly clear."

Metaphysical Breakdown

The name Rhine derives from <u>Gaulish</u> Renos, and ultimately from the <u>Proto-Indo-European root</u> *reie- ("to move, flow, run"), which is also the root of words like river and run.[4] ^ [a](b) <u>"Rhine"</u>. *Online Etymology Dictionary.* Douglas Harper. November 2001. Retrieved 2009-02-10.

The last part of Neo's bosses' name is Heart. When we breakdown his name we get, the flow or movement of the heart.

In ancient Kemet, the ability to transcend into higher consciousness was all based on the measurement of a person's heart. The Kemetic goddess, Maat weighed a person's heart to see if they would transcend in the afterlife. So for Neo to transcend to higher consciousness, he must pay attention to the level or position of his heart. This is where he will be judged. It comes down to the movement or flow of his heart.

Summary:

There is a slight tint of green in this scene as Neo is distracted by the men washing the windows outside his bosses' office.

Metaphysical Breakdown

The green tint of this scene refers to the color of the heart chakra. As we covered above, it is the position and level of the heart which Neo will be judged in his pursuit of higher consciousness. Coincidently, the heart chakra is the first level of higher consciousness.

Summary:

Neo receives a package. It is black phone with no keypad. Morpheus is giving him instructions on how to escape the agents. Neo must trust Morpheus if he wants to escape.

Metaphysical Breakdown

As we stated earlier, the black phone represents the activation of Neo's melanin. This is what guides Neo. He must trust his intuition no matter what his lower consciousness tells him if he wants to attain higher consciousness and escape the Matrix. Morpheus is simply the inner voice of Neo, represented by the activation of his melanin. It is Neo's intuition, faith, fearless instinct and perception of his reality that must guide him.

Summary:

Morpheus tells Neo, "I have been looking for you. I don't know if you are ready to see what I want to show you but unfortunately, you and I have run out of time."

Metaphysical Breakdown

Neo's melanin has been lying dormant in Neo's system. Neo must reach a level of consciousness in order for his melanin to be activated. It has been waiting for Neo to embrace it. It wants to guide Neo to higher consciousness.

Summary:

As Neo bends down in his cubicle to hide from the agents, you will notice his left lapel or jacket turned up in the back to resemble a golden pyramid.

Metaphysical Breakdown

This is a symbol paying homage to ancient Kemet as the foundation or birthplace of this knowledge or science. It is very subtle but undoubtedly deliberate. This is the science the elites have turned upside down in order to control and manipulate the masses.

Summary:

Morpheus speaking to Neo, "I can guide you but you must do exactly as I say."

Metaphysical Breakdown

For Neo to break free of his lower consciousness, he must trust his intuition no matter what his five senses tell him what his reality is. Neo must let go and trust his higher self. Neo must have no inhibitions or fears.

Summary:

Neo escapes to an office with scaffolding on the outside of it. He must make a left to get there.

Metaphysical Breakdown

Neo must make a left to escape to the outside of the building. The making a left, activates the right hemisphere of the brain which contains Neo's higher, spiritual consciousness. For Neo to escape the Matrix, which represents lower consciousness, he must activate the right hemisphere of his brain.

Summary:

Morpheus tells Neo that he can use the scaffold to get to the roof. Neo tells him, "No way, no way! This is crazy!"

Metaphysical Breakdown

In the Matrix or lower conscious world, things and behavior seem to be crazy if we based our perception in lower consciousness. Higher conscious behavior seems foreign or illogical to a person viewing their actions based on lower conscious thinking. They would not understand the behavior and thus label it as "crazy."

Summary:

Morpheus explains, "There are two ways out of this building. One is that scaffold the other is in their custody. You take a chance either way. I leave it up to you." Morpheus hangs up as Neo says, "This is insane!" When Neo was talking, he was holding up the phone to his left ear.

Metaphysical Breakdown

Kemetic philosophy suggests that all men are born of free will. All men are also born of two natures, their lower self and their higher self. Although, Neo's melanin has guided him to safety up until this point, he still lets his lower nature, in the form of fear, keep him from transcending. Fear is what keeps man from achieving higher consciousness. Neo has the free will to decide how he will interpret himself and his reality.

Summary:

Neo starts to doubt and question himself. He starts to play the victim role. He is in a state of fear and self-doubt as he opens the window to get to the scaffold.

Metaphysical Breakdown

Neo has now lowered his consciousness and is operating according to his lower self. Fear, self doubt and stress keep individuals locked into lower consciousness. This is why the elite ruling class through the media always perpetuates a constant state of fear to the masses.

Summary:

While climbing outside the ledge of the building, Neo is petrified. This causes him to drop the phone. Neo is arrested by the agents.

Metaphysical Breakdown

Neo refuses to embrace his melanin. This is displayed by Neo dropping the phone. Neo has fallen back into lower level consciousness. To activate one's melanin, they must get rid of all fear and walk out on faith. Neo is operating on the basis of his fear. If fear is present, one's melanin will shut down. Neo's fear has dominated his consciousness. Consequently, Neo is taken into custody by the Matrix agents who represent the protectors of his lower consciousness.

Chapter Six: Unable to Speak (16:48)

Summary:

Trinity looks in her left, rearview mirror of her motorcycle. She sees Neo being taken into custody by the agents.

Metaphysical Breakdown

By Trinity looking in her left, side mirror, suggests that she has activated her right hemisphere of her brain which contains her higher consciousness. This is why she must leave Neo behind because he is stuck in his lower consciousness because of the fear he has displayed when his melanin was trying to guide him to higher consciousness.

Summary:

Agent Smith interrogates Neo. He has an earpiece in his right ear. He tells him, "It seems like you have been living two lives. In one life you're Thomas A. Anderson program writer for a respectable software company. You have a social security number. You pay your taxes."

Metaphysical Breakdown

Agent Smith's earpiece is in his right ear because he is motivated and receives instructions from his lower consciousness. The right side of the body is activated by the left hemisphere of the brain. This side of the brain is responsible for man's lower level or animalistic consciousness.

As we covered earlier, in Kemet, they believed man had two natures. Man has a higher, spiritual self as well as a lower animalistic self. It is man's free will to decide which level he will define himself and his reality. Thomas A. Anderson is Neo's lower self and Neo is his higher self. The Agents try to make Neo believe that his lower self is the way for him to be successful and his higher self will lead him to failure.

Summary:

Agent Smith then turns the top page of Neo's file. On the front page is and identification card for Neo. You must look very closely because the ID is upside down and they only give the audience a quick glimpse. It has an expiration date of 09/11/01. Below the ID is a photo that we see upside down. If you look to the top right hand corner of the upside down picture, you will see a yellowish/orange object that is in the shape of an airplane. The object looks like it is headed towards two computer towers in the upper, right hand corner of the picture.

Metaphysical Breakdown

This is a very peculiar scene in the movie. The Matrix film came out in 1999. That was two years before 9-11 took place. But in this scene, we see interesting signs that predict the events of 9-11. The first clue is the expiration date of Neo's identification card. That date is September 11th, 2001. Is it a coincidence? I highly doubt it. Remember, everything in Hollywood films is put in the movie for a specific purpose or reason. Nothing is left to chance. So this date on Neo's identification is very suspicious.

Also, on the page below Neo's identification card, we see an upside down picture that looks like a room with computer equipment. It is very hard to make out as Agent Smith turns the page quickly. But, the top right corner, we see this yellowish-orange, elongated, missile like object. It is lying down on a type of shelf and is pointed at two, what it appears to be computer towers. Could this be a sign of the planes hitting the "twin towers" otherwise known as the world trade center? I personally believe it does. Hollywood is known for hiding things in the last place people would ever look, in plain sight. This is a communication from the elite, secret societies that can be deciphered by those who have been initiated into the inner circle of the group.

Summary:

Agent Smith continues, "The other life is lived in computers, where you go by the hacker name alias, "Neo." One of these lives has a future and one does not."

Metaphysical Breakdown

Agent Smith further explains the two conscious levels Neo can become. Accept he says them in reverse because he wants Neo to stay in the Matrix where he will define himself through his lower consciousness.

Neo or his higher consciousness is the life that has a future not his lower consciousness defined as Thomas A. Anderson.

Summary:

Neo demands his right to a phone call. Agent Smith replies, "Tell me Mr. Anderson, what good is a phone call if you are unable to speak?" Neo's mouth then proceeds to close itself shut.

Metaphysical Breakdown

This scene is speaking directly to the rights and laws of this country. Our laws are written in a language called, "legalese." One has to be a master of this language to understand the legalities and rights to which citizens are privy to. The law is written in such a language to confuse those citizens who believe they know their rights. Because we believe we know the law and our rights in it, we are susceptible to its unforgiving system of enslavement and confusion. In other words, what good are rights, you if you don't speak the language to understand them? Neo believes he knows his rights but he does not. This is why he doesn't have a voice to take advantage of his said "rights."

Summary:

Neo is then placed on the table by the agents and a bug is inserted through his navel.

Metaphysical Breakdown

We are all running around scared that the "New World Order" is going to make it mandatory for all citizens to be implanted with a computer chip, so that the government can trace and control the masses at all times. I have news for you, it has already been inserted. The elite have you focused on an arbitrary computer chip in one hand, as they have already implanted a tracking device in you in the other hand. If you keep focusing on the computer chip of the future, you will never be aware of the other means they use to track you right now.

Don't you know that your cell phone has a tracking device in it? They can triangulate your position wherever you try to go, as long as you have a cell phone. In this day and age, from the ages of six years old to ninety-nine years of age, it seems like everyone cannot live without their cell phones. Did you know that the same cell phone omits signals to your brain in order to manipulate and control your behavior depending on the frequency they broadcast? Did you know your car also has a GPS system that they can use to track your location? Did you know that a majority of these cars have a system like "On Star" that allows them to eavesdrop on your conversations without you knowing it? Did you know those supermarket discount cards keep track of the day, location and time you purchase groceries, as well as develop a profile on you providing the information on the foods and products you use and eat? Did you know My Space, Face Book, and Twitter are used to mine and collect data on you regarding your family, friends, interests, hobbies, employment, lifestyle, income, sexual orientation and religious denomination? All this information is collected and saved in a personal profile they have gathered on you. They will then sell this information to advertisers or use it in the future to manipulate and control you if deemed necessary. Rewards cards, gas cards, store cards and credit cards are all used on you for the same purposes.

So Neo being bugged is a graphic illustration of what is literally being done to us without our knowledge in the real world today.

Chapter Seven: Getting the Bug Out (21:34)

Summary:

Next scene, Neo is awakened out of a dream. The phone rings. Neo picks up the phone with his left hand and holds it up to his left ear. It is Morpheus. He explains to Neo that he is the "One." He says, "You may have spent the last few years looking for me, but I spent my entire life looking for you."

Metaphysical Breakdown

Neo picking up the phone with his left hand and putting it to his left ear signifies that Neo is operating with his higher consciousness. The left side of the body is controlled by the right hemisphere of the brain. This side of the brain is responsible for Neo's higher spiritual consciousness.

The phone represents the activation of Neo's melanin. Melanin is represented by the character, Morpheus. Neo must be operating at a higher consciousness level to enable his melanin to speak to him.

Morpheus tells Neo that he has spent his entire life looking for Neo. This refers to Neo's higher, spiritual consciousness. Neo's melanin, represented by Morpheus, has been lying dormant within Neo's body waiting for him to reach his higher consciousness so that it can be activated and thus communicate with him.

Summary:

Morpheus tells Neo to meet him at the "Adams Street Bridge."

Metaphysical Breakdown

Neo is about to be resurrected into higher consciousness. This is represented by the death of his lower consciousness and the birth of his higher consciousness. This is where Christianity got the term being "born again."

Adam, in the Bible represented the making of the first man. This is the process Neo will have to go through to reach his higher consciousness. He will be made a new man in higher consciousness. The bridge is an esoteric symbol that shows the transformation from one level to another, as in "crossing" the bridge to get to the other side, which is higher consciousness.

Summary:

Neo is under the bridge. It is raining. We can see the rain pouring over the opening of the tunnel.

Metaphysical Breakdown

If you look closely, you will see the oval opening of the tunnel. This symbolizes the female womb. We see the rain or water pouring over the opening of the tunnel. This scene signifies the "rebirth" of Neo into higher consciousness or Neo being born out of the womb becoming Adam.

Summary:

A black Lincoln Continental pulls up to Neo. It has suicide doors. Trinity tells Neo to get in.

Metaphysical Breakdown

The make of the car being a Lincoln Continental is significant. As you recall, we were told that Lincoln "freed" the slaves. Neo is being freed from being a slave to his lower level consciousness.

Also, this car is known for its "suicide doors." This represents what Neo must do in order to reach his higher consciousness. Neo, has to kill the lower level consciousness within him in order to reach his higher consciousness. In a sense, he has to "kill" his lower self

Summary:

Switch tells Neo, "We don't have time for 20 questions."

Metaphysical Breakdown

In numerology, the number twenty breaks down into the number two. Two represents division or separation. This scene is a precursor to Neo separating himself from his lower self, represented by the Matrix, and reaching his higher self.

Summary:

Neo threatens to leave as they stop the car. Trinity stops him. She tells him, "Please Neo, you have to trust me, because you have been down there, Neo. You know that road. You know exactly where it ends. And I know that's not where you want to be.

Metaphysical Breakdown

The road Trinity is describing to Neo is his lower consciousness. She tells Neo that he has been "down" there and knows where it "ends." All these adjectives symbolize a low place of existence.

Summary:

Neo rethinks his leaving as he looks out the car door looking back over his right shoulder. He closes the door and decides to stay with Trinity.

Metaphysical Breakdown

Neo looking over the right shoulder is a symbol of looking back or leaving behind his lower level consciousness. The right side of the body is controlled by the left hemisphere of the brain. This part of the brain holds man's lower consciousness. Neo is moving forward to his higher consciousness.

Summary:

The bug is extracted out of Neo's navel. Trinity drops it on the road as the car drives by. The red light goes off symbolizing the bug has been deactivated.

Metaphysical Breakdown

The navel represents Neo's lower level chakras. This is the place the bug was inserted by the agents to control Neo's lower level or animalistic behavior and consciousness without him knowing that he was being manipulated. The fact that the red light goes out in the bug symbolizes the death of Neo's lower level chakras. Red is the color of the lowest, root chakra responsible for animalistic behavior.

Chapter Eight: Morpheus Proposal (25:09)

Summary

Lightning strikes outside the building. We see water pouring down the sides of the skyscraper. We see an aerial shot of the winding staircase inside the building where Morpheus is at. There is a black and white, checkered floor pattern on all the floors.

Metaphysical Breakdown

These are occult symbols. Lightning is electric. It is known as masculine energy. Water is magnetic. It is known as feminine energy. This shot is basically showing Neo being "reborn" in the scene. Skyscrapers are phallic symbols and the water is the feminine principle. So one can use their imagination and see what is being displayed in this scene that represents the "rebirth" of Neo.

The checkered floor is a symbol in secret societies. It represents the Kemetic, universal law of polarity and duality. Opposites are really extreme expressions of the same thing. It is the ancient Chinese concept of the yin and the yang. If black represents the past and white represents the future, what makes up the present on the checkered floor? We are in a constant flow or change of the "now." If the "now" is made up of the coming together of the past and the future, then the past and the future are made up of the same substance. They are extreme expressions of the same thing or concept.

Summary:

Morpheus is seen by a window in the shape of a triangle or pyramid just as lightning strikes outside.

Metaphysical Breakdown

Morpheus represents the masculine principle of energy by standing by the triangular shape window as lightning strikes.

The triangle and lightning are symbols of masculine energy in the occult world. This energy gives out intent or instructions to the feminine energy that surrounds it.

Summary:

Morpheus introduces himself to Neo. Neo tells him that it is an honor to meet him. Morpheus tells Neo that the honor is all his.

Metaphysical Breakdown

Morpheus represents the activation of Neo's melanin. The honor is on Morpheus because if Neo never raised his consciousness, Morpheus or Neo's melanin, would have remained dormant in his system. Because of this, Morpheus owes his recognition to Neo's

Summary:

Neo and Morpheus both sit on red leather chairs facing each other. Each chair has a face of a lion carved into each arm rest.

Metaphysical Breakdown

The color red symbolizes the root chakra. This is man at his lowest level of consciousness. This scene shows that both men have controlled or mastered their lower selves and are now ready to transcend into higher consciousness. This is shown by them "sitting on top" of the red chairs. This is a sign of domination over it.

The lions on either side of the arms of the chair represent a Kemetic symbol called, "Aker." The lion on the left hand side represents the protection of the person in the seat past. The lion on the right represents the protection of the person in the seat future. Now the person can focus on the present and manifest what he wills. His present is now secure.

Summary:

There is a glass of water sitting on a round table between them. Morpheus has his hands clasped. The left hand is over the right.

Metaphysical Breakdown

Water in the occult world symbolizes life or the ability to create new life, as in the concept of baptismal. Neo is about to create a new life for himself. The round shape of the table represents 360 degrees of knowledge. In this case, Neo has the knowledge of his reality to be able to transcend into higher consciousness.

Morpheus' hand placement signifies his right brain or higher consciousness is master over his left brain or lower consciousness. Left hand is activated is activated by the right hemisphere of the brain, which contains higher, spiritual consciousness. The right hand is activated by the left hemisphere of the brain which contains lower level or animalistic consciousness.

Summary:

Morpheus talks to Neo. He says, "Let me tell you why you're here. Because you know something. What you know you can't explain. But you feel it." "It is this feeling that brought you to me."

Metaphysical Breakdown

The feeling that Morpheus is describing, is Neo's intuition. Neo is in a "state of knowing." These are the properties of Melanin. Morpheus, who is representing Neo's melanin, makes this point so that Neo will realize his melanin is activated.

Summary:

While Morpheus is talking to Neo, he is twirling an object in the shape of a rectangle or square.

Metaphysical Breakdown

In ancient Kemet, to stand on one's square was to stand in good moral, intellectual and spiritual standing. A square has 4 corners. Each corner is 90 degrees. So standing on one's square meant the mastering of 360 degrees of mental, physical and spiritual knowledge. Morpheus is initiating Neo into higher consciousness. It is now Neo's turn to stand on his square and be accounted for.

Summary:

As Morpheus is explaining the Matrix to Neo his left leg is crossed over his right. Coincidently, Neo's left arm is perched higher than his right arm.

Metaphysical Breakdown

Morpheus' leg placement signifies his right brain or higher consciousness is master over his left brain or lower consciousness. Left leg is activated by the right hemisphere of the brain, which contains higher, spiritual consciousness. The right leg is activated by the left hemisphere of the brain which contains lower level or animalistic consciousness. Morpheus' left leg is in a dominant position over his right leg. Same can be said true of Neo. Neo's left hand or higher self is higher than his right hand, which represents his lower self.

Summary:

Neo asks Morpheus, "What truth?" Morpheus explains to him, "That you are a slave Neo. Like everyone else you were born into bondage. Born into a prison that you cannot smell or taste or touch. A prison for your mind."

Metaphysical Breakdown

The world has been forced to adopt the culture of Western society or Eurocentric ideology, because of imperialism, colonialism and now capitalism. This culture gets people to define themselves and their reality through their lower level or animalistic consciousness. This culture caters and feeds the ego with ideas of individuality, materialism, shame, fear, greed and gluttony. Because of this, man does not realize that he is even capable of higher, spiritual consciousness. Man does not define himself or see his reality through the lenses of his higher self because he has no knowledge that he possesses such a thing. Because of this, man is locked into a prison of lower level consciousness. The "prison for your mind" that Morpheus is talking about is the lock down of the right hemisphere of the brain, which contains man's higher consciousness and the constant bombardment and activity of the left hemisphere of the brain , which contains man's lower self.

Summary:

Morpheus explains to Neo that no one can show you the Matrix, you have to experience it for yourself. Neo will have to make the decision for himself.

Metaphysical Breakdown

In order for a person to transcend into higher consciousness they must have the absence of fear. Every person must make a "leap of faith" when their lower consciousness is telling them that they are crazy for doing so. This is the threshold or initiation everyone must pass in order to operate at a higher consciousness level. People cannot do it for you. Every person as an individual must decide for themselves. It is a personal decision in everyone's lives. It is man's free will to decide for himself.

Chapter Nine: Down the Rabbit Hole
(28:51)

Summary:

Morpheus gives Neo the option of two pills. The red pill shows him a new reality and truth while the blue pill takes him back to the mundane life he is living in.

Metaphysical Breakdown

The red pill represents Neo's higher consciousness and the blue pill represents Neo's lower consciousness. It is Neo's free will to choose which one he will define himself and his reality through.

Summary:

Neo grabs the red pill with his left hand and swallows it.

Metaphysical Breakdown

The red pill, representing higher consciousness, is taking by Neo with his left hand, which also represents higher consciousness. The left hand activates the right hemisphere of the brain, which contains higher, spiritual consciousness.

Summary:

Trinity puts electrodes on Neo's left ear, arm and neck. None on his right side.

Metaphysical Breakdown

The left side of Neo's body represents his higher consciousness. The left side of the body is activated by the right hemisphere of the brain. This side of the brain is responsible for his higher, spiritual consciousness.

Chapter Ten: Slimey Rebirth (32:25)

Summary:

Neo is seen in a pod type structure. He looks like he is being awakened and born again. He reaches out with his left arm first to break the casing of the pod. The pod's liquid gel has a red hue to it.

Metaphysical Breakdown

Neo is represented in the womb. The liquid is red because it represents Neo's birth into the real material world. Neo is going through the process of his initiation into higher consciousness.

Neo reaches out and breaks the casing of the womb with his left hand to symbolize the activation of the right hemisphere of the brain which contains his higher, spiritual consciousness.

Summary:

Behind Neo's pod structure are six, six pointed stars or symbols.

Metaphysical Breakdown

As mentioned earlier in our Metaphysical Breakdown, the six pointed star represents the ancient Kemetic symbol Sephedet. It is the coming together of feminine and masculine energy to manifest the spiritual world or thoughts into the physical dimension.

Summary:

Neo looks all around him and sees several sky scraper structures with thousands of pods creating electricity for the robot machines.

Metaphysical Breakdown

Neo realizes that he has been asleep in his lower consciousness his whole life. He also sees the masses of people who have been asleep with him. The Matrix or the system has been using his energy and the other masses of people's energy, for their own benefit and have given them nothing in return but unattainable dreams and illusions of happiness. The is the master plan of the elite ruling class and secret societies.

Summary:

A robot machine confronts the awakened Neo. It looks like a scarab beetle. It instantaneously turns into a spiderlike creature. It then presumes to unplug Neo from the back of his neck and flush him down this pipe like structure, into a large body of water.

Metaphysical Breakdown

The scarab beetle in Kemet was called Khepera. It represented the ability for man to transcend from lower level of consciousness, to a higher level of consciousness.

When the robot realizes Neo is awake, he has no use for him. He flushes him down the toilet as to disregard him as waste. Once a person's conscious is raised, the system has no use for you. This is why they assassinate our leaders that expose the truth about the system we live in.

The back of the neck is where the Medulla Oblongata is located. This part of the brain is where thoughts are stored in the process of manifesting them into reality in the physical dimension. Because Neo discovers his higher consciousness, he now has access to this part of the brain that the Matrix was using to manifests its ideas into reality. Neo now has full access to his own Medulla Oblongata and can start using it for his own benefit and not the system that enslaves him. Neo can now create his own miracles instead of being used by the system that enslaves him.

The Scarab Beetle in ancient Kemet. Notice the three sections on top of the beetle's body. This configuration is the same as the fused bone plates on top of the human skull. This represented higher consciousness. The Scarab Beetle holds many other esoteric symbols and meanings as well.

Summary:

Neo struggles to stay afloat. Immediately, a window opens from above. A six armed, metal claw grabs Neo's lifeless body. Neo is spread out as the claw raises Neo towards the light up above him.

Metaphysical Breakdown

Neo is seen in this bottomless, dark pit filled with water. He is drowning. This is Neo's lower consciousness. This is how far he has fallen. The crane with six arms represents the six pointed star called the Sephedet. It represents the manifestation and the transformation of Neo from his lower consciousness to his higher consciousness. The crane "raises" Neo up to his higher consciousness. Neo has just been resurrected or "born again" into the real world. This is Neo's initiation into higher consciousness. It mimics the story of Jesus' resurrection from the Bible which stole it from Kemet.

Summary:

 The opening space Neo enters into resembles a square with three spotlights around its outside edges.

Metaphysical Breakdown

The square that Neo passes through is equal to 4 ninety degree angles. The angles add up to 360 degrees. They represent the knowledge needed for one to go from lower consciousness to higher consciousness. The three lights represent, in numerology, the perfection of God in the physical dimension. Just like the character of Jesus in the Bible was resurrected on the third day, our character Neo is resurrected with the three lights in the background.

Summary:

When Neo is raised into the Nebuchadnezzar, we see an "X" symbol behind his right side.

Metaphysical Breakdown

The "X" symbol is associated with the first god in Kemet who had the ability to resurrect himself, his name was Ausar. Neo has completed his resurrection.

In the picture above, we see the god Ausar, on the left in white, with the "X" on his chest, welcoming King Tut into eternal life.

Summary:

Morpheus tells Neo, "Welcome to the real world." The left side of Morpheus' face is illuminated while the right side of his face is in a shadow.

Metaphysical Breakdown

The shadowing of Morpheus' face emphasizes the activation of Neo's higher consciousness represented by the left side of Morpheus' face being illuminated while the right side of his face is in a shadow. Left side of the face represents the activation of higher consciousness housed in the right hemisphere of the brain. The right side of the face in shadow, represents the suppression of the left hemisphere of the brain, which houses lower consciousness.

Chapter Eleven: Nebuchadnezzar's Crew
(35:22)

Summary:

Morpheus speaking to Trinity says, "We've done it Trinity. We have found him." Trinity responds, "I hope you're right." Morpheus adds, "I don't have to hope, I know it."

Metaphysical Breakdown

Morpheus represents the activation of Neo's melanin. Once embraced in Neo's higher consciousness, Neo transcends into a "state of knowing." This enables him to understand the mysteries of the universe without thought or study. He knows that which he knows without equivocation.

Summary:

Neo awakens and ask Morpheus, "Am I dead?" Morpheus responds, "Far from it."

Metaphysical Breakdown

Neo has completed his resurrection. He has "killed" his lower consciousness and transcended to his higher self.

Summary:

Neo is lying on an operating table. The crew has inserted him with various needles throughout his body. Neo asks, "Why do my eyes hurt?" Morpheus tells him, "You've never used them before." "Rest Neo, the answers are coming."

Metaphysical Breakdown

In ancient Kemet the Pineal gland was called the first eye. This gland produces the melanin one needs to activate to have higher consciousness. Morpheus, representing Neo's melanin, tells him that he has never used his eyes before that is why they hurt. He is referring to Neo's Pineal gland. This is why he tells Neo that the answers are coming. Neo, in his higher consciousness, will be in a "state of knowing.

Summary:

Neo is seen resting in his bunk. He has both hands lying across his body. His left hand is higher than his right hand. The left hand is over his heart while the right hand is over his solar plexus.

Metaphysical Breakdown

The fourth chakra is the heart. It is the first chakra of higher consciousness. That is why Neo's left hand is placed on his heart. The left side of the body is controlled by the right hemisphere of the brain, which is responsible for higher consciousness.

His right hand is below his heart to symbolize that his higher consciousness dominates his lower self. The right hand is activated by the left hemisphere of the brain, which is responsible for lower level consciousness. The solar plexus is where the third chakra is located. This chakra is responsible for man's desires, passions and motivation.

Summary:

Neo proceeds to take the IV of out of his left arm so that he may get up and walk around.

Metaphysical Breakdown

Neo was being fed and sustained through the IV in his left arm. The left arm is activated by the right hemisphere of the brain, which higher consciousness was being nurtured or fed.

Summary:

Morpheus tells neo that the year is closer to 2199.

Metaphysical Breakdown

In numerology, 2199 breaks down to be the number three. Three represents the divine perfection of the God in the physical realm. In this case, it represents Neo's transformation and resurrection into higher consciousness.

Summary:

Morpheus introduces Neo to his crew as he takes a tour of the ship. He recognizes Trinity as she is seen with her hair covering her right eye.

Metaphysical Breakdown

The covering of Trinity's right eye symbolizes her suppression of her lower consciousness. The right eye is activated by the left hemisphere of the brain, which represents lower, animalistic consciousness.

Summary:

Morpheus introduces his crew. Switch has white hair and Cypher has a blood red tank top over his shirt. These two characters are the only ones that have features or characteristics that stand out from the others.

Metaphysical Breakdown

Switch's character represents homosexuality, or the going against the natural order of things. While everybody is dressed in black, she represents the opposite by wearing white.

Cypher represents Satan, the devil or man's lower self. He wears red because red is the color of the first, root chakra. This chakra represents man as an animal that is ruled by his physical desires and self-survival.

Summary:

Morpheus tells Neo, "The only way to find out what the Matrix is, is to see it for yourself." Neo's left side of his faces is illuminated and the right side is in a shadow.

Metaphysical Breakdown

Neo has to take the leap of faith himself from his lower consciousness to his higher consciousness. No one can do it for you. Each individual must do it on their own accord. No one can do it for you. It is a personal decision to define and change yourself and your reality.

The left side of Neo's face is illuminated because it is activated by the right hemisphere of the brain which represents man's higher consciousness. The right side of his face is in a shadow to represent the suppression or exclusion of his lower consciousness. The right side of the body is activated by the left hemisphere of the brain, which represents man's lower consciousness.

Chapter Twelve: The Real World (38:40)

Summary:

Morpheus and Neo are inserted in the construct. There is a close up of Neo's left eye before he goes in. Morpheus is seen posing with his left hand pointed up and his right hand pointed down.

Metaphysical Breakdown

The focus on Neo's left eye represents the activation of his higher consciousness.

Morpheus assumes the pose of the Free Masonry god called, Baphomet. But in Morpheus' pose he has his arms raised in the opposite direction of Baphomet. Morpheus left hand pointing up to the sky represents the promotion and activation of his higher consciousness. The left arm is activated by the right hemisphere of the brain which represents higher consciousness. Morpheus also points his right arm down to the ground. This represents the suppression and exclusion of man's lower consciousness. The right side of the body is controlled by the left hemisphere of the brain that represents man's lower consciousness.

Consequently, Baphomet has his arms positioned in the opposite direction as Morpheus, who represents the activation of Neo's melanin. That's because the ruling elite or secret societies want to suppress the masses ability to reach their higher consciousness and at the same time want to feed the lower consciousness of the masses so that they will be susceptible to manipulation, brainwashing, oppression and control.

President Obama and all others who take the "oath" in government or civil positions must assume the position of the Free Masonry god, Baphomet. This is where their true allegiance lies. It is in the conspiracy to keep the masses at a lower level of consciousness so that the secret, ruling elite can enslave, manipulate and control the masses.

Summary:

After this pose, Morpheus then puts his hands together, in the shape of an upside down triangle over his genital region.

Metaphysical Breakdown

This symbol represents the feminine principle of energy. This principle represents the spiritual or higher self of man. Morpheus, who represents the activation of Neo's consciousness, is "giving birth" to Neo's higher consciousness.

Summary:

Neo is wearing a dark green shirt and Morpheus is wearing a lime green tie.

Metaphysical Breakdown

Green is the color of the fourth chakra. It is the first level of higher consciousness. It is located at the heart. This is where both men are operating from. Their higher consciousness allows them access to this realm or dimension.

Summary:

We are shown the back of an old television. It also has the symbol of the upside down pyramid. It says, "Deep Image" over it.

Metaphysical Breakdown

As we covered earlier, this symbol represents the principle of feminine energy. It represents higher, spiritual consciousness. Because of this characteristic, everything view through higher consciousness will have a deeper meaning or understanding to that person.

Summary:

Morpheus asks Neo, "What is real? How do you define real? Real is simply electrical signals interpreted by your brain."

Metaphysical Breakdown

The brain deciphers a person's reality and how they define themselves. To be left brain dominant is to view and define reality and self through one's lower level or animalistic consciousness. To be right brain dominant is to view and define reality and self through one's higher or spiritual consciousness. These two views will give you opposite definitions of the exact same thing, depending on which hemisphere of the brain you are operating at.

117

Summary:

Morpheus picks up the remote with his left hand and turns on the TV.

Metaphysical Breakdown

The left hand represents Morpheus' higher consciousness. This is how Morpheus will interpret his environment and the world around him. This is shown by him turning on his reality, represented by the television, with his left hand. The left hand is controlled by the right hemisphere of the brain which represents higher consciousness."

Summary:

Morpheus sits down on the chair to the right of the TV. The chair is red and has a diamond-shape pattern on the back of it. Neo never sits down. He places his left hand on the chair only. Morpheus shows Neo what the real world really looks like. It is barren, gloomy and dark.

Metaphysical Breakdown

The two, red chairs represent the two hemispheres of the brain. The television, in the middle, represents the Pineal gland or first eye. Morpheus sits on the chair on the right, facing the T.V. This represents the right hemisphere of the brain which represents higher consciousness and the activation of Neo's melanin. When Neo views the world through his first eye or Pineal gland, he sees what the real world is really like. Neo never sits in the chair on the left of the T.V. because it represents the left hemisphere of his brain which represents his lower consciousness.

Summary:

They have now fallen into this gloomy abyss as Morpheus explains how the world has gotten to this point. Morpheus says, "Welcome to the desert of the real."

Metaphysical Breakdown

Morpheus, representing Neo's melanin, shows him how far he has fallen in regards to the reality that he chose to accept when he was imprisoned in the Matrix.

Summary:

Morpheus explains, "All of mankind was united in celebration. We marveled at our own magnificence as we gave birth to AI."

Metaphysical Breakdown

The term "mankind" refers to Caucasians in their imperialistic agenda to take over the world. All of Europe was united in oppressing the darker people of the world and controlling their resources through colonialism, slavery and religion.

A.I., meaning artificial intelligence, refers to the thinking of Caucasians. Because of their calcified Pineal gland and lack of melanin, they cannot view the world and their environment through the higher consciousness of the right hemisphere of their brain. Because of this, they are very analytical, logical and limited when it comes to spirituality. In Kemet, intelligence was measured by one's spirituality and their ability to decipher that God, wisdom, nature and intelligence were all housed in one universal law. So intelligence without spirituality or higher consciousness is called Artificial Intelligence. It is driven by man's lower consciousness in the form of the Ego.

Summary:

Morpheus explains, "A singular consciousness that spawned an entire race of machines."

Metaphysical Breakdown

This exclusive way of thinking, left brain dominant or artificial intelligence, was forced on the darker peoples of the world to enslave and oppress them in the effort to use their energy and resources for the betterment of their oppressor. They were made slaves or machines to the European throughout the world.

Summary:

He continues, "We know it was us who scorched the sky. At the time they were dependant on solar power and it was believed that they would be unable to survive without an energy source as abundant as the Sun."

Metaphysical Breakdown

People of Afrikan descent or people of color, have the highest concentrations of melanin. Melanin is activated by the Sun. The Sun supercharges the melanin in indigenous people, thus when you take away the Sun, you take away the people's ability to reach their higher, spiritual consciousness.

Summary:

Throughout human history we have been dependant on machines to survive. Fate, it seems, is not without a sense of irony."

Metaphysical Breakdown

Morpheus, speaking on the behalf of Caucasians, explains the dynamics of imperialism, colonialism and later, capitalism. Sooner or later this unbalanced system will turn against them. Darker peoples of the world will wake up and see their indigenous culture is the key to their freedom and happiness and not the Eurocentric culture that they were forced to accept.

Summary:

"There are endless fields where human beings are no longer born, we are grown."

Metaphysical Breakdown

The fields Morpheus is talking about is the environment or community that Black people and darker people of the world are subjected to. These communities are infested with poverty, drugs, guns, substandard housing, education, health care, nutrition, false religion and hopelessness. The product of all this lower level energy is a group of people or population that can be used and manipulated to serve the purposes of those who control their reality.

Summary:

"I watched them liquefy the dead so that they could be fed intravenously to the living." They show a white baby, lying on its left side, as the metallic liquid is fed to him.

Metaphysical Breakdown

This scene symbolizes the Secret Society agenda of sacrificing Black lives and resources, for the consumption, betterment, power of the Illuminati, through the implemented and sustained system of white supremacy.

Summary:

Morpheus continues, "What is the Matrix? Control." He then turns off the TV with the remote in his right hand. "The Matrix is a computer generated dream world. Built to keep us under control, in order to change a human being into this." Morpheus holds up a battery with his left hand.

Metaphysical Breakdown

Morpheus shows by turning off the T.V. with the remote in his right hand and saying the word "control", how the system manipulates and controls the masses. The control Morpheus is talking about is the promotion and activation of the left hemisphere of the brain which is controlled by the right hand. This part of the brain is responsible for lower level, animalistic consciousness. The "powers that be" control the masses by manipulating, feeding and nurturing their lower level, animalistic consciousness housed in the left hemisphere of their brains. This way they can predict and manipulate their behavior as well as, inhibit their potential for higher, spiritual consciousness.

Summary:

Neo wants out of the construct. He starts to panic and starts to hyperventilate. He does not believe what he has seen and cannot face the truth. He eventually passes out.

Metaphysical Breakdown

Neo is having a difficult time of switching his consciousness. Neo is struggling with defining his reality and self image. He is transitioning from being left brain dominant, which is lower level consciousness to becoming right brain dominant, which represents his higher consciousness.

Chapter Thirteen: The Search is Over
(44:23)

Summary:

Morpheus apologizes to Neo. Neo is lying on his left side. He explains, "We never free a mind once it has reached certain age. It's dangerous. The mind has trouble letting go."

Metaphysical Breakdown

The position of Neo lying on his left side symbolizes that he is suppressing his higher consciousness. Neo's right side is on top of his left side. Neo's right side of his body is activated by the left hemisphere of the brain which represents lower level or animalistic consciousness, thus Neo's lower consciousness dominants his higher consciousness.

Neo doubts his decision to transcend into his higher consciousness. Fear is a trait of lower consciousness. Neo is letting his fear keep him from attaining his higher consciousness.

Summary:

Morpheus says, "As long as the Matrix exists, the human race will never be free."

Metaphysical Breakdown

As long as this system promotes man's lower consciousness and suppresses man's higher consciousness, the human race will always be enslaved. It is the mindset that will set man free, not the freedom of the physical body, for as the mind goes, the body must follow. Not the other way around.

Summary:

Morpheus tells Neo that he believes his search is over in finding the one the Oracle has talked about that would end the war and free his people. Neo turns over from his left side and looks at Morpheus.

Metaphysical Breakdown

Morpheus, representing Neo's melanin, now tells him that he is the key to the people's freedom. Neo has internalized this statement by Morpheus. He shows his belief by getting up from his left side and looking up at Morpheus. This movement shows that Neo has raised his consciousness. The left side of Neo's body is activated by the right hemisphere of the brain, which represents his higher consciousness. Neo is now operating in his higher consciousness displayed by repositioning of his body.

Chapter Fourteen: Training Begins (46:33)

Summary:

Neo is seen sitting in a fetal position. Tank opens the round door to this small room and introduces himself to Neo as his operator.

Metaphysical Breakdown

This scene represents Neo's "rebirth" into his higher consciousness. The room Neo is sitting in represents the womb. Neo is in the same fetal position as a new born baby. Tank opens the round door which represents the birth canal. Neo is being "reborn" into higher consciousness, which allows him to soak up information at an alarming rate.

Summary:

Tank explains to Neo that he and his brother Dosier are the only ones left that were not born in the Matrix.

Metaphysical Breakdown

Tank and his brother are of Afrikan descent. This a clue and key point that suggests the original man on Earth, was the Black man. All knowledge and civilizations around the world started in Afrika.

Summary:

Tank downloads program after program into Neo's brain. Neo is insatiable. His appetite for knowledge cannot be satisfied.

Metaphysical Breakdown

The human being only uses 15% of their brain power. Neo, having activated his dormant, higher consciousness in the right hemisphere of his brain, can now access a higher percentage of his brain capacity.

Chapter Fifteen: Morpheus/Neo Matchup (48:57)

Summary:

Morpheus explains to Neo that certain rules in the Matrix can be bent while others can be broken.

Metaphysical Breakdown

When one operates according to their higher, spiritual consciousness activated in the right hemisphere of the brain, they are not subjected to the rules and physics of the lower, physical dimension. Because they define themselves through their spiritual self and not their physical self, they can bypass the laws of the physical dimension. The spirit world is more powerful than the physical world. Laws of the physical dimension do not apply to spiritual beings.

Summary:

Morpheus kicks Neo in the gut. Neo is beaten. Morpheus tells Neo, "How did I beat you?" Morpheus looks down at his left hand with his right hand behind his back.

Metaphysical Breakdown

Morpheus is showing that he is using his higher consciousness to defeat Neo who is still learning to transcend from lower consciousness to his higher self. By Morpheus, looking down at his left hand, he is hinting to the activation of the right hemisphere of his brain, which represents his higher, spiritual consciousness. The fact that he hides his right hand behind his back, symbolizes the suppression of the left hemisphere of his brain, which represents his lower consciousness.

Summary:

Mouse looking at Neo fighting comments, "Jesus Christ, he is fast!"

Metaphysical Breakdown

Mouse is calling Neo by the name of Jesus Christ. Jesus the Christ represents the ancient Kemetic level of higher consciousness called, Kerast. Kerast represents man who has mastered his physical, lower self in order to achieve his highest, spiritual consciousness. This is what allows Neo to breaks the laws of physics in the physical dimension. He is starting to operate and define himself and his environment based on his higher, spiritual self.

Summary:

Morpheus tells Neo, "What are you waiting for. You know you are faster than this. Don't think you are, know you are." He waves to Neo to come on with his left hand.

Metaphysical Breakdown

The act of Morpheus waving to Neo to come on with his left hand, is signaling to Neo to use his higher consciousness which is represented by the right hemisphere of his brain. Once he is operating according to the perception of his higher consciousness, he will be in a state of "knowing." In this state, one does not have to practice or study concepts over time in order to master them. They just know instantaneously.

Summary:

Morpheus tells Neo, "C'mon stop trying to hit me and hit me!"

Metaphysical Breakdown

Morpheus is urging Neo to operate in his higher consciousness. In his higher consciousness, Neo doesn't have to try, he just does.

Summary:

Neo holds back from striking Morpheus with his left fist.

Metaphysical Breakdown

The left fist represents the activation of Neo's right, hemisphere of the brain which the activation of his higher consciousness.

Summary:

Morpheus, "I'm trying to free your mind Neo, but I can only show you the door. You're the one that has to walk through it."

Metaphysical Breakdown

This scene represents the process from which one has to raise their consciousness through their own accord; no one can do it for you.

Chapter Sixteen: First Jump (53:30)

Summary:

Morpheus and Neo are transported to the roof of a tall skyscraper. Morpheus tells Neo, "You have to let it all go Neo, fear, doubt and disbelief. Free your mind"

Metaphysical Breakdown

Neo's fear, doubt and disbelief are by products of his lower consciousness housed in the left hemisphere of the brain. These character traits, keep him from transcending into higher consciousness. He will have to let go of these traits if we chooses to transcend into higher consciousness.

Summary:

The crew doubts that Neo will make his first jump. They concur that nobody ever makes their first jump. Cypher says, "Everybody falls the first time."

Metaphysical Breakdown

Remember, Cypher represents Lucifer or the lower consciousness in man. Higher consciousness, represents man as a spiritual being first, before he "fell" to the physical dimension, to become man. The Biblical story of Lucipher, being the "fallen" angel, represents this Kemetic ideology. For the spiritual man to become a physical being, he must first "fall" from the etheric or spiritual realm, thus all men in the physical body must "fall" their first time, just as Lucifer did.

Chapter Seventeen: The Gatekeepers
(56:31)

Summary:

The opening scene shows a crowd of people, waiting at a cross walk. The red signal shows a man standing still to signify stop. The green signal is a man walking to signify it is okay to go.

Metaphysical Breakdown

This scene shows how easily the masses can be controlled and maintained. All these people automatically stop and go according to the change of color of the light from red to green. It is the same conditioning as Pavlov's dog and nobody questions this conditioned, human behavior.

Summary:

Morpheus and Neo are going against the flow of human traffic. Neo keeps bumping into people.

Metaphysical Breakdown

We see Neo, "going against the grain." The masses of people are stuck in lower level consciousness. When Neo looks to raise his consciousness, he realizes he must do the exact opposite of what the general population is programmed to do. A person of higher consciousness in a lower consciousness society, will bump heads, stick out and will be labeled or viewed as crazy.

Summary:

Morpheus tells Neo, "The system is our enemy." "You have to understand, many of these people are not ready to be unplugged. And many of them are so inert, so hopelessly dependant on the system, that they will fight to protect it."

Metaphysical Breakdown

The system promotes and nurtures the lower consciousness of the masses. Many people only know themselves and their reality through the lenses of their lower consciousness. Because of this, they have embraced this level of existence. They live by fear and control and will try to destroy or discredit anyone who challenges the way they define their reality, even when the system they live in controls, manipulates and oppresses them.

Summary:

While Morpheus is talking to Neo, he is distracted by a woman wearing a red dress. Just then, an agent holds a gun up to Neo's head.

Metaphysical Breakdown

The woman in red, represents the first chakra in Neo's body. This chakra is also red. It represents Neo's lowest level of consciousness. Because Neo is distracted by his carnal or sexual urges, he is vulnerable to fall into lower level or animalistic consciousness. Neo must master his lower, animalistic or carnal urges in order to transcend into higher, spiritual consciousness. If he does not, he is subject to one of the many pitfalls in the system that wants to keep him at a lower level and "kill" Neo's higher consciousness, in order to enslave him.

Summary:

Morpheus explains to Neo,"That means anyone who we haven't unplugged can potentially be an agent." "Every man and woman who has stood up against an agent has died."

Metaphysical Breakdown

Because everyone in the system embraces and defines their reality through their lower consciousness, they all have the potential to destroy anyone who seeks to have higher consciousness.

Morpheus alludes to the fact that anyone who stood up to an agent has died. He is relating to all the men and women who have spoke out against this system in order to free the people from lower level consciousness. People like Malcolm X, Martin Luther King, Che Guevara, Patrice Lumumba, Marcus Garvey, Huey P. Newton, John F. Kennedy and many others.

Summary:

"They are the gatekeepers. They're guarding all the doors and holding all the keys. "Yet their strength and speed are still based on a world built on rules. Because of that, they will never be as fast or as strong as you can be."

Metaphysical Breakdown

When one bases their reality on their lower level consciousness, they lock themselves into the rules and laws of that dimension. When one raises their consciousness, they liberate themselves from the rules of the lower level consciousness and can bypass and liberate themselves from the laws and physics it contains.

Summary:

Neo answers, "What are you trying to tell me, that I can dodge bullets?" Morpheus replies, "No Neo, I'm trying to tell you when you are ready, you wont have to."

Metaphysical Breakdown

Neo is still speaking in terms of his left hemisphere of his brain which represents his lower level consciousness. Morpheus wants him to view his reality in terms of the right hemisphere of the brain which represents his higher consciousness. In this mindset, he will discover that he doesn't have to adhere to any physics or laws of the lower dimension. If he thinks of dodging bullets, he is still locked into describing his environment based on physical laws. He is still empowering the lower level dimension by moving out of harm's way of the bullet. Morpheus wants him to understand that he can control the laws of physics when he raises his consciousness, thus there is no threat of being injured by the bullets. So there is no need to dodge them.

Chapter Eighteen: Running Silent & Deep (59:00)

Summary:

The crew is being followed by a Sentinel. Trinity explains that the only weapon they have against them is an EMP. This stands for an Electro-Magnetic Pulse that disables the machines.

Metaphysical Breakdown

Let us breakdown Electro-Magnetic energy. Electric energy is positive energy. That means it must post up or stay still in order for it to be utilized. Positive energy "gives out" energy. It is represented by the masculine principle. It is the part of the battery that protrudes like the male erection.

Magnetic energy is labeled negative. It has to be in motion for it to be utilized. Negative means, to have no gates or restrictions. Negative energy is labeled feminine. It is the end of the battery that has an indentation. Negative energy "receives" energy.

The coming together of masculine energy and feminine energy produces electro-magnetic energy. This energy can be used to manifest the spiritual realm into the physical dimension. The two people must be operating at their highest consciousness in order to manifest these miracles. This science has been kept from the masses to keep them locked in the system. If they understood this science, It could be used to defeat the system of lower level consciousness. This is the only weapon that Morpheus uses that has an effect on the Sentinels in the Matrix.

Summary:

When Morpheus asks Tank how they are doing we immediately see a part of a room shaped like a triangle or pyramid.

Metaphysical Breakdown

Tank is representing positive or male energy. The triangle or pyramid is an esoteric sign for masculine energy. Masculine energy "gives out" energy.

Chapter Nineteen: Dealing for Bliss
(1:01:07)

Summary:

Opening scene we see Cypher in front of fifteen computer screens. The camera seems to pan in from a room shaped like a pyramid or triangle.

Metaphysical Breakdown

In numerology, the number 15 is broken down to the number 6. This number represents the lowest, animalistic consciousness level of man. Cypher represents man's lower consciousness. His name is short for Lucifer or the Devil.

We see the esoteric symbol for masculine energy being revealed by the pyramidal shape of the room.

Summary:

Neo sneaks up on Cypher from his left side. He does not see him. Cypher tells Neo, "You scared the Bejesus out of me!"

Metaphysical Breakdown

The left side of Cypher is activated by the right hemisphere of the brain which represents his higher consciousness. The fact that Neo was allowed to sneak up on Cypher's left side, lets us know that he has neglected or has ignored altogether his higher consciousness. We can assume that Cypher operates exclusively, according to his right side which represents his lower level consciousness.

Summary:

Cypher explains to Neo how to decipher the Matrix codes. Cypher tells Neo while looking at the codes, "All I see is blonde, brunette, redhead….."

Metaphysical Breakdown

When Cypher looks at the Matrix codes he only focuses on the different types of women that are revealed to him. This suggests that Cypher is operating at a lower level of consciousness containing his carnal or sexual desires. This is all he sees. This is the reality he chooses to recognize.

Summary:

Cypher introduces and offers Neo a drink of makeshift alcohol.

Metaphysical Breakdown

Cypher, just like the devil in the Bible tries to tempt lower Neo's consciousness by offering him mind altering substances that enhance the embracing of his lower self..

Summary:

Cypher tells Neo, "Why oh why didn't I take the blue pill." Cypher takes a drink holding the cup with his left hand.

Metaphysical Breakdown

Cypher expresses that he wishes he could descend back into his lower consciousness. He poisons his higher consciousness by drinking the alcohol from his left hand which represents his higher consciousness

Summary:

Cypher tells Neo, "Do you know why he did it? Why you're here? Neo nods his head yes. Cypher replies, "Jesus! What a mind job."

Metaphysical Breakdown

Cypher subliminally calls Neo, Jesus. He refers to the concept of Neo being Jesus as a "mind job." That is because the Kerast or Christ consciousness can be achieved by switching from being left brain dominant, to being right brain dominant. It is a job for his mind or brain.

Summary:

Neo thanks Cypher for the drink. Cypher tells Neo, "Sweet dreams."

Metaphysical Breakdown

Cypher is referring to Neo's higher consciousness. He is implying for Neo to keep his higher consciousness asleep or to keep it dormant.

Summary:

Next scene Cypher is at a restaurant eating a steak with the agents. The agent says, "Do we have a deal Mr. Reagan?"

Metaphysical Breakdown

The name used to describe Cypher's last name is very significant. Reagan means impulsive. Impulse is a character trait that exemplifies man's lower consciousness. This is what Cypher represents, man's lower self.

The name Reagan was also used by the girl whose character was possessed by the devil in the movie The Exorcist. This is another clue to decipher Cypher's true identity.

Summary:

He holds up his fork and says, "I know this steak doesn't exist. I know that when I put it in my mouth the Matrix is telling my brain it is juicy and delicious. After nine years, you know what I realized, ignorance is bliss."

Metaphysical Breakdown

[Cypher gives a clue to the nutritional value and state of the food we eat. With genetically modified foods, processed foods, steroids, additives & preservatives, in our foods, we really do not know what we are really eating and we don't want to know the process it takes to get the food on our plates. Also, foods that we know are not good for us, we still consume because they are designed and engineered to appeal to the part of our brain that has been manipulated to control our appetites.

In numerology the number nine represents man's judgment. If man passes his test, he can move on to higher consciousness because he has learned from his life lessons. If man does not pass his judgment, he must keep repeating his life lesson until he is able to transcend into higher consciousness Cypher has failed his judgment and must repeat his life lesson in the Matrix which represents his lower consciousness.

Summary:

Cypher tells the agent, "I don't want to remember nothing, nothing. You understand? And I want to be rich. You know someone important, like an actor."

Metaphysical Breakdown

Cypher is displaying his lower level consciousness by trying to appease his ego. His ego wants to be rich and famous. His ego views these things as being important in his life. His ego also doesn't want to know the truth if it is going to affect his ability to attain these things.

Summary:

Cypher is seen smoking a cigar with his left hand after he makes the deal to give up Morpheus to the agents.

Metaphysical Breakdown

The left hand of Cypher represents his higher consciousness. The left hand is controlled by the right hemisphere of the brain, which represents his higher consciousness. The cigar is symbolized as polluting or poisoning his higher consciousness by holding it in his left hand.

Chapter Twenty: Off to See the Oracle (1:05:17)

Summary:

The crew is sitting around the table eating this oatmeal-like substance. Dozier explains to the group what they are eating, "It's a single-celled protein combined with synthetic amino acids, vitamins and minerals. Everything the body needs."

Metaphysical Breakdown

Dozier is describing that real food may not appeal to our lower consciousness but, food was made to sustain the health and strength of the body, not appeal to our lower consciousness.

Summary:

Mouse replies, "It doesn't have everything the body needs. To deny our own impulses, is to deny they very thing that makes us human."

Metaphysical Breakdown

Mouse is relating to the needs and wants of our lower, animalistic consciousness. Mouse wants to embrace the lower consciousness in man. Higher consciousness defines man as a spiritual being having a human experience. Mouse only wants to define man as a physical or lower level being.

Chapter Twenty-One: There is No Spoon (1:07:45)

Summary:

As the crew exits the building after being uploaded into the Matrix, we see Switch wearing an all-white leather outfit. All the other members are wearing all-black. Switches sunglasses are even lighter than the rest of the crews.

Metaphysical Breakdown

Switch represents homosexuality. Switch goes against or is the opposite of our crew. In ancient Kemet, practicing homosexuality was to go against the natural order of the universe. Switch represents this concept. She has "switched" her role in nature from woman to man.

Summary:

Cypher calls the agents and drops the phone in the trash so that they can be tracked down.

Metaphysical Breakdown

The black phone represents the activation on Cypher's melanin contained in his higher consciousness. To drop the phone signifies his intention to lower his consciousness and define himself and his environment through his lower self.

Summary:

Neo is in disbelief as he sees the neighborhood through his newfound consciousness. He exclaims, "God!" Trinity answers, "What?"

Metaphysical Breakdown

Neo subliminally calls Trinity God. In Afrika, the first concept of God was a woman. This is a well-known fact in the world of the occult and secret societies. This fact has been hidden by the masses to promote a male dominated ideology and superiority.

141

Summary:

Trinity follows up and says, "That the Matrix cannot tell you who you are." Neo responds, "But the Oracle can?" Trinity answers, "But that's different."

Metaphysical Breakdown

The Matrix represents one's lower consciousness, thus it will define you in terms of your lower self. The Oracle sees Neo in terms of the potential of his higher consciousness or higher self. This is the difference between the two.

Summary:

Morpheus and Neo arrive at the Oracle's building. They see an elderly, blind man of Indian descent sitting in the lobby. Morpheus nods at him as if to greet him. The blind man acknowledges Morpheus' gesture by nodding back even though he is presumably blind and cannot see.

Metaphysical Breakdown

The original indigenous people of India were Black from Afrika. This is the connection Morpheus, a Black man, has with this elderly man from India. These original Black men taught them the mystery systems of Kemet. The Indians would later develop their own spiritual philosophies based on this Afrikan science as the foundation.

The fact that the elderly man from India acknowledges Morpheus even though he is blind, is also a Kemetic character trait.

In Kemet, true sight came from one's Pineal gland, not their eyes. In fact, the Pineal gland was called the "first eye." The Pineal gland is responsible for producing melanin. One must lose their sight which sees the world in terms of one's lower consciousness. They must open their first eye which sees the world through their higher, spiritual consciousness. This is why the blind man can see and acknowledge Morpheus when he looks and nods at him.]

Summary:

Morpheus and Neo enter the elevator. Morpheus presses the ninth floor button.

Metaphysical Breakdown

The number nine, in numerology represents man's judgment he must pass to reach a higher level of consciousness. Neo going up to the ninth floor to meet the Oracle, symbolizes Morpheus' judgment he must pass in order to achieve higher consciousness.

Summary:

Neo speaks to Morpheus in the elevator the letters K, Y & M are carved on the elevator wall behind him.

Metaphysical Breakdown

The letters K, Y, & M in numerology, breakdown to the number 13. The number thirteen represents resurrection. In Kemet, resurrection meant to "put to death" lower level consciousness to be "reborn" into higher or spiritual level of consciousness. The individual must lay to rest animalistic ideas and behaviors and raise himself up to his godlike self.

Summary:

Morpheus responds to Neo. There is graffiti behind him and Neo, on the elevator wall. It spells out "STBY."

Metaphysical Breakdown

The graffiti in the background comes out to equal the number 12 in numerology. This number represents completion. Neo is nearing his completion into resurrecting himself from his lower consciousness, into his higher consciousness.

Summary:

Morpheus explains to Neo that the Oracle is not to be looked upon as right or wrong. He further explains to him that she is a guide that can help him find his path.

Metaphysical Breakdown

The concept of right and wrong is interpreted by our lower consciousness. Morpheus is telling Neo to raise his consciousness and perceive the Oracle's words using his higher consciousness. Neo's higher consciousness will give him the code from which to decipher truth from reality and the simple, immature principles of right or wrong that do not apply.

Summary:

Morpheus and Neo arrive at the Oracle's door. There is graffiti on the wall on the left of Morpheus. It spells, "MOL."

Metaphysical Breakdown

In numerology, these letters add up to the number 40. This number represents the completion of man's test to master his lower self in an effort to achieve his higher consciousness.

Summary:

Morpheus tells Neo, "I can only show you the door. You have to walk through it."

Metaphysical Breakdown

This concept has been covered earlier in the film. Man has the free will to define himself through his lower consciousness or his higher consciousness. No one can decide for him. Neo must "open the door" himself.

Summary:

Just as Neo reaches for the door knob to open the door, a Black woman opens it before him. She tells him, "Hello Neo, you're right on time."

Metaphysical Breakdown

The first concept of God in Afrika was a Black woman. The occult and secret societies are familiar with this concept and choose to keep it a secret. Also, Neo must embrace his feminine self, which represents his higher, spiritual self, if he wants to "open the door" to his higher consciousness.

Summary:

As they enter the Oracle's house, we see a sun clock on the Morpheus' left side, as they stand in the entrance way.

Metaphysical Breakdown

In Kemet and the occult world, the Sun is a symbol of higher, universal knowledge or consciousness. The fact that it is seen over Morpheus' left side, suggests the activation of his higher consciousness. The left side of Morpheus' body represents the activation of the right hemisphere of the brain, which symbolizes his higher, spiritual consciousness.

Summary:

As the hostess takes Neo inside the living room, we see a woman holding a baby as she exits the room. She appears white but has the hair of a Black woman.

Metaphysical Breakdown

I believe this woman represents the high jacking of this Afrikan knowledge and mystery systems by the European. They now lead others to believe, that they were to originators of this. It is well known that the Greeks went to Kemet to study and receive all their philosophies and mathematical knowledge. They then went back to Greece and presented their own inferior version of this Afrikan knowledge to the world, as if they were the originators of it.

Summary:

The living room has several prominent copper fixtures throughout the room.

Metaphysical Breakdown

Copper is well known in Kemet for its purifying qualities. In order to achieve higher consciousness, one must 'purify' themselves from lower level behavior and thinking. This is done by raising one's consciousness.

Summary:

Two white children are levitating blocks. The blocks have a picture of an helicopter on them as well as the numbers 9 and 3. They also have the letters, J, Z & V.

Metaphysical Breakdown

In numerology, these letters and numbers add up to the number 7. This number represents God's divinity in the physical dimension. This is the goal of achieving higher consciousness. It is to become as close to God as possible.

Summary:

On the T.V. behind the girls is a show that shows giant rabbits roaming the street.

Metaphysical Breakdown

The rabbits pay homage to the story of Alice in Wonderland. Neo has now emerged himself into another world or consciousness.

Summary:

The blocks are suspended in the air. They reveal the letters; W, I & L.

Metaphysical Breakdown

These blocks spell out the word WIL. This is referring to man's free will to define himself through his lower consciousness or his higher consciousness. It is a man's definition of himself and the environment around him that determines his reality. The children are able to defy the laws of physics because they are operating according to their higher, spiritual consciousness.

Summary:

Neo sees a white boy sitting on the ground bending spoons. He tells Neo, "Do not try to bend the spoon. That is impossible. Instead, only try to realize the truth. Neo answers, "What truth?" The boy responds, "There is no spoon." The boy says, "Then you will see that it is not the spoon that bends. It is only yourself."

Metaphysical Breakdown

The boy saying this knowledge and showing Neo how to bend spoons, demonstrates the Caucasian always inserting himself and taking credit for knowledge and philosophies he has stolen from indigenous people throughout the world and more specifically, Kemet.

The boy is suggesting to Neo to interpret himself and his reality through his higher consciousness which is represented by the right hemisphere of the brain. He is telling Neo that if he "sees" his reality according to his higher consciousness, he can create his own rules and not be subjected to the laws, rules and physics of the lower consciousness and physical dimension. So it is not the spoon Neo is trying to bend but Neo's Mind! He needs to "bend" his mind to the right hemisphere of his brain, in order for him to create his own reality. For then he will understand that the spoon does not exist if he doesn't validate its existence. In this state of higher consciousness, Neo can create his own truth.

Summary:

Neo concentrates on the spoon. He moves his head to the left and the spoon bends in the same direction.

Metaphysical Breakdown

By moving the body to the left, symbolizes the activation of the right hemisphere of the brain which represents higher consciousness. The left side of the body is controlled by the right hemisphere of the brain. Neo is able to bend the spoon because he is operating according to his higher self or consciousness.

Chapter Twenty-Two: Choices & a Cookie (1:12:31)

Summary:

Neo enters the kitchen to meet the Oracle. She is wearing all green.

Metaphysical Breakdown

The color green represents the fourth chakra located at the heart. It is represented by the color green and is the first level of higher consciousness.

Summary:

The Oracle can predict every move Neo makes before he makes it.

Metaphysical Breakdown

A person who operates according to their higher consciousness, like the Oracle, accepts their feelings of intuition as fact or truth. This allows the Oracle to predict Neo's behavior. It is her keen sense of intuition that she interprets as her reality.

Summary:

The Oracle asks Neo if he thinks he is the One. Neo responds by saying he honestly doesn't know.

Metaphysical Breakdown

When one truly reaches their higher self, they begin to transcend into a "state of knowing." This is the ability to master and know things without practice or previous experience or knowledge. If Neo does not know, he obviously has not reached this higher state of consciousness.

Summary:

Immediately, the Oracle tells Neo to look up at a sign above the doorway he just walked in. It is written in Latin. She tells Neo it means, "Know Thyself."

Metaphysical Breakdown

The inscription, "Know Thyself" was a Kemetic term that they put above all the temple doorways in ancient Kemet. They believed the answers of all the mysteries of the universe, were contained inside oneself. It directly correlates to a person reaching their higher self or spiritual consciousness. If one was to transcend into their higher self, the secrets of the universe would be revealed. This is why they put the sign above the doorways. This meant a person had to look up in order to read the sign. The act of the person looking up would reinforce the ideology of pursuing and identifying himself through their higher self or spiritual consciousness.

This goes against Western or European philosophy and religion, which has placed the idea of God outside of man and not reachable, whereas in ancient Kemet, God was attainable from within, if one was willing to raise their consciousness and master their lower, physical self. This theory is promoted by having the individual bow down to pay homage to the God, instead of looking up. This act instills in a person to define themselves through their lower selves or consciousness. This is the act of someone ashamed of their lower level behavior and reaffirms the principle that they are not worthy of higher consciousness or spirituality.

Summary:

The Oracle explains, "Being the One is just like being in love. No one can tell you you're in love, you just know it."

Metaphysical Breakdown

The Oracle is referring to the "state of knowing" one manifests when they have reached a level of higher consciousness. In this state, person knows that which he knows without confirmation from outside sources or experiences.

Summary:

The Oracles plays like she is giving Neo a physical examination to see if he is the One. She asks Neo to tell her what she is going to say. Neo tells her he is not the One.

Metaphysical Breakdown

If Neo had reached a level in his higher consciousness and said that he was the "One," then the Oracle would have confirmed his answer. She asks Neo if he was the "One" to test him to see if he was in a "state of knowing." He failed his test because he did not believe in himself.

Summary:

She tells Neo that she is sorry. She says that he has the gift but that Neo is waiting for something. She tells Neo maybe in his next lifetime.

Metaphysical Breakdown

Neo is apprehensive in making the claim that he is the "One." It is this fear that keeps him from attaining his higher self. Kemetic philosophy tells us that we are born in the physical dimension for a reason and a specific purpose. If we do not acquire or learn the life lesson we specifically came down here for, we will be reincarnated until we do. This is how we are able to transcend into other dimensions in the afterlife.

Summary:

Neo tells the Oracle that Morpheus almost had him convinced that he was the One. She tells Neo without Morpheus, we are lost.

Metaphysical Breakdown

Morpheus represents Neo's melanin which is activated in Neo's higher consciousness. If Neo fully embraced his melanin or what Morpheus revealed to him, he would have passed the test and been claimed the One by the Oracle. It is Neo's fear or lower level consciousness that keeps him from fully embracing his melanin, thus keeping him away from being the "One."

Summary:

The Oracle explains to Neo, "Morpheus believes in you Neo. And no one not you, not even me can convince him otherwise. He believes it so blindly that he is going to sacrifice his life to save yours.

Metaphysical Breakdown

Morpheus representing the activation of Neo's melanin in his higher consciousness has no doubts about what he perceives as his reality. Fear and doubt have no place in a person's higher consciousness or self. This is why Morpheus is willing to give his life for what he believes.

This selfless act is also the threshold a person must overcome to achieve higher consciousness. One must display the ability to sacrifice their own life for a cause they view as more important than their own lives. This is where the Biblical story of Jesus comes from.

Summary:

The Oracle elaborates, "In the one hand you will have Morpheus' life. And in the other hand, you will have your own. One of you is going to die. Which one will be up to you."

Metaphysical Breakdown

Morpheus represents the activation of Neo's melanin contained in his higher consciousness. Neo must sacrifice his own life, which represents his lower self, in order to save Morpheus, who is represents Neo's higher self or consciousness. This is why the Oracle says that each life will be in each one of Neo's hands. Remember, the left hand symbolizes Morpheus and higher consciousness. The right hand represents Neo and his lower consciousness. Neo must kill or sacrifice his lower self in order to transcend into his higher self. This is Neo's initiation into his higher consciousness. The Oracle is explaining the procedure for his resurrection.

Summary:

She tells Neo as soon as he steps outside he will feel better. She tells him that he doesn't believe in any of this fate crap. You're in control of your own life.

Metaphysical Breakdown

Neo, because he is being controlled by doubt and fear, is activating according to his lower consciousness. Because of this, Neo will live his life without acknowledging or recognizing his higher self. He will begin to believe the lie that his lower self tells him to embrace.

Summary:

The Oracle offers Neo a cookie. There are six on the plate. She tells him he will feel better after he eats it.

Metaphysical Breakdown

In numerology, the number six represents man's lower self. By Neo ingesting the cookie suggests that he will be comforted by his ego and his lower self. For Neo, ignorance in his lower consciousness is bliss. With higher consciousness comes responsibility. This may discourage people from knowing truth. People do not want the responsibility that comes with knowing the truth. Neo is no different.

Chapter Twenty-Three: Glitch in the Matrix (1:17:46)

Summary:

In this scene we see Mouse lying down with his feet up looking at a poster of the woman in red he created in a computer simulation program. Mouse is the last one to realize it's a trap. Mouse dies first.

Metaphysical Breakdown

The woman in red, represents man's lower level or carnal desires. Red is the symbol of the first or root chakra in man. It represents man's consciousness as a beast or controlled by his animalistic desires. Mouse is preoccupied with this lower level consciousness. This distraction causes him to be killed by the Matrix, which represents man's prison of lower level consciousness. This scene relates to man's many distractions that keep him locked into lower, level or animalistic consciousness. It is man's test to overcome his lower consciousness in order to transcend into higher consciousness.

Summary:

Neo, Morpheus and Trinity pull up in their Lincoln Continental with the license plate number AA034.

Metaphysical Breakdown

In numerology, these numbers and letters add up to equal the number nine. Nine represents man's judgment. This sign is a prelude to this scene representing a test of some sort for the main characters involved.

Summary:

Cypher is seen wearing red tint sun glasses while the others are wearing black.

Metaphysical Breakdown

Cypher represents Lucifer or man's lower self or nature. Red is the color of the lowest chakra. It represents man motivated by his animalistic or lower level desires. This is what Cypher represents.

Summary:

Neo looks to his left and sees a black cat walking across the threshold of a door. He sees the same cat and has déjà vu.

Metaphysical Breakdown

Neo looking to his left, symbolizes the activation of the right hemisphere of the brain which represents his higher consciousness. In his state of higher consciousness, he sees a black cat. In Kemet, the house cat represented protection. The color black, represented Melanin. The house cat was represented by the goddess, Bast or Bastet. The fact that Neo sees Bast by activating his higher consciousness, suggests that he is being protected in a time where his environment does not tell him he is in danger. Neo is using his higher consciousness, through his intuition, to navigate his reality.

The Kemet, goddess Bast or Bastet. She was the god of protection. House cats have very keen sense of smell, sight and intuition. These characteristics are beneficial for someone whose job is to look out for someone else. This is why our ancestors selected the cat to symbolize these character traits.

Summary:

The floor in the building is white and black checkered linoleum.

Metaphysical Breakdown

The white and black checkered floor is a Masonic symbol. This symbol that communicates to the initiates of that secret society. We discussed about this in an earlier chapter.

Summary:

The agents realize that they are on the eighth floor.

Metaphysical Breakdown

The number eight in numerology, represents the concept of eternity or infinity. This number has no beginning or no ending. This concept symbolizes the longevity of the Matrix if one does not raise their consciousness. That person will be enslaved forever.

Chapter Twenty-Four: One Left Behind
(1:21:00)

Summary:

Tank tells our crew to make a left to find the wet wall to escape.

Metaphysical Breakdown

The symbol of "making a left," to escape the agents, represents the activation of the right hemisphere of the brain which represents higher consciousness. The left side of the body is controlled by the right hemisphere of the brain.

Summary:

When Morpheus attacks the agent to save Neo, Trinity grabs Neo's left foot to pull him down to save him.

Metaphysical Breakdown

The grabbing of Neo's left foot by Trinity, who represents Neo's spirituality, symbolizes the procedure he must implement in attaining higher consciousness. The left side of the body is controlled by the right hemisphere of the brain which represents higher consciousness.

Chapter Twenty-Five: Heroes Unplugged
(1:25:02)

Summary:

Trinity escapes coming up from a manhole cover. A truck with a green tarp passes over her before she appears.

Metaphysical Breakdown

This scene relates to Trinity raising her kundalini energy or consciousness represented by her chakras. She is going from lower consciousness, which is represented by her being underground, to higher consciousness, which is represented by her emerging up from the man hole. The green tarp on the truck that passes over her represents the heart chakra. This is the first chakra in higher consciousness.

Summary:

Tank tells Trinity that they can escape at the corner of Franklin & Erie.

Metaphysical Breakdown

The name, Franklin, in Etymology, means "free man." The name Erie means, "a place for." When we put the two meanings of these names together, we get "a place for free men." This is where Trinity must go to escape the Matrix or lower level consciousness.

Summary:

Cypher tells Trinity that he thought he was in love with her for a long time. He regrets that he has to kill her. He tells her that he is tired of the war, the fighting, the ship, etc.......

Metaphysical Breakdown

Cypher, representing man's lower consciousness, looks to himself as a victim. He feels sorry for himself. This is a product or point of view of lower level consciousness.

Summary:

Cypher jumps on Morpheus's lap and tells him, "God, I wish I can be there, when they break you. So right then you know it was me."

Metaphysical Breakdown

The fact that Cypher is on top of Morpheus, signifies that lower consciousness is dominating higher consciousness. Cypher, incidentally calls Morpheus, god.

Summary:

Cypher continues, "You call this free, if I have to choose between this and the Matrix. I choose the Matrix." "I think the Matrix can be more real than this world."

Metaphysical Breakdown

People who operate and define themselves and their reality through lower consciousness, would rather not know the truth, if acknowledging the truth takes them out of their comfort zones. Living a lie is much easier to deal with for them.

Summary:

Cypher tells Trinity to say good bye to Switch. Switch responds, "Not like this. Not like this." Cypher pulls the plug and she dies.

Metaphysical Breakdown

Switch, who represents homosexuality, does not want to die in her present state. This scene implies that she wants more time to change her sexual orientation before she dies by pleading, "Not like this."

161

Chapter Twenty-Six: Cypher's Burnout (1:29:42)

Summary:

Cypher asks Trinity to reaffirm her faith in her belief that Neo is the One. She tells him yes. All of a sudden Tank appears on the scene and kills Cypher saving Neo's life. He tells Cypher that he is "Going to burn!"

Metaphysical Breakdown

Trinity must reaffirm her beliefs to Cypher, who represents lower consciousness. Our lower consciousness will always try to convince us through fear, doubt and ego, that our undertaking to transcend into higher consciousness is a futile act. It will always try to discourage us. So it is very important to reaffirm ourselves and the thoughts we want to manifest.

Tank, telling Cypher that he is going to burn, suggests that he really represents the devil or Satan.

Chapter Twenty- Seven: Matters of Belief (1:31:24)

Summary:

The beginning of this chapter at the (1:31:38) mark, one sees a panoramic scene of city skyscrapers. One building has the name, "Mulpha" and another building shows the letters, "NORWICH." Agent Smith says, "Have you ever stood and stared at it?"

Metaphysical Breakdown

I believe this scene in the movie contains very important hidden messages and symbols. They flash this panoramic view of a downtown view of a city for about three seconds. The agent's comment, "Have you ever stood and stared at it?" signifies to me that he is referring to this particular scene in the movie. I have not yet deciphered the meaning or symbols of this scene, but I am certain of its significance. I would love to hear your interpretation.

Summary:

Agent Smith tells Morpheus, "Billions of people just living out their lives. oblivious."

Metaphysical Breakdown

Oblivious, refers to the fact that they are defining themselves and their reality through their lower level consciousness. They do not know that they have access to their higher selves from which to define themselves and their reality.

Summary:

Agent Smith continues, "I believe that human beings define their reality through misery and suffering."

Metaphysical Breakdown

This is proof that man's exists on a lower level of consciousness in the Matrix or system by defining himself and his reality through pain and misery.

Summary:

Agent Smith speaks, "The Matrix was redesigned to this. The peak of your civilization. I say "your civilization," because as soon as we started thinking for you, it became our civilization, which of course is what this is all about."

Metaphysical Breakdown

We are in the peak of European or Caucasian civilization. People of color were forced to adopt this culture of defining themselves and their environment through lower level consciousness. So Agent Smith referring to "your civilization" really means European or Western culture that dominates people of color throughout the world.

Summary:

Agent Smith continues, "Evolution. Like the dinosaur, you had your time. The future is our world, Morpheus. The future is our time."

Metaphysical Breakdown

Agent Smith representing the white man's system is telling Morpheus, a Black man, that his time, Kemet, has passed. The future belongs to the white man.

Summary:

Morpheus is seen with and electrode on the right side of his head and on the back of his neck.

Metaphysical Breakdown

The right side of his head represents the right hemisphere of his brain. The agents are trying to break Morpheus' higher consciousness and have him define himself and his reality through the left hemisphere of the brain, which contains his lower consciousness.

The back of Morpheus' neck is where his "reptilian brain" is located. This represents man's lowest level of animalistic consciousness.

Summary:

Trinity tells Neo, "Morpheus, sacrificed himself so that he can get you out." Neo tells her he must attempt to save Morpheus.

Metaphysical Breakdown

The final step to reaching Kerast or Christ consciousness, is the willingness to sacrifice your life for a cause or person you deem greater than yourself. This is the principle character of Jesus represented in the Bible. He died for our sins so that you would have eternal life.

Summary:

Neo says to Tank, "Morpheus believed in something and he was ready to give his life for it. I understand that now. That's why I must go." Trinity tells Neo that she is going with him. Trinity tells Neo, "If you don't like it, I believe you can go to hell."

Metaphysical Breakdown

Hell is not a place but a lower level state of consciousness in man. Trinity represents Neo's spirituality or higher consciousness. Neo will go to his lower state of consciousness if he doesn't acknowledge his spirituality or higher self. Neo needs to take Trinity with him to succeed.

Chapter Twenty- Eight: Virus to be Cured (1:37:20)

Summary:

Agent Smith lectures Morpheus, "Every mammal instinctively develops equilibrium with the surrounding environment, but you humans do not. You move to an area and you multiply until every natural resource is consumed. The only way you can survive is to spread to another area. There is another organism on this planet that follows the same pattern. A virus."

Metaphysical Breakdown

The Agent is describing the imperialistic system of white supremacy. Everywhere the white man has encountered people of color, the people of that region ended up losing everything they had before the white man came. The white man's greed and lust for power and control is insatiable, just like a virus.

Summary:

"Human beings are a disease. A cancer of this planet. You are a plague and we are the cure."

Metaphysical Breakdown

He is directly speaking to the Caucasian race. Remember Agent Smith is white and Morpheus is Black. This is the mindset of white supremacy.

Summary:

Agent Smith speaks to Morpheus, "I hate this place, this zoo, this prison, this reality or whatever you want to call it. I can't stand it any longer. I must get out of here. I must get free."

Metaphysical Breakdown

This is where things get interesting. Because of the white man's lack of melanin, he cannot transcend into higher, spiritual consciousness. He is trapped in the system that he has created. This is his legacy and reality which he, himself cannot escape. He is trapped in his own system of lower level consciousness. Whereas, people of color can transcend in the afterlife to higher dimensions, Caucasians are relegated to being permanently trapped into this lower dimension. Without melanin, one cannot "cross over."

Summary:

Agent Smith continues, "And in this mind is the key. My key. Once Zion is destroyed there is no need for me to be here. I need the codes. I have to get inside of Zion and you have to tell me how. You're going to tell me or you're going to die."

Metaphysical Breakdown

The white man must use the Black man's science, labor, creativity, spirituality, resources etc.... to create a world with some semblance of higher consciousness for himself. Agent Smith, representing the white man and his system of white supremacy, must use the Black man's mind, which contains higher, spiritual consciousness, which he does not have the capacity to internalize, in order to try to get out of lower level consciousness. This is the big secret that white people do not want Black people to recognize. Caucasians have set up a system where Black people seem to be dependent on them for all facets of life. They set the image of darker people of the world needing white folks to look after them. This is further from the truth. It is the other way around. They need people of color to maintain and internalize this system of white supremacy that steals their resources, ideologies and sciences and oppresses the people.

Zion, represents heaven or higher, spiritual consciousness. Agent Smith, representing the white man, believes he can somehow force his way or manipulate his way into achieving higher, spiritual consciousness. If the white man cannot reach higher, spiritual consciousness, he threatens to kill everyone else. He has the mindset, if I can't have it, nobody else will either.

Chapter Twenty-Nine: Lobby Shooting Spree (1:41:00)

Summary:

As Neo enters the metal detector, the light goes from green to red.

Metaphysical Breakdown

In the chakra system, the lowest level of consciousness is red. The first level of higher consciousness is green. Neo, representing higher consciousness, is about to display lower, animalistic behavior indicated by the light of the metal detector. The light goes from green, higher consciousness to red, lower consciousness.

Summary:

Neo and Trinity head to the elevator. Trinity presses the "Up" button which resembles a triangle. The elevator goes to floors 40 to 92, as marked on the left side of Neo.

Metaphysical Breakdown

The triangle symbol on the elevator button, is the esoteric symbol that represents masculine principle of energy. Masculine energy gives out energy. This is a sign of aggression which will be displayed by Neo and Trinity.

The number of the floors, 40 and 92, in numerology break down to the number 6. Six represents man's lower, animalistic level of consciousness. This is the behavior the two will display when trying to free Morpheus.

Chapter Thirty: Dodge This (1:44:16)

Summary:

Neo and Trinity stop the elevator on the 41st. floor.

Metaphysical Breakdown

Forty-one, in numerology, breaks down to the number five. This number represents God's grace or God having favor in one's undertaking. Even though Neo and Trinity will be displaying lower level consciousness, God is pleased with their intentions to right that which is wrong.

Summary:

Neo rigs the elevator to fall as he and Trinity grab its cable to fly up the elevator shaft. Neo grabs the cable with his left hand. Before Neo shoots the cable he says, "There is no spoon."

Metaphysical Breakdown

The elevator represents Neo's consciousness. For him to ascend, he needs his spirituality, represented by him holding on to Trinity. He also needs to activate the right hemisphere of the brain which represents his higher consciousness. Neo reminds himself of this procedure by quoting the young boy who taught him how to "bend spoons" or activate the right hemisphere of his brain, while he was visiting the Oracle. He puts this mindset at work as he believes in himself.

Summary:

Neo calls for Trinity before he is able to dodge bullets like the agents can.

Metaphysical Breakdown

This relates to the fact that in order to achieve higher consciousness, one must embrace their spirituality. Trinity represents Neo's spirituality, his sacred feminine. This is what allows him to defy the laws of physics in the lower, physical dimension. Without her, he could not accomplish these amazing feats.

Summary:

Neo is lying on the ground. An agent is ready to shoot him. In the background, we see letters on a sky scraper that say, "ACW."

Metaphysical Breakdown

In numerology, these letters break down to the number nine. Nine represents man's judgment or test he must pass n order to reach higher consciousness. This scene represents one of Neo's many tests he must pass to achieve higher consciousness.

Summary:

Trinity kills the agent from point blank range. The body turns back into a pilot named Kim. He has a blood stain in the middle of his forehead.

The name, Kim in etymology means "royal fortress." This man or agent that Trinity kills represents the protector of the Matrix or royal fortress. He is an agent of the Matrix

The blood in the middle of his forehead represents the destruction or dysfunction of his Pineal gland which produces the melanin needed to attain higher, spiritual consciousness. The agent can only operate at a lower level of consciousness because of the damage or calcification to his Pineal gland.

Chapter Thirty-One: Gotcha (1:46:56)

Summary:

Trinity picks up Neo using a "Lion's Paw" handshake with their left hands.

Metaphysical Breakdown

In secret societies, the symbol of the initiate going from lower consciousness to higher consciousness is represented by a handshake called the Lion's Paw. It is a sign of resurrection.

The "Lion's Paw" grip used in secret societies to show the "resurrection" of the initiate from lower consciousness into higher consciousness. Notice the grabbing of the left arms to represent higher consciousness.

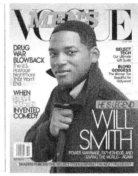

Occultist Pat Robertson, representing religion; Al Gore, representing politics and Will Smith, representing the entertainment industry, all displaying the "Lion's Paw" a gesture that demonstrates Masonic dominion and control over their perspective fields.

The lion was the symbol for the first degrees of initiation, the sign which allowed the opening of the book, so to speak. It possibly represented the royalty of initiation, the status that comes with being aware of what is concealed

- Tony Bushby(*Secret in the Bible*)

Summary:

As Morpheus runs towards the helicopter to be saved, the agents shoot his left ankle before he can jump.

Metaphysical Breakdown

The Agent is trying to "kill or injure" Morpheus' higher consciousness so that he cannot escape the Matrix which represents, lower consciousness. The left side of the body is controlled by the right hemisphere of the brain which represents higher consciousness.

174

Summary:

Neo jumps after Morpheus so that he doesn't fall.

Metaphysical Breakdown

In order for Neo to reach Kerast or Christ consciousness, he must be willing to give his life for a cause or person he deems greater than himself.

Summary:

Neo uses the same "Lion's Paw" grip with his left hand to keep Morpheus from falling.

Metaphysical Breakdown

In secret societies, the symbol of the initiate going from lower consciousness to higher consciousness or a higher degree is represented by a handshake called the Lion's Paw. It is a sign of resurrection. See photo above.

Chapter Thirty-Two: Rooftop Rescue
(1:50:13)

Summary:

Neo saves Trinity by pulling her up by a rope as the helicopter crashes into a building. He uses the "Lion's Paw" grip to help her up.

Metaphysical Breakdown

In secret societies, the symbol of the initiate going from lower consciousness to higher consciousness or a higher degree is represented by a handshake called the Lion's Paw. It is a sign of resurrection.

Summary:

Morpheus explains to Neo, "There is a difference between knowing the path and walking the path."

Metaphysical Breakdown

Morpheus is explaining the level of higher consciousness when one is in a "state of knowing." This is what Morpheus was waiting for Neo to discover and claim within himself. Every man must internalize this consciousness within themselves. No one can do it for you."

Summary:

Tank says the nearest exit for our crew is at State & Balboa. The crew consists of Morpheus, Trinity and Neo.

Metaphysical Breakdown

In etymology, the word State means constant, firm or steadfast. The name Balboa is Spanish meaning pleasant valley. So when we put the definitions of these two words together we get, constant or steadfast, pleasant valley. These two words identify the feeling one has in higher consciousness. This is the state of mind one achieves when they escape the Matrix, which represents lower consciousness.

Chapter Thirty- Three: Subway Showdown (1:55:52)

Summary:

They arrive at the subway station. Neo hands Morpheus the phone and tells him he is first. Morpheus puts the phone to his left ear and is transported to the ship. Trinity also puts the phone to her left ear and is transported also.

Metaphysical Breakdown

Trains and train stations in occult movies represent the system that oppresses the masses without them even knowing it. Trains can only go where the tracks are laid. They can only travel according to the person who lays the tracks for the train. The train represents the mindset of the people. The secret societies or the elite, are represented as the ones who lay the track from which the train to travel. They are the ones that are in control of the masses without the people knowing that they are being manipulated and controlled. The train has no choice but to stay on its tracks. If there is a film with a train or train station, chances are it is an occult movie with hidden symbols and messages.

Putting the phone to the left ear signifies Neo and Trinity operating according to their higher consciousness. The left side of the body is controlled by the right hemisphere of the brain, which represents higher consciousness.

Summary:

Agent Smith shows up and confronts Neo. Neo turns around as if to contemplate running. There are eighteen steps that lead to the exit of the subway.

Metaphysical Breakdown

In numerology, the number nine represents man's judgment or test in his quest from lower consciousness to attaining higher consciousness. Neo contemplates running from Agent Smith by looking at the steps that lead to the exit of the subway. He conquers his fear of Agent Smith. The feeling of fear is in man's lower consciousness. Neo stands up to Agent Smith and believes in his ability to defeat him. These are characteristics of Neo operating according to his higher consciousness. Neo has passed his test when he masters his fears and stands up to Agent Smith.

Summary:

Neo starts to fight the agent. He kicks him in the face and breaks the left lens of his sun glasses.

Metaphysical Breakdown

The breaking of the left lens of Agent Smith's sunglasses represents the agent's inability to activate his higher consciousness. The left eye is activated by the right hemisphere of the brain which represents man's higher consciousness. If the eye is broken or damaged it cannot attain higher consciousness.

Summary:

There is a sign of the number three in back of the agent.

Metaphysical Breakdown

In numerology, the number three represents God's divine perfection. This number represents Neo's ascension into Kerast or Christ consciousness.

Summary:

Neo blocks a punch to his heart from Agent Smith. Neo's hands are put into a position that looks like the letter "X."

Metaphysical Breakdown

In Kemet, the first god to resurrect himself was named Ausar. He had a symbol of an "X" on his chest. In the occult world, the letter "X" symbolizes resurrection or the ability to transcend from

178

lower consciousness to higher consciousness. The position of the heart is the first chakra of higher consciousness. Neo is assuming this role or position.

Summary:

Neo is struck by Agent Smith and starts to spit blood. Trinity says, "Jesus, he is killing him."

Metaphysical Breakdown

Trinity is really calling Neo, Jesus. She is referring to his Kerast or Christ consciousness. In order for Jesus to be raised from the dead, which represented his lower consciousness, he had to die and be resurrected into higher consciousness on the third day.

Chapter Thirty-Four: My Name is Neo (1:56:31)

Summary:

Neo gets up after taking a beating from Agent Smith. He seems rejuvenated. He raises his right fist up and points his left fist down.

Metaphysical Breakdown

Neo has risen into higher consciousness just like the character of Jesus in the Bible. He assumes the position of the free mason god, Baphomet. This pose shows the initiates the power they possess in dominating and manipulating the world's populations. They are basically bragging to one another about how powerful they are.

Notice the positioning of the arms. This is the same position Neo assumes when he realizes the strength and power he possesses.

Summary:

While Neo is beating up Agent Smith, you will notice a sign on the back of the subway wall that says, "Sol."

Metaphysical Breakdown

The word Sol is Spanish for Sun. The Sun is represents higher consciousness or enlightenment. It also symbolizes the character of Jesus as the "Sun" of Man. This is the level of consciousness Neo is transcending to. The Sun also represents raw and powerful masculine energy.

Summary:

On the wall to Neo's left, is graffiti that spells, "ISA."

Metaphysical Breakdown

The Arabic name for Jesus in the Quran is Isa. This is another clue as to who Neo represents. Neo is the Kerast or has attained Christ consciousness. Neo is the Christ that every man and woman can achieve when they decide to raise their consciousness By mastering their lower selves.

Summary:

Agent Smith has Neo on the train tracks he tells Neo, "Goodbye Mr. Anderson." Neo responds by saying, "My name is Neo!"

Metaphysical Breakdown

Neo has made the transition from his lower self to his higher self. Neo has been resurrected. Mr. Anderson represents his lower self and Neo represents his higher self.

Chapter Thirty-Five: Sentinels Attack
(1:58:44)

Summary:

Tank tells Neo to go to Wabash & Lake to escape the agents and get out of the Matrix.

Metaphysical Breakdown

Lake- To send or a servant. Source: An Etymological Dictionary of Family and Christian Names With an Essay on their Derivation and Import; Arthur, William, M.A.; New York, NY: Sheldon, Blake, Bleeker & CO., 1857.

Wabash- "it shines white." When you put the meaning of these two words together you get, "to send a servant that shines white." In the Biblical story of Jesus' resurrection he was described as shining with a bright white glow when he was seen after his resurrection. He was also sent by his father to save humanity. This is the same description of the place of Neo's exit from the Matrix, which represents man's lower level consciousness.

Summary:

In order for Neo to escape the agents when he is running through the apartment, Tank tells him to go through the door on his left. He repeats this by saying, "Your other left."

Metaphysical Breakdown

The direction of going to the "left" represents the activation of the right hemisphere of the brain which represents higher consciousness. The fact that Tank tells Neo to go to his left and then tells him his other left, signifies that he has two left hands. In Kemet, several of the Metu Neter or hieroglyphics portray characters as having two left hands. This signifies that this character was operating exclusively in their higher consciousness. This is how Neo has ascended in his higher consciousness. Remember higher consciousness is represented by the feminine principle of energy which "receives" energy. This characteristic represents higher, spiritual consciousness.

By having two lefts or two left hands, Neo cannot activate the left hemisphere of his brain, which represents his lower, animalistic consciousness. The right hand, which Neo does not have, signifies the activation of the left hemisphere of the brain.

 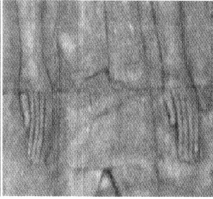

The picture on the left is from Kemet. It displays the figure in the center as having two left hands. He is being guided by the gods Heru on the left and Anpu on the right. Notice he has his left foot forward to activate the right hemisphere of his brain.

Picture on the right, is a close up of two left hands from another Kemetic scene.

Summary:

The door Neo breaks through is apartment 3C.

Metaphysical Breakdown

In numerology, 3C breaks down to the number six. This number represents man at his lower level or animalistic consciousness. The viewer can gather from the room number that some type of killing, maiming or torturing will be happening in this room.

Summary:

Neo runs back into the "Heart O' the City" hotel.

Metaphysical Breakdown

This is the same hotel Trinity was in at the beginning of the movie. In Kemet, a person was judged according to their heart. It was the heart that the goddess Maat weighed when a person died to see if they would go on in the afterlife. So it makes perfect sense that Neo's final battle with lower consciousness would take place inside a hotel described as the "Heart O' the City."

Summary:

Tank tells Neo that he can escape if he gets to room #303.

Metaphysical Breakdown

In numerology, this number breaks down to the number six. Six represents man's lower level, animalistic consciousness. This is the level of consciousness Neo must put to death in himself for him to be resurrected into higher consciousness. This is the room where Neo's lower self will be put to death.

Chapter Thirty-Six: "He is the One."
(2:02:20)

Summary:

Neo rushes into room #303, only to find Agent Smith waiting for him. Agent Smith shoots him at point blank range, in the heart ten times.

Metaphysical Breakdown

In numerology, the number 303, breaks down to the number six. Six represents man's lower level, animalistic consciousness. This is the level of consciousness Neo must put to death within himself for him to be resurrected into higher consciousness. This is the room where Neo's lower self will be put to death.

The heart is where the battle for higher consciousness is fought.

Summary:

Neo appears to have died. His hearts monitor flat lines.

Metaphysical Breakdown

Same Metaphysical Breakdown as above.

Summary:

Neo is laying on the ground dead, on his right side. The light is shining on the left side of his face.

Metaphysical Breakdown

By Neo lying on his right side denotes that he is suppressing his lower consciousness represented in the left hemisphere of the brain. The fact that the left side of his face is illuminated signifies the activation of the right hemisphere of the brain which is represents his higher self.

185

Summary:

Trinity talks to Neo's body, while she lies on top of him. She says, "Neo, I'm not afraid anymore. The Oracle told me that I'd fall in love, and that man I loved would be the One. So you see, you can't be dead. You can't be because I love you. You hear me? I love you." She then proceeds to kiss Neo. In the background, sparks begin to fly. Neo's heart monitor begins to beep. It shows the number two on the screen. Trinity then tells Neo to get up!

Metaphysical Breakdown

In Kemet, the god Ausar was the first god to resurrect himself. He was able to do this by the help of his wife Auset. Auset was the one that put him back together once he was dead and breathed life back into his dead body. Auset, even straddles Ausar's body just as Trinity climbs on top of Neo. This scene is taken directly from that Kemetic story of resurrection.

Summary:

Neo stands up. The three agents see him and start shooting at him. Neo is able to stop there bullets in the air. There are twelve bullets that are right in front of him.

Metaphysical Breakdown

Neo now emulates the story of Jesus from the Bible. The three agents represent the three kings that came bearing gifts to the new born Jesus or savior. The twelve bullets that seem to follow Neo represent the twelve apostles that "followed" Jesus. Neo picks one of the bullets out of the sky, he examines it and then discards it. This action represents the unveiling and discovery of the apostle Judas, who betrayed Jesus.

Summary:

Neo looks up at the agents. The left side of his face is illuminated as the right side of his face is shaded.

Metaphysical Breakdown

Neo has completed his resurrection from his lower, animalistic consciousness to his higher, spiritual consciousness. He is the Kerast or as achieved the Christ consciousness.

Chapter Thirty-Seven: Final Connections
(2:05:34)

Summary:

Neo now sees everything in the Matrix code. Agent Smith runs towards him. Neo stands his ground.

Metaphysical Breakdown

Neo has no sense of fear. Neo sees the Matrix according to his higher, spiritual consciousness. The green shade he sees in the symbols represents the heart chakra, which is the first level of higher consciousness. Neo has completed his transformation.

Summary:

Neo literally fights him with his right hand behind his back. He then kicks him down the hall with his left foot.

Metaphysical Breakdown

Neo's right hand being placed behind his back symbolizes his void of lower consciousness. He doesn't use his right side of his body, thus he cannot activate the left hemisphere of his brain which represents his lower consciousness. All of Neo's movements are located on the left side of his body which exclusively activates the right hemisphere of the brain which represents higher consciousness.

Summary:

Neo literally jumps into Agent Smith and destroys him from the inside out.

Metaphysical Breakdown

The only way to destroy one's lower consciousness, which Agent Smith represents, is to go within and attack it from the inside out. The battle is an internal struggle of the individual, not external.

Summary:

Morpheus pushes the electro-magnetic pulse button to kill the invading Sentinels

Metaphysical Breakdown

In the occult, electric energy is masculine and magnetic energy is feminine. The combination of the two coming together, electro-magnetic energy, produces a "gateway" to bring the spiritual dimension into the physical realm. In other words, the coming together of a man and woman in higher consciousness creates the ability for them to manifest miracles together and be self-sufficient from a system that looks to oppress them. This is the only "weapon" Morpheus uses against the machines.

Summary:

The next scene we see a computer screen that reads, "9-18-99 14:32:21"

Metaphysical Breakdown

In numerology, these set of numbers break down to the number 13. This is the number of resurrection. This is the number that represents Neo, which means new. Neo is born again and has a "new" life because of his higher consciousness.

Summary:

Neo says, "You're afraid of us. You're afraid of change. I don't know the future. I didn't come here to tell you how it's going to end. I came here to tell you how it's going to begin. I'm going to hang up this phone and then I'm going to show these people what you don't want them to see. I'm going to show them a world without you. A world without rules and controls, without borders or boundaries. A world where anything is possible. "

Metaphysical Breakdown

Neo is speaking to the elite and the secret societies that control the world and the masses from behind the shadows. They are the ones that are afraid. Neo states that he doesn't know how it will end but he came to tell how it will begin. The beginning of this revolution is the activation of man's higher consciousness housed in the right hemisphere of the brain. Once man translates and defines himself and his reality through his higher consciousness, he initiates the beginning of the process of setting himself free.

Neo states that he will show the people a world without you. The "you" he is referring to is the same elite, secret societies that control the world. Their main objective is to control all of the world's resources, wealth and power by providing an environment that feeds people's lower level consciousness. If this entity was eliminated, the people would be able to see the world and define themselves through their higher consciousness. Once this was achieved, there would be no means of control on the masses. The people would be liberated from the prisons of their minds.

Once this is achieved, anything is possible. Neo speaks of a world without borders, rules, control or boundaries. Man would live in harmony with himself, his fellow man and his environment. This is what the secret societies fear. They fear the reawakening of man discovering his higher consciousness.

Summary:

The camera focuses in on the words "SYSTEM FAILURE." The camera proceeds to go between the "M" in system and the "F" in failure.

Metaphysical Breakdown

The left side of the tunnel the camera focuses in on has the letter "M." The letter "M" in numerology represents the number thirteen. This is the number of resurrection. Resurrection is the putting to death of one's lower consciousness and being reborn into one's higher, spiritual consciousness. The left side symbolizes the activation of the right hemisphere of the brain which contains man's higher consciousness.

The right side of the tunnel has the letter "F." In numerology, this letter breaks down to represent the number six. This number represents one's lower level or animalistic consciousness. The fact that the letter "F" is on the right of the tunnel represents the activation of the left hemisphere of the brain which represents one's lower consciousness. So the message of the scene represents man's own free will. Man has the ability to choose to either define himself and his environment through his lower self or he can define himself and his environment through his higher self.

Chapter Thirty-Eight: End Credits (2:08:42)

Summary:

Next scene, Neo is seen using a phone with his left hand inside a phone booth. He says, "Where we go from there is a choice I leave to you." He exits the phone booth, turns to his left, puts on his sun glasses, looks up in the sky and flies away!

Metaphysical Breakdown

As you know by now, the symbolism of Neo putting emphasis on moving to his left is very significant in representing his higher consciousness by activating the right hemisphere of the brain. This symbolism has been used several times throughout the film. Because of its frequency, this lets the viewer comprehend the significance and relevance of this ideology. This must be a very important concept to be repeated over and over again in regards to Neo breaking out of his lower level consciousness and transcending to higher consciousness or spirituality.

Neo than states that where we go from here is a choice I leave to you. Again, the focus and interest is in man having free will or a choice to operate in regards to his lower or higher self. The solution to all of man's problems lies within. Man's freedom is predicated on how he defines himself and his environment.

Neo steps out of the phone booth. The phone booth symbolizes the system or Matrix which promotes man's lower level consciousness. By Neo choosing to "step out of the box," signifies his commitment and his faith in operating at his highest level of consciousness. Neo chooses not to accept the reality that has been given to him to enslave him. He has made a conscious choice to activate his higher consciousness and define his own reality as he sees fit. He has reclaimed his mind, body and spirit.

Next, Neo puts on his sunglasses on and flies away. In Kemet, the Pineal gland which produces melanin was known as the "first eye." It was the activation of this "eye" that connected man to his higher consciousness. Neo's sunglasses represent the activation of his "first eye." The sunglasses being black represent the melanin produced by his Pineal gland or "first eye." When his melanin is activated, Neo can fly or ascend into his higher consciousness. This is man's solution to overcoming his lower consciousness, represented by Neo's ability to fly and be free.

In this Kemetic, Metu Neter we see the Sun hitting the figure on the right on it's Pineal gland. This symbolizes the activation of Melanin to achieve higher consciousness. Notice the body of a lion and the head of a man. The animal body of the figure represents the lower consciousness one has to overcome to reach the higher consciousness in the brain or head of the individual.

THE END

Contents

DVD Chapter One: A New World (0:00)

Commentary:

Opening scene shows Jake flying in a dream sequence. When Jake was mortally wounded, he had dreams of flying. He was free. Jake says, "Sooner or later you always have to wake up."

Metaphysical Breakdown

The symbol of "flying" refers to man's higher self or consciousness. The act of Jake "waking up," refers to recognition of his higher, spiritual consciousness and not defining himself through his lower or physical self. This alludes to the Afrikan concept that we are all spirits having a human experience. We should not define or place too much value on the physical dimension. Life begins when the body dies as the spirit is free of the constraints of the body and the physical realm. Life, in the physical dimension is for preparation for the spiritual realm. It took Jake to be mortally wounded before he viewed himself as spiritual being with no physical limitations.

Commentary:

When Jake is seen waking up, there is a close up of his right eye.

Metaphysical Breakdown

Right eye symbolizes the activation of the left brain. This hemisphere of the brain represents man's lower or physical self as he wakes up from the spiritual dimension or the dream world. The background color is Indigo, which represents Jake's higher consciousness in the spiritual dimension. This is the color of the 6th chakra which represents the activation of the Pineal gland or "first eye." This chakra represents the acknowledgement and awareness of the higher or spiritual self.

Commentary:

Next we see two drops of water floating in the air. The two drops emerge as one.

Metaphysical Breakdown

In numerology, the number two represents division or separation. In this scene the two drops represent man's twin personalities. Man has a higher or spiritual self and a lower or physical self. It is man's freewill to decide how he will define himself and the life he lives. Our conscious thoughts define our reality. It is an internal interpretation of our external circumstances. The two drops emerging as one represents the duality of man and his conscience.

Commentary:

In the background of the cushion Jake is lying on, is stitching in a diamond pattern.

Metaphysical Breakdown

The geometric shape represents the gateway to higher consciousness. You see it in the middle of the Freemasonry symbol. It is the space between the compass, which represents the woman on top and the square on the bottom, which represents the man. The coming together of the man and woman opens up a "gateway" to manifest infinite possibilities. This symbol permeates throughout all Hollywood movies.

http://www.lexingtonlodge1.org/images/Masonic-symbol-white.png

Commentary:

Jake mentions that he has been in "Cryo" (suspended animation) for six years.

Metaphysical Breakdown

In numerology, six is the number of lower man. Jake is going through a transformation process into resurrecting himself from his lower or animalistic self into his higher or spiritual self. This is what this whole sequence is about. Jake is being initiated into higher consciousness. Jake being in "Cryo" or asleep, represents the state or unawareness of his higher or spiritual consciousness.

Commentary:

He even mentions, "It feels like 1/5th of tequila and an ass kicking."

Metaphysical Breakdown

In numerology, 1 + 5 = 6. Six is the number of lower self or animalistic consciousness. This lower level behavior and understanding is what Jake is rising above and leaving behind him.

Commentary:

Jakes sleeping quarters, which resembles a coffin, is now opened as he is being "raised from the dead." Jake further states that his brother Tommy was a scientist and not himself.

Metaphysical Breakdown

Tommy is the nickname for Thomas. In etymology, Thomas means twin. In actuality, Jake didn't have a brother. His twin brother is just a symbol of Jake's lower or animalistic self. Tommy is Jake's lower self that was controlled by the left hemisphere of his brain, which is logical and analytical. That's why Tommy was said to be a scientist. All scientists a very skeptical, logical and analytical. They seek physical proof in order to substantiate their theories. Jake has now put to death his lower self, represented by his brother Tommy, and is now operating with the right hemisphere of his brain, in order to define his reality through his spiritual or higher self. Being "raised" is part of the initiation process in secret societies. They all have rituals of a mock funeral of the initiate and then his "resurrection" from the dead, into a higher level or degree in the organization. They get this ritual from Kemet.

Commentary:

Jake asks the attendant, "Are we there yet?" The attendant tells him, "Yeah, we're there sunshine."

Metaphysical Breakdown

The attendant calls Jake, Sunshine for a reason. Men are represented by the Sun in Kemetic or esoteric knowledge. The Sun is electric. The Sun gives out energy. These are properties of the masculine or positive principle of energy. Women are represented by the moon. The moon is magnetic. The feminine principle of energy receives energy. The moon receives and reflects the Sun's energy. This is the Kemetic Law of Gender. All energy is either positive, which means to give out or negative, which means to receive. The Sun or masculine principle, "gives out" energy and the Moon or feminine principle "reflects or receives the energy or light from the Sun. This is why the attendant refers to Jake as having properties of the Sun and why male babies are called sons.

Commentary:

Jake's attendant also grabs Jake by his left wrist or forearm.

Metaphysical Breakdown

This handshake is called the "Lion's Paw" in secret societies. It also symbolizes the resurrection of the initiate into higher consciousness. In the occult world, resurrection means to "put to death" lower level consciousness of the left hemisphere of the brain and rise to higher, spiritual consciousness by activating the right hemisphere of the brain. The left side of the body activates the right hemisphere of the brain which represents man's higher spiritual consciousness. The fact that he grabs his left arm represents the activation of his right brain or higher spiritual self. He also taps Jake on his left shoulder to further this point. Jake is being "raised" from the dead. Death of lower level consciousness.

The lion was the symbol for the first degrees of initiation, the sign which allowed the opening of the book, so to speak. It possibly represented the royalty of initiation, the status that comes with being aware of what is concealed

- Tony Bushby(*Secret in the Bible*) |

Occultist Pat Robertson, representing religion; Al Gore, representing politics and Will Smith, representing the entertainment industry, all displaying the "Lion's Paw" a gesture that demonstrates Masonic dominion and control over their perspective fields.

Commentary:

Jake's compartment is numbered H-6. You can see it on top of the screen.

Metaphysical Breakdown

In numerology, this number and letter sequence breaks down to equal the number five. The number five can be interpreted as God sees favor in your undertaking. Jake is in God's graces. Jake is taking a major step in his life in achieving and believing in the best of himself, which is his higher, spiritual consciousness by putting to "death" his lower or animalistic consciousness.

Commentary:

There is a man directly underneath Jake's compartment facing the opposite direction.

Metaphysical Breakdown

This symbolizes the Kemetic law of, "As above, so below." It represents the macrocosm and the microcosm of the Universe that all matter must adhere to the same laws no matter how big or small. It also symbolizes Jake's choice to define himself through his higher self, as Jake is seen on top of the man below him. All things in nature have the exact opposite represented. Like hot and cold or up and down. Esoteric knowledge teaches us that what seems like opposites or two different things, are really extreme expressions of the one thing. For instance, hot and cold are both extreme expressions of the one thing, which is temperature, a unit of measurement.

Commentary:

Next scene, Jake's brother Tommy, is seen in a casket getting ready to be cremated. Jake is seen watching. He is wearing a T-shirt with an eagle on the front.

Metaphysical Breakdown

This scene symbolizes Jake's lower self being put to rest. The bird on Jake's T-shirt also represents Jakes initiation into higher consciousness. In ancient Kemet, the hawk or god Heru, represents man's resurrection into higher consciousness. The hawk flies highest in the sky and can rise above and see all lower lever behavior from its vantage point. No one flies higher than the hawk in ancient Kemet. The hawk is "above" the behavior of lower consciousness.

Commentary:

The attendant announces, "You been in cryo for 5 years, 9 months and 22 day."

Metaphysical Blueprint

In numerology, these numbers add up to the number nine. Nine symbolizes man's judgment or life lesson that he must overcome in order to transcend. Jake is being tested or judged in his pursuit of higher consciousness.

Commentary:

Jake starts to float outside of his compartment. He reaches his locker. He then proceeds to open it with his left hand.

Metaphysical Blueprint

The left side of the body, in this case the left hand, represents the activation of the right brain. This hemisphere of the brain symbolizes higher or spiritual consciousness. Jake is opening a new definition of reality in a new world of higher consciousness.

Commentary:

Jake explains how his twin brother died. "A guy with a gun ends his journey, for the paper in his wallet."

Metaphysical Blueprint

This cause of death is the most common cause for the majority of people. Not the act of being shot but the motivation for money. We are all living and dying for paper that we call money. We never are concerned about investing and reaching our higher, spiritual selves. In ancient Kemet, life was lived as preparation for the spiritual realm after we have crossed over. It was about living a moral and righteous life. Not about how much material things one could surround himself with. Life in the physical realm was only considered a blink of an eye, opposed to the spiritual realm we all will return to for eternity. So based on a person's life that was dedicated to achieving righteousness, humility and overcoming the ego in the physical realm, was in direct correlation to how high he can ascend to in the spiritual realm. Life was motivated by achieving one's higher spiritual consciousness not motivated by paying bills, owning a house or driving a nice car.

Commentary:

Coroner covers Tommy's body with his left hand before they close the lid.

Metaphysical Blueprint

Again, the left hand symbolizes the activation of the right brain or man's higher, spiritual self. Jake's lower self is being destroyed.

Commentary:

The next scene they show a wide shot of the space ship they are on. If one was to look closely they will see the bottom of the ship is identical to the top of the ship.

Metaphysical Blueprint

This image further displays the law of, "As above, so below." This concept can is also displayed in the Asian yin and yang symbol. This principle is one of the Universal Laws in ancient Kemet. It is the universal balance of everything. On cannot put out lower level energy and think it won't come back to them. On the other hand, if one puts out higher conscious energy, they shall witness the results of that energy as well. Our life and experiences are mere reflections of the thoughts and actions we put out.

Commentary:

The next scene, we see Tommy's coffin being loaded into the incinerator. The number on the coffin is 976323.

Metaphysical Blueprint

In numerology this number adds up to the number 3. In the Bible, the character of Jesus rose from the dead on the third day. Three represents divine perfection. This is Jake's crucifixion and resurrection. The story of Christ's crucifixion is really an example of how man can overcome his ego, in an attempt to reach is higher self. To kill the ego, one must go through the trials and tribulations that the character of Jesus went through. These include; being accused of something you did not do and accepting the burden for it, stripped down naked or humiliated, tortured, ridiculed and reprimanded without complaining, perseverance, overcoming exhaustion, forgiveness, faith and humility. To sacrifice yourself for the good of others. This is the road man must take to higher consciousness.

Commentary:

This point is further made by the coroner pushing the coffin in the incinerator with his right hand.

Metaphysical Breakdown

This act symbolizes the death of left brain dominant thinking, which represents man's lower or animalistic self. The right hand activates the left hemisphere of the brain. The left brain activates our lower self.

Commentary:

The men around Jake offer him a job to take over his brother's position. They say, "You can step into his shoes, so to speak." And "It will be a fresh start on a new world."

Metaphysical Blueprint

All this signifies confirmation that Jake is now venturing into a whole new reality because he chose to operate according to his higher self. If one changes their thinking, they can change their reality. There was really only one pair of shoes to begin with. Jake and Tommy are one in the same. The shoe analogy is a clue to this point.

Commentary:

The coroner pushes the fourth button, which is the furnace incinerator, with his right hand.

Metaphysical Blueprint

The number 4 in numerology represents creation. In this case the new creation of Jake operating at his higher consciousness. Again the coroner uses the right hand to push the button to further point out the death of left brain dominant thinking. This button turns on the flames to cremate Tommy's body which represents Jake's lower self.

Commentary:

As they incinerate Tommy's body, one can see the torches are lined up in relation to each other to form an "X." This "X" is completed once the incinerator is ignited and the body is burned.

Metaphysical Blueprint

This also is a Kemetic symbol of resurrection. The "X" represents the god Ausar, who was the first god to resurrect himself. When the flames are lit they connect with each other through the body. This is not a coincidence, but a symbol meant to show, Jake's resurrection into higher consciousness.

Burial chamber J: rear wall (left part) - KV 62
Valley of the Kings East Valley, Thebes West Bank, Thebes

New Kingdom, Dynasty 18, Tutankhamen

The god Ausar who the Greeks called Osiris, is represented by the figure on the left with the "X" on his chest. King "Tut", in the middle, is be greeted by Ausar to welcome him to eternal life after his physical death.

Commentary:

Next scene they show the spaceship getting ready to land on Pandora. Pandora is not a planet but a moon.

Metaphysical Breakdown

As we mentioned earlier, the moon represents feminine energy. This energy represents man's higher, spiritual self. Feminine energy is also activated in the right hemisphere of the brain. Pandora represents a world of higher spiritual consciousness. This is where Jake will be reborn and transcend to higher consciousness. This is where Jake will live now and define his reality.

Commentary:

As the ship lands the soldiers inside get ready to disembark. The soldier in charge says, "Exo packs on. If you lose that mask your unconscious in 20 seconds and your dead in 4 minutes."

Metaphysical Breakdown

The numerology, 20 + 4= 6. Six is the number of lower man. Again this is another sign of Jake's initiation into higher consciousness by putting to death his lower self or consciousness. Jake is not defining himself through the physical limitations of his body. That's why he is in a wheel chair. For him to truly transcend, he must define himself through his spiritual self, not his lower physical body.

Commentary:

Another significant sign is the man giving out instructions is Black.

Metaphysical Breakdown

Hollywood is always putting Black people in strategic positions, saying specific lines, in movies to make a point or suggest as to where the true knowledge comes from. That place is Afrika. In this case, Afrikan knowledge is what is being expressed to not only keep the soldiers alive, but to give secret homage to where this esoteric knowledge comes from.

Commentary:

Next scene the pilots of the ship are communicating with the control tower. They say, "Hell's Gate tower this is TAV-16 on approach."

Metaphysical Breakdown

These set of numbers and letters in numerology add up to the number 5. Five represents that God sees favor in your undertaking. Jake is now making the commitment to "land" on Pandora, which represents defining his reality through his feminine, spiritual and higher self. The name of the base of Pandora is called Hell's Gate. On must figuratively "go to Hell and back." To attain higher spiritual consciousness. It is the struggle of all men. This is the system of white supremacy. This is the hell people of color face every day. It is a system designed for men to view and define themselves through their lower selves. It promotes and is driven by the ego, not man's spiritual nature.

Commentary:

As they fly over a mining field, the image resembles the shape of the Asian Yin & Yang symbol.

Metaphysical Breakdown

This is another example of the Kemetic law of "as above, so below."

Commentary:

Jake, "One life ends, another begins.

Metaphysical Breakdown

As he states this, they show his twin brother's body burning in the incinerator. This suggests his initiation into higher consciousness by "putting to death" his lower or animalistic consciousness.

Commentary:

As the soldiers exit the ship, they show 6 Marines before they show Jake, who is the seventh.

Metaphysical Breakdown

Seven in numerology represents God's divinity in the physical dimension. Jake, being the seventh Marine, is now singled out as the one who will represent God's personality or divinity in Hell's Gate.

Commentary:

As Jake rolls out in his wheel chair, he has to swerve out the way to avoid a giant, robot machine, called an Amp suit with the number 18 on it. Jake makes a left to avoid being injured or killed.

Metaphysical Breakdown

18 in numerology breaks down to the number 9. Nine represents man's judgment or life lesson. Jake turning left represents the activation of the right brain. This is the answer to Jake's lessons in life. Do not be analytical or logical in your view of the world, use your intuition, faith and spirituality to face the perceived dangers and pitfalls of life.

Commentary:

A giant dump truck rolls by with arrows piercing it's tires. Pay attention to the rims they have a particular pattern. They have 6 major marks or points on them.

Metaphysical Breakdown

These marks are laid out as an outline to the Sephedet, Seal of Solomon or what is now known as the Star of David. This symbol represents masculine and feminine energy coming together to open a gateway where infinite possibilities are manifested.

This symbol is the coming together of two triangles. The upside down triangle represents feminine energy and the right side up triangle, super imposed over the other, represents masculine energy. The hexagon shape, in the middle represents the gateway of infinite possibilities.

DVD Chapter Two:
You Are Not in Kansas Anymore (6:17)

Commentary:

Flash to next scene, which shows Col. Quaritch walking with his right foot stepping forward first. On the sixth step, the camera zooms in on his firearm.

Metaphysical Breakdown

The character of Col. Quaritch, by walking out with his right foot forward is activating his left brain, which represents the activation of his lower or animalistic self. By zooming in on his gun on his sixth step, further reveals his lower level or destructive consciousness. This lets the audience know, this character is a potential villain in the movie.

Commentary:

The Colonel has major scars on the right side of his face.

Metaphysical Breakdown

This image further suggests his sole activation of his left brain exclusively. All of his decisions and view of reality come from his lower consciousness which is activated in the left hemisphere of the brain. He has no heart, no compassion and no humility. As one can view, the left side of his face is free of any scars.

Commentary:

Col. Quaritch states, "Out there, beyond that fence, every living thing that crawls, flies or squats in the mud wants to kill you and eat your eyes for Jujubes."

Metaphysical Breakdown

Renowned author and scholar, Dr. Francis Cress Welsing has a theory to the white man's psychology when it comes to white supremacy. She suggests that white people operate on a level of fear when they come into contact with people of color or nature in general. Because melanated people or people of color have the genetic potency and capacity to destroy the white race genetically, white people subconsciously go into attack mode or operate on the defensive. They subconsciously internalize that everything around them, including nature, is trying to kill them. Col. Quaritch's comments support this theory. The only place they feel safe is in the confines of their "white" walls or fences called Hell's Gate. So Caucasians live in a constant state of fear. This is the basis for the colonist, imperialist, war mongering, racism, genocide and preemptive strike behavior and ideology.

Commentary:

Jake now rolls into the military briefing. Super imposed over his head is a sign with the number 5 and an arrow pointing directly down on him.

Metaphysical Breakdown

Five in numerology represents God has favor in your undertaking. This is another esoteric sign that Jake is operating according to his higher or spiritual self.

Commentary:

As the camera pans around to pick up the Colonel, you see the number six super imposed behind him.

Metaphysical Breakdown

Six is the number of lower man or the beast in man. This esoteric sign lets you know that this character is operating according to his lowest self, which is man as a human animal.

215

DVD Chapter Three:
This is Your Avatar Now, Jake (4:11)

Commentary:

The character of Norm is introduced for the first time. He catches up with Jake on the sixth level of the base. You can see the number six on the right beam right next to Norm.

Metaphysical Breakdown

Six again in numerology represents man's lower self. This is the level where the Avatars are stored. Jake must give up his physical body and define himself by his higher self which is represented by the Avatar. The Avatar's body is Indigo which is the sixth chakra. It represents man's ability to see and define himself through the spiritual realm or his higher consciousness.

Commentary:

Jake makes a left in his wheel chair leaving Norm behind.

Metaphysical Breakdown

This symbol is played over and over again in this movie. The making of the left with the body or the use of the left side of the body, symbolizes the activation of the right hemisphere of the brain or Jake's higher or spiritual consciousness.

Commentary:

Jake meets his Avatar for the first time. His Avatar is sleeping on the right side of his body in the incubator.

Metaphysical Breakdown

Many Afrikan rites of passage have the initiate lay on their right sides. This is also common in secret society rituals. This

216

symbolizes the suppression of left brain function, which is the lower self. The left side of the body is now on top of the right. The left side of the body is now free to move. This symbolizes the activation of the right hemisphere of the brain, which represents higher consciousness.

Commentary:

Jake speaking on how the Avatars are made, "They are grown from human DNA mixed with the DNA of the natives.

Metaphysical Breakdown

The natives or Avatars represent Black people or people of color. The mixing of the DNA means the comingling of the white race with people of color. This is the only way white people can acquire melanin. They have to give birth to a child whose father or mother was Black or a person of color. The point being made here, is that white people, because their lack of melanin cannot achieve the level of higher consciousness Black people or people of color can achieve naturally. This does not mean that people of color are superior. They can also operate at the lowest level of man being a beast. What is does suggest, is the potential people of color have in regards to achieving a higher spiritual level of consciousness that Caucasians do not have access to because of their lack of melanin. White people intermingling with their own race, cannot produce melanin on their own. It needs to be introduced into their gene pool.

Commentary:

Next scene Jake is seen giving his video diary about his experiences. The date on the video screen is 5/19/2154.

Metaphysical Breakdown

In numerology, these numbers add up to 3. It relates to the character of Jesus in the Bible being resurrected on the third day. This is who Jake represents or who he symbolizes.

Commentary:

Grace Augustine is now introduced into the movie. Norm explains to her that he has been studying the Na'vi language for five years.

Metaphysical Breakdown

Five in numerology represents God being pleased with your undertaking. The fact that Norm has taken time to communicate and define himself through his higher self, is pointed out by the number five. Remember, anything belonging to the Na'vi, symbolizes man's activation of his higher consciousness and thus he is closer to God.

Commentary:

Jake introduces himself to Grace. He extends his right hand out for her to shake. She rejects it. She also mentions that she needs his brother, who has trained three years for this mission.

Metaphysical Breakdown

This is a symbol of rejecting left brain or lower consciousness behavior. The extension of the right hand when meeting an individual, is a subtle form of defining one's reality through their lower selves. In ancient Kemet, they emphasized the walking out or extension of the left side of the body first. This simple act activated the right hemisphere of the brain, which defines reality through one's higher self. Since Jake's hand was rejected, further exemplifies the rejection of lower consciousness and behavior. Coincidently, the number three also comes up to symbolize Jake's resurrection or his defining reality through his higher self.

Commentary:

Dr. Max Patel tells Jake to be here tomorrow at 0800 hours to start is Avatar training.

Metaphysical Breakdown

The number 8 in numerology represents infinity or eternity. Jake will be making a permanent change in his life once he becomes his Avatar. He has made a life commitment to define and live his life through his higher self.

DVD Chapter Four:
This Is Why We're Here (1:55)

Commentary:

Grace goes up to see Selfridge to discuss the presence of Jake in her department. Selfridge is practicing his putting. Grace kicks the cup before Selfridge's ball can go into it.

Metaphysical Breakdown

The white ball represents Eurocentric culture or white supremacy. Whenever Europeans encountered people of color in their travels, they always subjected and forced the natives to adopt their ways. The Europeans always believed cultures that were not their own were always inferior to them. Grace is protecting the cup which represents Afrocentric or Na'vi culture, by moving it out the way of the white ball that is trying to infiltrate it. Grace is protecting the Na'vi or indigenous people from lower level, European invasion.

Commentary:

Selfridge moves over to a 3D monitor. In the center of the monitor is three pentagons stacked on top of each other. These pentagons represent the outer perimeter or walls of Hell's Gate.

Metaphysical Breakdown

The pentagon represents the middle of a five pointed star. The star in ancient Kemet represented man at his highest level of consciousness. The Sun is a star which represents masculine energy. Now when you turn the star or pentagon upside down, it has the opposite definition. It now represents man at his lowest state of consciousness. The inverted star represents man defining himself through his lower or animalistic nature. Selfridge represents the assets of the corporation without regard to human life or higher consciousness. The corporation is motivated exclusively by money and power for its shareholders and nobody or anything else. This thinking makes the Selfridge character a beast or a demon in lower level consciousness. He is the upside pentagon or star.

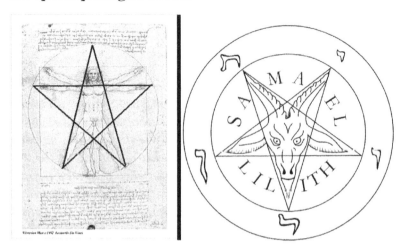

This is a Advance drawing of man being represented by the 5 pointed star, on the left. The picture on the right, is a picture of the Free Mason god, named Baphomet. He is represented as the upside down star. This is the symbol, of promoting and defining man through his lower self. This is how man is able to be manipulated and controlled. This is done by feeding man's ego or lower nature that is used to define himself and his reality.

Commentary:

All of Col. Quaritch's soldiers have a patch of a pentagon logo on their right shoulders. The patch is colored red on the left side.

Metaphysical Breakdown

The pentagon patch being on the right side of the body represents the activation of the left brain or man's lower consciousness. The fact that the patch is colored red on the left side, symbolizes that man's potential for higher consciousness is blocked by his lower self. Red symbolizes man's lowest chakra or consciousness. This is the culture of the military industrial complex and the multi-national corporations, represented by the characters of Col. Quaritch and Parker Selfridge.

Commentary:

Selfridge takes Grace into his office and shows her a black, metallic rock. He tells her, "This is why we are here. Unobtainuim. This little gray rock sells for $20 million a kilo. That's the only reason."

Metaphysical Breakdown

This is the jest of the movie. Selfridge is displaying and revealing the privileged mentality white people or Eurocentric ideology they have when it comes to dealing with people of color. They feel that it is the duty of people of color to worship, think, act and serve white people like it is part of the natural order of things. Unobtainuim is really Melanin or the chemical that makes people of color not only dark but spiritually enlightened. Selfridge carefully picks up and holds the Unobtainuim in his left hand, symbolizing its higher consciousness. Remember left hand activates the right hemisphere of the brain which represents man's higher consciousness. Since white people cannot produce Melanin on their own, they must oppress and high jack the spiritual ideologies and concepts of the darker people of the world. Even with this stolen science and knowledge from Black people, Caucasians still have a difficult time communicating on a spiritual realm. They cannot seem to live with one with nature without destroying the natural order of things.

What the corporation, which represents Caucasians in Avatar is seeking, is the access to the darker people of the world, not some imaginary substance in the ground. They are actually mining the PEOPLE! Black people are white people's most precious resource!

The numerology behind 20 million breaks down to the number 2. The number two represents division or separation. In this case, the separation or division of Melanin or higher consciousness, from people of color high jacked by the European, for their own purposes motivated by their lower, animalistic behavior and thinking.

DVD Chapter Five: First Awakening (1:13)

Commentary:

Grace is questioning Norm about how many hours he has logged in. Norm answers 520 hours.

Metaphysical Breakdown

520 in numerology breaks down to be the number 7. Seven represents God's manifestation in the physical dimension. Norm is operating at a high conscious level by taking time to do the work to communicate with his higher self.

Commentary:

Jake is then escorted to his machine, called a "Link" that will transfer him to his Avatar body. Jake touches the inside of the machine with his left hand first.

Metaphysical Breakdown

Again left hand signifies the activation of the higher conscious, right brain. Jake is preparing to transfer into his higher consciousness. The machine is named "Link" because it links Jake to his higher, spiritual consciousness.

Commentary:

Grace states to Jake, "So you just figured you would come out here, to the most hostile environment known to man, with no training of any kind, and see how it went? What was going through your head?" Jake replies, "Maybe I was just sick of doctors telling me what I couldn't do."

Metaphysical Breakdown

Jake is not operating on fear or logic, which are attributes of the left hemisphere of the brain. Jake is walking out on faith, trusting his own intuition and imagination to guide him in unforeseen territory which everyone tells him that he has no business even being there. This mindset is housed in the right hemisphere of the brain. This thinking is the fuel that manifests miracles in the right brain that become our reality. Jake is trusting his instincts and not letting lower level thoughts discourage him from pursuing his dreams. Being fearful is a direct sign of one operating according to their lower consciousness.

Commentary:

The operators of the links pronounce that link 3 is ready.

Metaphysical Blueprint

Link 3 is Jake's link. Three in numerology represents the perfect trinity. Jesus rose on the third day to symbolize the completion of his resurrection. This is Jake's resurrection into higher consciousness.

Commentary

Dr. Max Patel states, "Launch sequence in 3, go."

Metaphysical Breakdown

Again this further explains the significance of the number 3 representing Jake's resurrection into higher consciousness.

Commentary:

The next scene Max compliments Jake on his brain scan. He says, "That's a gorgeous brain. Nice activity."

Metaphysical Breakdown

Again, relating to Jakes activation of the right hemisphere of his brain. This part of the brain houses our higher selves and is the place where dreams and miracles are born.

Commentary:

Next, the link operator replies, "Phase lock- 40%."

Metaphysical Breakdown

In numerology, the number 40 stands on its own. Forty is the number of trial, struggle or lesson. Jesus was tempted in the desert for 40 days, after which, he passed his test and was able to transcend on the cross later. This is Jake's test. He must pass this stage of the transformation before he can assume his Avatar body.

Commentary:

The operator then proceeds to announce, "Phase lock- 99%. Link is stable."

Metaphysical Breakdown

In numerology the number 99 comes out to be 9. Nine is the symbol of judgment. Jake is being judged as to whether he can proceed to enter the realm of higher consciousness. His consciousness is being tested to see if he has mastered his lower self.

Commentary:

Let's take this moment to breakdown the machine or link that transfers Jake and others into their Avatar bodies. The person lies down in a compartment that looks like a high tech coffin. The lid is then closed on them and it slowly moves into another machine that looks like a donut.

Metaphysical Breakdown

Basically, this is the act of sex. The elongated, coffin-type machine represents the male penis or masculine energy. The donut-like machine, the coffin goes into represents the woman's vagina or feminine energy. Just like in the "Star of David" symbol mentioned earlier. The combining of male energy, which is

225

electric, with female energy, which is magnetic, creates an electro-magnetic field, which produces a "gateway" to manifest a person's thoughts into becoming reality in the physical dimension. Our Kemetic ancestors used the sacred science of sex to astro-project their thoughts into reality. In order to activate the gateway, the couple needs to have melanin. When the lid is shut on Jake, one can see a lens that is placed over the middle of his forehead. This is the area that houses the Pineal gland. This is what our Kemetic ancestors described as the "First Eye." For one to truly see and manifest, in the spiritual realm, one's Pineal gland must be activated. The Pineal gland produces melanin. Europeans have a calcified Pineal gland which cannot produce Melanin at all or produces a very weak grade of Melanin. This is the secret science that has been kept from the masses. This is why institutions want you to internalize that sex is dirty and should be stigmatized as lower level consciousness. This mindset keeps you from manifesting anything on your own. These secret societies want the masses to constantly depend on them for answers and solutions to the problems they have inevitably given to us in the first place. For if we only recognized the gift and power of Melanin, we would not need or participate in their system of white supremacy. As a result of being victims in this system, we are placed in a constant state of dependency and fear, which keeps us from our higher consciousness.

Commentary:

Next scene, the camera zooms in and focuses on the space between Jake's eyes, relative to his forehead. A tunnel appears that looks like it is made up of electricity with many colors and bright lights. Jake seems to be traveling at a high rate of speed through this tunnel. The screen becomes blurry and Jake is then seen in his Avatar body.

Metaphysical Breakdown

The space between Jake's eyes, in the middle of his forehead, represents his "first eye" or the location of his Pineal gland. This was called the first eye by our ancient, Kemetic ancestors because it allowed them to see into and recognize the spiritual realm or

226

unseen energy. The Pineal gland is the gland that produces the chemical called Melanin. Melanin is the fuel that opens up higher consciousness in order to travel into higher, spiritual dimensions. Without Melanin, an individual cannot reach higher realms of consciousness. In order for Jake to activate his Melanin, he must put to death lower level consciousness and behavior that is housed in the left hemisphere of the brain. This is where the ego dwells. Jake has reached a level of consciousness where he can activate his Pineal gland to produce the Melanin he needs to attain higher realms of consciousness. This is the threshold into Jake defining himself as an enlightened being.

Commentary:

Next scene, Jake is seen in his Avatar body. He has wires hooked up to the left side of his head as the doctor's flash a light into his left eye first.

Metaphysical Breakdown

The wires connected to Jake's left side and the flashing of the light in his left eye represents Jake's activation of the right hemisphere of his brain, which symbolizes higher consciousness. The left side of the body activates the right hemisphere of the brain which represents man's higher, spiritual consciousness.

Commentary:

Jake now rushes into exploring his new body. The doctors want to sedate him with a drug called, "Supitocam."

Metaphysical Breakdown

The reason Jake is rushing and doesn't want to wait for the doctors to fully check him out is because Jake is in the "state of knowing." This means Jake is operating at a level of mastery where he understands all aspects and mysteries of life without trying to do it. His concept is not based on logic, he just is. He needs no practice or no instruction. He has the capacity to know all things because he is operating at a high level of consciousness.

*** I do not understand the meaning of the drug that they want to use to sedate Jake with, "SUPITOCAM." I am very curious to know any readers interpretation of the word. It is a made up word, so this furthers my curiosity as to what it symbolizes or represents. It must have a very significant, esoteric meaning, as it was suggested to stop Jake from leaving. ***

Commentary:

Jake rushes out the lab. He is temporarily blinded by the Sun. He meets two other Avatars that are playing basketball with red clothing on.

Metaphysical Breakdown

In ancient Kemet, the Sun represented higher consciousness. This is why Jake is blinded initially when he sees the Sun. The two Avatars playing basketball in red, represents the tragedy of Black athletes, who possess all these God given, physical gifts but spiritually and mentally they are operating on the lowest level of consciousness. The color red represents man defining himself at his lowest level, the physical body. This is the color of the first chakra that represents man's lowest level of consciousness. These Black athletes literally have the potential to reach higher consciousness, but they choose to define themselves by their lower, physical consciousness and how well they play a child's game for the duration of their adult lives.

Commentary:

The female playing basketball further states, "I don't even have to play defense on you."

Metaphysical Breakdown

This suggests that Black people, who define themselves by their lower selves, are not a threat to the system that enslaves them.

228

For they are the slaves that don't even know they are slaves. Remember this system feeds and encourages our lower level consciousness. Many of us don't want the responsibility of attaining higher consciousness. The system is not threatened by Black people waking up and understanding what is being done to them. Therefore, no "defense" is necessary for people who are not a threat to achieving higher consciousness.

Commentary:

As Jake is running at full speed, Norm cries out to him, "We are not supposed to be running!"

Metaphysical Breakdown

This is proof that Jake is no longer operating according to his left brain. He is dismissing logic, rules and people telling him what he can't do. He is now walking or running out on faith and is in the state of knowing, with no fear to hold him back.

Commentary:

Jake almost collides with an Amp suit or a mechanical robot, which has the number 26 on it. Jake yells out, "Jesus!" as he jumps out the way.

Metaphysical Breakdown

In numerology 26 breaks down to the number 8. Eight is the number of infinity or eternity. This represents Jake's constant struggle to raise his consciousness in a system that is constantly trying to keep him mentally, physically and spiritually dead. When Jake yells out the name Jesus, he is literally talking about himself and his ability to resurrect himself into attaining higher consciousness. Remember Jake is a Black man. The character of Jesus in the Bible, was taken from the Kemetic god Heru, who is Afrikan or Black.

Commentary:

Jake is then seen sliding and curling his toes in rich, dark and fertile soil.

Metaphysical Breakdown

The soil represents the rich, dark and fertile characteristics of the chemical Melanin that Jake used to activate his Avatar body. It is the foundation under his feet. Without it, none of this would be possible.

Commentary:

Grace suddenly appears in her Avatar body. She is wearing a Stanford University shirt. She then throws Jake a fruit that is deep purple in color. Jake takes a bite and comments on how good it taste.

Metaphysical Breakdown

Stanford University's mascot is a pine tree. The pine cone in the occult world represents the Pineal gland which produces Melanin. The Pineal gland has the same shape of a pine cone thus that is where it gets its name. The color purple represents the highest or seventh chakra located above the crown of the head. This level of consciousness allows Jake to have out of body experiences. Jake is now a master or shaman. Jake eating of the purple fruit is his initiation into the highest level of consciousness. This fruit or consciousness was given to him by the Pineal gland represented by God's Grace in the Stanford University shirt.

Commentary:

Jake goes to sleep as an Avatar and wakes up as a human.

Metaphysical Breakdown

Jake is now operating back into the realm of his lower, physical self. Jake seems to be disappointed when he sees he cannot walk again. Jake is limited at this lower level of consciousness, which he finds himself confined to. Jake now understands the difference between higher and lower consciousness and prefers to operate and define his reality according to his higher self. This is why Jake is so disappointed to return back to his human body, which represents his lower self.

DVD Chapter Six:
Colonel Quaritch (4:46)

Commentary:

Trudy is now introduced in the movie. She is shown getting her helicopter ready for combat. She has a tiger painted on its right side. She informs her gunner that they are leaving at zero-9 tomorrow.

Metaphysical Breakdown

The tiger on her helicopter symbolizes the lion goddess Sekhmet. In ancient Kemet, this deity represented God's wrath or justice. The lion represented the power, swiftness and finality of God's vengeance. The tiger and lion are both represented in the cat or feline family. The cat being on the right side of the helicopter represents its purpose and designed for destruction in war. War is man's lower self. It is the lowest level man can descend. The number nine in numerology represents the judgment Trudy is about to be tested on her next sortie run. Trudy will battle her conscience and the aspects of what is right and wrong. Her morality will come into play. In other words, she will be tested on how she views herself and her environment. Will she embrace her lower self or higher consciousness?

Commentary:

As Trudy and Jake are walking to see Col. Quaritch, a shuttle with missiles labeled NPB-9, almost runs into Jake. Trudy shouts out, "Watch it!"

Metaphysical Breakdown

In numerology, these numbers and letters add up to the number 5. This number suggests God has favor in your undertaking or you are in God's graces. This scene foreshadows Jakes run in with these weapons of mass destruction later on in the film. The hidden message given here is that no military weapon will harm Jake because he has God on his side.

Commentary:

Jake meets Col. Quaritch. He acknowledges Jakes previous military tours. He tells him, "Venezuela that was some mean bush."

Metaphysical Breakdown

The letter "V" is a symbol for the sacred feminine. It represents the womb or the upside down pyramid that represents feminine energy. As in the zodiac sign of Virgo, the virgin Mary and the Holy Grail being described as the womb and not a real cup. The shape of the letter "V" suggests that it is made to hold, contain or receive energy. So Venezuela represents the female being described as, "mean bush." This is a hidden and sexist insult towards women. It describes the sacred feminine as "mean bush."

Commentary:

Quaritch then explains to Jake that he had three tours in Nigeria.

Metaphysical Breakdown

The number 3 in numerology represents God's divine trinity. Nigeria, of course, is a country in Afrika. The hidden message here is giving Black people homage for the sacred knowledge or God consciousness that they use to manipulate the masses today.

Commentary

Quaritch jumps in his Amp suit and leaves Jake. The number of Quaritch's Amp suit is 11.

Metaphysical Breakdown

Eleven in numerology is a master number. It means different things according to the consciousness level of who it is representing. In this case, Col. Quaritch represents the lowest level of consciousness. It implies that too much of a good thing can be bad for you. Eleven is one more than ten which is the number of perfection. Quaritch has power and resources to make great changes but because he is operating at the lowest level of consciousness, he abuses his power and resources.

Commentary:

Next scene Jake is back in Link-3 getting ready to transcend into his Avatar body. Link tech says, "Phase lock at 40%. I have 5 congruencies. Phase lock 90%.

Metaphysical Breakdown

Numerology: 3 symbolizes divine perfection, 40 represents the test or struggle; 5 symbolizes God has favor in your undertaking; and 9 represents man's judgment or life lesson he must pass to transcend into higher consciousness. So according to the numbers Jake's divine perfection will be tested, but because God sees favor in his undertaking, he will eventually prevail over his adversity.

DVD Chapter Seven:
First Sortie (3:59)

Commentary:

Next scene, the crew is in the helicopter. A flock of purple birds are flying on the right side of them in unison.

Metaphysical Breakdown

In ancient Kemet, the bird represents knowledge or higher consciousness. Flying on the left side of the helicopter symbolizes the activation of the right hemisphere of the brain, which also symbolizes higher consciousness. The color purple also represents higher consciousness. It is the color of the highest crown chakra.

Commentary:

Trudy lands her helicopter in the middle of Pandora's jungle. The number on her helicopter is 16. All the crew gets out on the right side of the helicopter. Jakes is the only one to exit the helicopter from the left side.

Metaphysical Breakdown

Sixteen in numerology breaks down to the number 7. Seven represents God's divinity in the physical plane. This translates to signify the crew is operating at a high frequency and is working with nature or God. The fact that Jake was the only one to exit the helicopter on the left side symbolizes the activation of his right brain where higher knowledge dwells. Jake is singled out in this scene as assuming the role as a savior, although it hasn't been revealed yet.

Commentary:

Grace tells the marine to stay behind with the helicopter. He replies, "You the man, Doc."

Metaphysical Breakdown

Women in high positions in western society must lose their femininity in order to be successful in the business world. Western society views these women as liberating or breaking the barriers of sexism. In ancient Kemet, the women embraced their femininity because they knew that is where their true power and strength lies. Remember, feminine energy receives energy as masculine energy gives out energy. So the woman must lose her natural, feminine principle and adopt masculine ways to be considered successful. Grace has adopted and defines herself through the nurturing of her masculine energy. This is the only way women can compete and "climb the corporate ladder" in business or corporate culture.

Commentary:

While the group is exploring the jungle they encounter these creatures called Prolemuris. They resemble lemurs but with six arms and legs.

Metaphysical Breakdown

There is a common theme in the movie that all creatures have six arms and legs. The number 6 in numerology represents the lower self or beast in man. This symbol further exemplifies this concept by having all beasts or animals on Pandora, have six arms and legs.

Commentary:

Prolemuris picks fruit from the vine with his left hand while Jake is observing. Grace explains to Jake that the creature is not aggressive.

Metaphysical Breakdown

The left hand of the lemur represents the activation of the right hemisphere of the brain or higher consciousness. People of higher consciousness do not act out of fear, thus they are non-aggressive or non-violent.

Commentary:

Grace and Norm are seen taking samples of a plant that displays consciousness. Grace tells Norm, "You've contaminated the sample with your saliva." Norm responds, "Right."

Metaphysical Breakdown

Melanated people or people of color are closer to nature because of the Melanin content they possess aids in their understanding of a holistic and spiritual connection that nature encompasses. Caucasians, because of their lack of Melanin, cannot decipher or communicate with nature at the level people of color can. Norm's saliva, which contains traces of his DNA, contaminates nature because it cannot communicate with it. To communicate with nature, which our Kemetic ancestors called God, one needs to possess Melanin. Melanin is the receptor to God or nature. Non-Melanated people or Europeans maintain a left brain concept of nature or God. Eurocentric view of nature is dominated by the left brain or the lower self. He further adds to this point by responding by saying, right. Again, the right side of the body activates the left hemisphere of the brain, which contains man's lower consciousness.

DVD Chapter Eight:
Thanator Chase (2:52)

Commentary:

Next scene Jake runs into Rhino-type creature called a, "Thanator." Jake must stand his ground. If he displays any fear or retreats, the animal will attack him.

Metaphysical Breakdown

This is another test for Jake in his initiation into higher consciousness. Jake must overcome his fears in his efforts to transcend. Fear, is housed in the left brain. Jake must overcome his fear as his test that he has defeated his lower self. This is part of his test and initiation.

Commentary:

As Jake stands up to the Thanator, he begins to act cocky. He starts to brag and boast about his accomplishments. He states, "Yeah, come on! What you got? Oh yeah, who's bad? That's right! Yeah, that's what I'm talking about, bitch! That's right; get your punk ass back to mommy! Yeah, yeah, you got nothing. You keep running." "Yeah, and why don't you bring back some of your friends, huh?"

Metaphysical Breakdown

Jake starts to feel too good about himself. This is Jake's ego, which represents his lower self. Jake has now switched to his left brain which houses the ego and lower consciousness. Humility kills the ego and the lower self. Jake did not remain humble. For this he must learn a very valuable lesson. Any self-gloating, praise or arrogance feeds the ego. One must kill the ego in order to reach and stay at a higher level of consciousness. It is an ongoing, lifelong, struggle of man.

Commentary:

Just then a giant panther-like creature comes on the scene. It is called a Viperwolf. Jake is told to run for his life to avoid certain death from this creature. Jake takes off running.

Metaphysical Breakdown

This scene would have never taken place if Jake remained humble in his accomplishment of overcoming his fear, by standing up to the Thanator. Universal law will always come back around to balance our reality and give us the life lesson we need. This is Jake's life lesson. Always show humility. Never let your ego get in the way of achieving and maintaining higher consciousness. Jake's consciousness has fallen and now he must learn the hard way in order for his consciousness to climb back up. The arrival of the Thanator is his next lesson.

Commentary:

Jake is now being attacked by the Viperwolf. The creature bites his backpack. Jake's left arm is stuck in the strap, as the Viperwolf slings him, Jake falls to safety.

Metaphysical Breakdown

Again the focus of this scene is the left arm being stuck in the strap of Jake's backpack. This event is what helps Jake escape his certain death. The left arm represents the activation of the right hemisphere of the brain where higher consciousness dwells. This is how Jake escapes his death, by switching over to higher consciousness and not defining himself through his fear or ego housed in his left brain.

Commentary:

Jake then has to jump off a cliff in order to escape the creature. Jake jumps with his right first and crosses his arms close to his chest as he hits the water.

This scene is a little confusing to me. I would have expected Jake to jump of the cliff with his left foot first to symbolize his higher consciousness and no fear. The right leg first symbolizes a man's moral standing in his physical body. It does not represent his spirituality or higher consciousness. It represents man defined by his physical body or his character and moral standing. The crossing of the arms to make the symbol of the "X" when he lands in the water symbolizes Jake's resurrection into higher consciousness, just as the water is used as a symbol of baptism. The "X" symbol stands for the first god that was able to resurrect himself. His name was Ausar. However, I do know that this positioning of the arms is standard procedure for high jumps in military training. Now you understand its hidden meaning. It's more than just a safety position. Such a high jump these soldiers make would surely lead to certain death. So the crossing of the arms represents the new life they receive by surviving such a death defying leap.

The Kemetic god, Ausar is on the left. He is represented by the "X" on his chest, which symbolizes resurrection. He is greeting the young pharaoh who has just died. Ausar is granting the pharaoh new life in the after world.

DVD Chapter Nine: A Sign (2:29)

Commentary:

Next scene Jake is seen sharpening a spear he has made for his protection. He is very nervous and jumps at any movement or sound that he encounters.

Metaphysical Breakdown

Jake is now operating at a lower frequency. His main motivation for his behavior is fear and self-survival. These are properties of his lowest chakra or conscience level. Jake has fallen from his higher consciousness to his lowest consciousness. He now defines himself through his ego or lower self. Jake feels everything is trying to kill him. He goes into defense mode, which is lower consciousness. This is where the Caucasian operates and defines his reality. This is the psychology behind his imperialistic, colonialist, and white supremacist world view. Jake feels that he is validated by his self-survival at the expense of the rest of his environment.

Commentary:

Neytiri is now introduced in the movie. She is perched on a tree limb looking down at Jake. She is attempting to kill him with her bow and arrow until, she suddenly, looks to her left and witnesses a seed from the 'Sacred Tree" falling harmlessly on the tip of the arrow. She changes her mind, as she sees this as a sign that must be respected.

Metaphysical Breakdown

This "seed from the Sacred Tree" is in the shape of the Kemetic Lotus flower. This flower grew along the muddy and swampy banks of the Nile River. This plant would somehow grow through several feet of mud and murky water and break through to bloom a beautiful, purple flower on top of the water. Purple, is the color of the highest chakra. Because of these characteristics, the Lotus flower was a symbol of resurrection in Kemet. Man has

241

the ability to overcome his lower self and bloom a beautiful flower of higher consciousness. By Neytiri, looking to her left to see the sign, further exemplifies the activation of the right hemisphere of the brain which represents her higher consciousness.

The Lotus flower in ancient Kemet. In the picture on the right, it is located at the god Ausar's feet, who represents resurrection. It shows four figures standing on top of the flower, which represents that person's resurrection in the afterlife.

The picture on the left shows a woman holding the Lotus flower with her left hand to represent the activation of her higher, spiritual consciousness.

Commentary:

Trudy and the rest of the crew are seen looking for Jake in the helicopter. They are all looking out the right side of the helicopter. Trudy is also circling to the right. Trudy tells Grace that they are not allowed to run night ops and that they just have to wait until the morning. Grace replies, "He won't make it till morning." They head back to the base by banking to the left and flying off into the sunset.

They are all sitting on the right side of the helicopter while the pilot is banking to the right to symbolize the activation of the left hemisphere of the brain. Trudy comments that they are not allowed to do "night" ops because the left brain only deciphers reality that they can see, touch, taste, smell or hear. It takes the activation of the right brain to decipher reality through intuition, clairvoyance, imagination and instincts. If Jake is operating with the left brain he will not survive the night, but if he uses his right brain, he will be fine.

DVD Chapter Ten: Viperwolves (2:18)

Commentary:

It is dark now. Jake is all alone. He frantically makes a spear for a weapon and makes a torch so that he can see in the dark. He can hear strange sounds of wild animals all around him. He is in a panic of desperation. His main motivation is fear predicated on self-preservation.

Metaphysical Breakdown

Jake is now operating at his lowest level. His main purpose is survival. His motivation is fear. Jake has dropped to the lowest level man can descend to. Jake perceives his environment as a threat so it becomes a threat. If Jake was operating at his highest consciousness, he would embrace his environment. His motivation would be to blend in with his environment, not be fearful of it. If he understood this concept, his environment would never have perceived him as a threat. Thus, no one would have been attacked. In theory, Jake attacked his environment first by operating at a lower level consciousness.

Commentary:

Jake gets his torch to light. He sees several Viperwolves have surrounded him. Jake feels threatened and starts to lunge out. The Viperwolves are black in color and have faint red and green stripes down their sides. They resemble dogs. Jake taunts them to come on and attack him. The Viperwolves after being provoked start to attack Jake. Jake is outnumbered and is quickly overwhelmed.

Metaphysical Breakdown

Jake disturbs the natural order of the environment by lighting his torch. This act is perceived as an act of violence towards his dark, natural surroundings. Jake is now representing the white man. The white man enforced his culture and ideology on

Afrika. He disrupted the "natural order" of Afrocentric ideology in Afrikan culture.

Jake is surrounded by Viperwolves which represent Black people. Red, black and green are the colors of the Black Nationalism flag or Black power. Jake perceives that they are a threat to him. He also realizes he is outnumbered. The Viperwolves resemble dogs. The concept being represented by the second half of their name, "wolf." The wolf is a cousin of the dog. They are both in the canine family. The dog refers to Anpu, the Kemet god who was represented as a black Jackal. Anpu was the anthropomorphic symbol of the properties and characteristics of Melanin.

The Black jackal or dog in Kemet, is represented by the god Anpu. Anpu represented the properties of Melanin that people of color possess to navigate the unseen or spiritual realm. Anpu was represented as a dog or jackal because it can detect sights and sounds that are invisible to humans. The detection of energy they we cannot decipher with our senses, demands for us to activate our Melanin and right brain consciousness. To put it simple, for higher consciousness, one cannot rely on what they see, hear feel, taste or smell, but more on how they "feel." Anpu represents the concept of "feeling" with your mind and "thinking" with your heart.

The European or white man's psychology, views the world and Black people as a threat to his very existence. He feels he is constantly being attacked by nature and the genetic potency of the Melanin the Black man carries to wipe him out as a race. Melanated or people of Afrikan descent carry dominant genes. Europeans or white people carry recessive genes. If Black people were to have sex with white people, all their offspring would be considered Black because of the dominant, Melanated genes and traits that would be passed down to the children. This was witnessed in slavery when the white man raped his female, Afrikan slave. Her children, even though they were fathered by a white man, were still considered Black and treated like slaves. White people cannot produce color. They can only reproduce white offspring. Black people can produce all colors. So Jake representing the white man's gene pool must lash out or what is

245

called a preemptive strike on Black people, to assure the survival of his recessive or white gene pool. As Francis Cress Welsing states, this is the foundation for white supremacy. It is the white man's psychology that tells him his environment and the darker people of the Earth are trying to destroy him. The white man lives in a constant state of fear. Coincidently, one cannot attain higher consciousness or spirituality if they are operating on the lower frequency of fear. This is the white man's dilemma. The name Viperwolf can be broken down as such; Viper pertains to the snake. The snake, in ancient Kemet, was a symbol of unseen energy or spirituality. All energy moves in waves just like the snake slithers in his movement. So the snake or viper stands for the recognition and acknowledgement of unseen energy or spirituality, which can only be interpreted if one has higher consciousness. More than 90% of all energy cannot be deciphered by our five senses. So in order to be able to recognize and use this energy, one must attain higher consciousness. This explains the first part of the name in "Viper" wolf.

The wolf has always been seen as some sort of mascot to represent European masculinity. That's why the canine is, "Man's best friend."

DVD Chapter Eleven: Neytiri (1:51)

Commentary:

Jake is being overwhelmed by the Viperwolves. He is close to defeat. Out of nowhere, Neytiri shows off to fend off the rest of the Viperwolves. The Viperwolves eyes glow in the dark a green color.

Metaphysical Breakdown

Green is the color of the heart chakra. It is the first level of higher consciousness. Although the Viperwolves may look ferocious and menacing, they operate from a state of love. It is Jake's perception that operates on fear that tells him the Viperwolves are dangerous.

Commentary:

After the Viperwolves are chased away Neytiri immediately puts out the torch Jake has made.

Metaphysical Breakdown

The fire was seen as a violent act against the natural order of the jungle at night. Jake because he was operating at the low consciousness of fear and self-preservation did not recognize what he had done. Same holds true, with the Caucasian when dealing with nature or indigenous people of color. Throughout the world, his culture and mindset is the "violent act" unleashed on people with Melanin. He does not understand this concept because he operates and defines his reality in a lower consciousness point of view. Thus whenever he encountered people of color throughout history, he forcefully changed the indigenous into adopting his worldview and culture. This act destroyed people of color throughout the world and we see the repercussions of this violence today.

Commentary:

Immediately after the torch is put out, the whole jungle seems to glow an iridescent color.

Metaphysical Breakdown

If Jake was operating with his right brain of higher consciousness, he would have been able to see the jungle for what it was and would not have felt threatened. The whole jungle would have been "lit up" because he would have relied on his first eye or Pineal gland to "see" and interpret his surroundings. Because Jake was fearful, he could not "see" in the dark.

Commentary:

Next, Neytiri is seen praying over the animals that she killed or wounded. Jake thanks her for killing them to save his life. She says, "Don't thank. You don't thank for this. This is sad. Very sad only. All this is your fault. They did not need to die." Jake responds, "But they attacked me. How am I the bad guy?" Neytiri responds, "Your fault! Your fault!"

Metaphysical Breakdown

Because Jake is operating in a state of fear and self-preservation, he feels justified in his actions to do whatever he has to do to survive. Again, Jake representing the white man, feels that he is constantly under attack. Neytiri knows that he is too immature as far as his consciousness to know and be accountable for his lower level behavior. Jake doesn't realize that he was responsible for the Viperwolve's response towards him.

Commentary:

Neytiri reiterates this point to Jake by saying, "You're like a baby. Making noise and don't know what to do."

Metaphysical Breakdown

Babies are not conscious of their higher selves. All babies operate at the lowest level of consciousness. They cry when they are hungry, scared, sad, angry, irritated, uncomfortable and sick. This one emotion is the only reaction they know how to do to communicate with the world. This is the white man's reaction when he faces any situation that he is not comfortable in. All he knows how to do is lash out and cry that his consciousness or ego is being tested.

Commentary:

Next scene Jake asks Neytiri why she saved him. She explains to him, "You have a strong heart. No fear. But stupid! Ignorant like a child!"

Metaphysical Breakdown

Neytiri acknowledges the white man's strong will and no fear when it comes to setting his mind on something he wants. This is something all people of color have witnessed when dealing with him. He will jump out of airplanes, climb mountain tops, deep sea dive, tie a rubber band to his feet and jump from tall places, try to tame wild animals, jump out of airplanes, build enormous cities in places they have no business being, strap a rocket to his back and go into outer space, etc............... The white man has always pushed the limits when it comes to his dealings with nature and universal law. The white man is the "extreme sport." Neytiri, representing Black people, are fascinated in some way by this peculiar behavior. The Caucasian goes against and tries to defy nature and he never apologizes for his actions. People of color are intrigued by this mindset.

Commentary:

As Neytiri walks away, Jake follows her and begs her to teach him her ways. Neytiri responds, "Sky people cannot learn what they cannot see." Jake responds, "Well teach me how to see?" Neytiri, "No one can teach you to see."

Metaphysical Breakdown

The Sky people represent the Caucasian. They are called Sky people because they feel they are on "top of the world." White supremacy feeds their egos. Neytiri informs Jake that he cannot see. This relates to the ancient Kemetic concept of the "first eye." Remember, the first eye is the Pineal gland which produces Melanin. It is this chemical that allows darker people of the world to reach higher spirituality and consciousness. Without Melanin, one's Pineal gland cannot be activated. As a result, white people cannot "see." Melanin cannot be acquired after one is born. Your Melanated parents must pass it down to you. The Caucasian race cannot learn how to see and define reality through the eyes of people of color. Thus, no one can teach them to see. They do not have the capacity or the equipment. Neytiri furthers this point by telling Jake that he should not be here, i.e. that place being, the spiritual dimension of higher consciousness on Pandora.

Commentary:

Neytiri then yells out at Jake to go back. She raises her left hand while holding her bow or weapon in her right hand. Jake almost falls off the tree limb. Neytiri saves him by grabbing his left arm. She then tells him, "You like a baby!"

Metaphysical Blueprint

Left hand symbolizing right brain higher consciousness and right hand symbolizing left brain lower consciousness. Neytiri is telling Jake that he is not ready or capable of higher consciousness by telling him to go back to his world of lower consciousness. Jake being saved by Neytiri grabbing his left arm and then calling him a baby relates to the fact that he is very

250

ignorant when it comes to higher consciousness held in the activation of his right brain. Neytiri carries her weapons in her right arm to symbolize her lower consciousness is held in the left hemisphere of her brain. Right side of the body activates the left hemisphere of the brain and vice-versa.

Commentary:

Just as Neytiri tells Jake to go back, seeds from the "Sacred Tree" cover Jake's body. Jake spreads his arms out as the seeds land on him. He attempts to knock them off, but Neytiri stops him.

Metaphysical Blueprint

Jake's first reaction is to lash out in fear of these strange objects. This act shows Jake's lower level consciousness. Neytiri scolds him for his actions and tells him to stay still. This is Jake's initiation. The spreading of Jake's arms in this position represents Jake's initiation into higher consciousness. He assumes the same position as Jesus did, in the Bible, when he was "crucified on the cross" or crossed over into higher consciousness. Jake is in the same position as Jesus was on the cross. The symbolism behind the crucifixion is really about switching from lower level consciousness in the left hemisphere of the brain to transcending into higher, spiritual consciousness housed in the right hemisphere of the brain. The symbol of the cross represents man in the middle of the two hemispheres of the brain. Man is born of free will to decide which level of consciousness he will embrace when it comes to how he views himself and his environment. Jake must decide to kill his lower consciousness so that he can be resurrected into higher consciousness. Jake is now being reborn into higher consciousness. Remember the seed from the Sacred Tree is in the shape of the lotus flower, which represents resurrection into higher consciousness in ancient Kemet.

Commentary:

Neytiri immediately grabs Jake's left arm and tells him to come with her. On the way, Jake is taken down by a weapon used to trip him. Three warriors appear out of nowhere, having followed Jake, riding these "horse-like" animals.

Metaphysical Breakdown

This further supports my theory that Jake is representing the Christ figure in the Bible. The appearance of three horses coincides with the Biblical arrival of the three wise men that showed up at the birth of Jesus. This story is being retold and its true meaning is being revealed. Every person has the ability and the freewill to achieve their higher selves or what is known as Christ consciousness. This is where Christians get the concept of being "born again" but they don't understand its true meaning.

Commentary:

Tsu'Tey is introduced in the film. He is the tribe's top warrior. He tells Neytiri, "These demons are forbidden here."

Metaphysical Breakdown

This statement reiterates the point of the white man and his lower level consciousness cannot "see" or reside in a higher consciousness environment. All indigenous people around the world have referred to the Caucasian as a devil, demon or lower level entity, when referring to their historical relationship with them. The white man has always been described in these terms when coming in contact with darker people of the Earth.

All the devil or demon description means is a man defining himself and his environment at his lowest animalistic behavior. In Kemet, man could aspire to be a god or lower himself to the point of a demon.

DVD Chapter Twelve: Omaticaya Klan (2:10)

Commentary:

Jake is brought into the village called, "Home Tree." The warriors hold a knife to his braid as if to subdue him. Home Tree is a gigantic tree that spirals up in the air. The villagers live and sleep in the tree.

Metaphysical Breakdown

In ancient Kemet, the hair braid was a symbol of the chakra system in the body. Each knot where the three strands of hair come together represents a level of consciousness or energy vortex along the spinal column. So the fear of cutting off the braid, was the fear of cutting the individual off from higher consciousness. This act was considered worse than death. Home Tree is in the shape of a DNA strand. It represents the genetic blueprint of Na'vi or Black people. This is where the Melanin is found. It is in one's genes. It can only be passed down if one were to "join" one's gene pool. This is why Jake wants to "join" the Na'vi people. He wants the Melanin or he wants to be Black.

Commentary:

Neytiri introduces herself to her father, the chief tribal leader named Eytukan. She touches her forehead with her left hand and responds, "I see you."

Metaphysical Breakdown

The touching of the Pineal gland with the left hand and saying I see you, demonstrates the activation of her Melanin and right brain higher consciousness. She is aware of the unseen energy or spiritual realm her father's aura is emulating. She sees his spirit, which represents a person's true or higher self.

253

Commentary:

Eytukan who is dressed in South Afrikan, Zulu, traditional dress states, "This creature, why do you bring him here? No dream walker will come here. This alien smell fills my nose!" His Pineal gland is decorated with some type of shell. Jake tries to approach the chief and is immediately stopped.

Metaphysical Breakdown

When Europeans first met indigenous people throughout the world a common theme amongst the natives was the peculiar stench the Europeans emitted. Eytukan gives his disapproval of Jake, representing the white man, being in their higher conscience world. Jake, oblivious to nature's laws and the natural order of the universe has the audacity to approach the chief without adhering to the proper protocol of respect and propriety.

Commentary:

Moat, Neytiri's mother and spiritual guide of the people is introduced. She states, "I will look at this alien." Moat inspects Jake's hair braid, tail and takes a sample of his blood with her left hand.

Metaphysical Breakdown

She wants to make sure Jake is not one of them, since he displays the same physical features. She checks the braid, which symbolizes his consciousness level or chakras; His tail, as we know Black people are known for their behinds and his blood, which represents the level of Melanin found in his DNA. She does all this by using her left hand to decipher her physical reality through her right hemisphere of the brain which represents her higher consciousness.

Commentary:

Moat states, "Why have you come to us?" Jake responds, to learn. Moat replies, "We have tried to teach other Sky people. It is hard to fill a cup which is already full."

Metaphysical Breakdown

This statement represents white people defining their reality through their left brains which houses lower consciousness. This is where the ego resides. On cannot attain higher consciousness if one defines themselves and their reality through the ego. If one does not attain a place of humility, one cannot see or be taught higher consciousness. Killing the ego is the threshold one must pass in order to open the door to higher consciousness. Because of the white man's lack of Melanin, he defines himself and the world through lower consciousness. This is why she says that his cup is full. Caucasians are already full of themselves because the system of white supremacy tells them that they are superior in every way to people of color.

Commentary:

Moat assigns her daughter to teach Jake their ways. Moat further states, "Then we will see if your insanity can be cured."

Metaphysical Breakdown

The tribe is curious if the white man can attain higher consciousness just by learning their ways. Every incidence where darker or indigenous people opened their doors to white people, their culture and way of life was destroyed.

The Na'vi define lower level consciousness as insanity. Insanity is a dysfunction of the brain. Insanity is defining yourself and your reality exclusively with the left hemisphere of the brain. This is Eurocentric ideology.

Commentary:

Neytiri leads Jake to a tree where they sleep at night. Jake falls asleep and returns back to his physical body.

Metaphysical Breakdown

Melanin is activated at night in the form of Melatonin. It is what our dreams are made of. It allows us to travel in other dimensions to help us interpret life lessons and acquire the tools we need in the physical realm. The dream state is not limited to the laws of the physical dimension. Because of that, it can be interpreted as more real than when we are awake. This is the state of existence that Jake has tapped into to achieve higher consciousness.

DVD Chapter Thirteen: Covert Report (7:47)

Commentary:

Parker Selfridge is introduced. Jake tells him that he has infiltrated the Na'vi village. Selfridge replies, "Just find out what the blue monkeys want. You know, I mean we try to give them medicine, education, roads. But no, no, no. They like mud. And that wouldn't bother me, its just that there, uh. Their damn village happens to be resting on the richest Unobtanium deposit within 200 klicks of any direction."

Metaphysical Breakdown

Selfridge displays the history of European behavior when in contact with the darker people of the world. They always maintain a superior attitude when it comes to their relationships with the indigenous. They treat them like children and try to swindle the natives out of their resources with promises of better technology and a better way of life. The point that is never addressed is that the natives never asked for anything from the invaders. They were always forced to comply. In numerology 200 becomes the number two. Two is the number of separation or division. This refers to separating the Na'vi from their Unobtanium, which is their most precious resource. Unobtainium is really the Melanin in the Na'vi or people of color's DNA. Melanin holds the ability to reach higher consciousness and manifesting your thoughts into the physical dimension. The goal of the white man is to keep the darker people of the world from reaching higher consciousness because the white race cannot function there. So the object is for the darker people of the world to define their reality through the white man's lower consciousness in an effort to keep them enslaved and oppressed. The system, in turn, steals the properties and attributes that Melanated people manifest and falsely portrays them to the rest of the world as European knowledge, science, spirituality, philosophy and history. This is the system of white supremacy in a nut shell. Laid out in not-so plain sight in this scene.

257

Commentary:

On Selfridge's video display, we see three pentagons that represent the parameters of Hell's Gate. It is in Sector 12. Selfridge then pans the virtual map to position 94k. This is the location on Home Tree. He says, "Jesus!" when the operator stops the map at this location.

Metaphysical Breakdown

The number 12 in numerology, signifies completion, as in the completion of their plans to destroy Home Tree. Home Tree is located at 94 kilometers. 94 in numerology breaks down to the number thirteen. 13 is the number of resurrection. This symbolizes Home Tree as a place of higher consciousness. Selfridge yells out the name Jesus to point out that the Biblical character represents man's ability to transcend into higher consciousness. Jesus is taken from the Kemetic god Heru. He represents man's higher self. He put to death the lower consciousness in himself in an effort to be resurrected into higher consciousness. Jesus, represents the Black man's ability to raise his consciousness. Or in this case, is referred to the Na'vi people.

Commentary:

Col. Quaritch tells Jake he has 3 months to get the Na'vi to move before they come in and annihilate their village.

Metaphysical Breakdown

Three months is 90 days. This comes out to be the number nine in numerology. Nine represents man's judgment. Jake's lesson he must learn first is to move the Na'vi out of harm's way or have their blood on his hands. This is what Jake will struggle with. This is his test to pass or fail into higher consciousness.

Commentary:

Next scene Jake is learning to ride a horse-like creature with six legs. Jake connects the end of his braid to the animal. Jake and the animal can now communicate telepathically.

Metaphysical Breakdown

Black people have a unique hair structure. It is the best form for sending and receiving energy in nature. All energy travels in spirals or waves. Afrikan hair structure is a spiral or wave archetype. Black people have a built-in antenna to communicate with seen and unseen energy in nature, represented by the structure of their hair. The connecting of the hair to communicate with this animal in nature, is an example of this unique characteristic of people of Afrikan lineage.

Commentary:

Jake tells the horse like animal to go forward. He falls flat on his face in the mud.

Metaphysical Breakdown

When Jake gets up, only the left side of his face is covered in black mud. This symbolizes the Black man's natural instinct to operate the right hemisphere of his brain. The mud on the left side of his face shows his blackness or Melanin and how it operates the right side of his brain where higher consciousness can be experienced. An example of this trait is the ability to communicate with nature telepathically. The right side of his face remains free of mud. This right side represents his lower consciousness. It has no mud or Melanin.

DVD Chapter Fourteen: The Hallelujah Mountains (1:41)

Commentary:

Grace informs Jake that they will be "getting out of Dodge" and moving camp to the Hallelujah Mountains.

Metaphysical Breakdown

The name of the car company that makes the Dodge car line is Chrysler. The logo for Dodge is not a ram, but a goat. The goat in the occult, symbolizes the powers that be that understand and use this Kemetic knowledge to manipulate and oppress the unsuspecting masses. The goat also represents the Free Mason god called, Baphomet. He has the head of a goat and the body of a human. The goat lives in the hills looking down on all the sheep that are manipulated and controlled. So the goat sees the system for what it is as opposed to the ignorant sheep that follow their masters blindly.

Chrysler which sounds like Christ, comes from the root word Chrysalis. This is the cocoon like structure the caterpillar encases itself in before it metamorphoses into a butterfly. This is also an occult symbol of resurrection or higher consciousness. This is why our Kemetic ancestors wrapped the deceased in cloth. It symbolized the metamorphosis from the physical dimension to the higher spiritual dimension. This consciousness was called Kerast. This is where we get the title Jesus Christ from. So our group in the movie, "getting out of Dodge," symbolizes their awakening of the system and freeing themselves from it by working outside of its control.

Commentary:

Our group is in the helicopter flying to the Hallelujah Mountains. Grace acknowledges that they are in the "Flux Vortex." In this area, no electronic equipment works. Their instruments are out of commission and they have to fly on instincts.

Metaphysical Breakdown

This is an example of relying on your right brain to guide you. One must walk out on faith and trusts one's intuition in order to achieve higher consciousness. You must rely on your instincts, which is a pretty scary thing to do you when one has been conditioned to operate and define reality through their left brain. Our group is transcending. They are not operating on fear. Fear has been used on the masses as a method of control and manipulation. Overcoming one's fear and trusting one's intuition, is the threshold one must pass to achieve higher consciousness.

Commentary:

Norm responds upon seeing the beauty of this region, "Oh my God!"

Metaphysical Breakdown

Norm, being activated into higher consciousness has seen God or nature for the first time, through the lens of his "first eye," the Pineal gland. Norm is using his right brain to define his reality.

Commentary:

The group is now in the facilities of the camp. Grace is telling everyone where they will sleep. She tells Norm to take the bottom bunk and Trudy to take the top one.

Metaphysical Breakdown

In Kemet, feminine energy is always represented coming down from the heavens (spirituality) while male energy is always portrayed is coming from the Earth (physical realm). This is part of the secret science and the law of gender in the universe.

Commentary:

She further tells Jake to hang a left.

Metaphysical Blueprint

Referring to the left side of the body activates the right hemisphere of the brain where higher consciousness dwells. Jake is an enlightened being.

Commentary:

Jake's unit is named Beulah.

Metaphysical Breakdown

Beulah is the symbolic name for Israel or the Promised Land. It also means to marry. Jake is now married to the Promised Land, which is higher consciousness. He has made a lifetime commitment to define himself and his environment through his higher self or spiritual consciousness.

Commentary:

The next scene, Jake and Neytiri are high in the tree tops. You will notice mushrooms growing on the limbs of the trees at their feet.

Metaphysical Breakdown

In the occult, mushrooms were used by ancient, holy men to travel into spirit or higher dimensions. Many secret societies worshipped the mushroom for this reason. This scene pays homage to this practice. Notice these mushrooms only grow "high" in the trees.

Commentary:

Neytiri tells Jake not to look in the eye of her Ikran, her dragon like flying beast.

Metaphysical Breakdown

"The eyes are the windows to your soul." Since the Ikran will only let one person ride her for the duration of their lives, it is only fitting that the Ikran only connects with one soul for this purpose. Thus the Ikran is only allowed to witness one soul or the one rider it will be committed to for the duration of its life.

Commentary:

Neytiri puts her headgear on before she flies off on her Ikran. Jake asks when he will be able to choose and ride his Ikran. Neytiri replies to him when he is ready.

Metaphysical Breakdown

The head gear covering the forehead and the lenses over the eyes, represent the activation of the Pineal gland and the production of Melanin needed to transcend into higher consciousness. Higher consciousness is displayed by Neytiri's ability to "fly." Jake has not reached this level of consciousness so it is not time for him to "fly." He must keep working to raise his consciousness level.

DVD Chapter Fifteen: Learn fast or Die (4:10)

Commentary:

Jake equates learning to speak the Na'vi language with field stripping a weapon. He thinks it is all about repetition. Neytiri scolds him by hitting him on his face. The word they are trying to learn is "Nari" but it sounds like "naughty."

Metaphysical Breakdown

Learning to speak Na'vi, is equivalent to defining nature and communicating with higher knowledge. It is not an actual language in this sense, but a worldview on how to define one's reality. Jake still equates the Na'vi way of life by definitions of his lower self. Field stripping a weapon or a tool one uses to take lives is not the proper analogy for learning how to speak Na'vi. It is in direct contrast to the Na'vi way of life. Because of this thinking, Neytiri scolds Jake by hitting him on the right side of his head, which represents left brain, lower consciousness. She even tells him he is "naughty" for speaking in such terms.

Commentary:

Jake is now doing his video log. He is very tired and irritated. He does not want to do it. He makes excuses as to why he needs to do it later. Jake starts out by saying, "Video log 12 time's 2132."

Metaphysical Breakdown

Jake is battling with his lower self. He is at a weakened stage at this time. He is displaying lower level behavior by complaining that he is tired, irritable and needs rec. Jake is even sarcastic. The numerology of 12 x 2132 = 25,584. This breaks down to the number 6. The number of the beast or the lower of man. This is the behavior Jake must overcome to reach higher consciousness. One must master their lower selves. This is the side of man that makes excuses, gives in to weaknesses and plays the victim role. These feelings must be mastered.

Commentary:

Jake is seen with Norm practicing the Na'vi greeting of "I see you." Norm explains to Jake that it means much more than to physically see someone. He explains to Jake that it means, "I see into you. I'm accepting you. I understand you." They both touch the middle of their foreheads with their hand as part of the greeting.

Metaphysical Breakdown

This scene points directly to the ancient Kemetic philosophy of the "first eye" or activated Pineal gland. It is only through the Pineal gland's production of Melanin that one can see into the spiritual realm of higher consciousness. It is to acknowledge a person's energy or spirituality and not their physical bodies. Seen energy that we can decipher with our five senses only makes up 10% of our reality we call energy. There is 90% of unseen energy or reality that is unaccountable for if we only rely on our five senses. The activation of the Pineal gland is able to decipher the other 90% of energy we cannot see. Therefore, higher consciousness is where true "reality" can be seen, deciphered and experienced.

Commentary:

Next scene Jake is following Neytiri at a blistering pace as she puts him through the motions not unlike an obstacle course. Just as Jake is about to grab and swing on a limb with his left hand, he says," I have to trust my body to know what to do."

Metaphysical Breakdown

Jake is learning higher consciousness. He is finally catching on. He is walking out on faith and has put fear aside. Taking the "leap of faith" and grabbing the limb with his left hand shows that he is operating in the right hemisphere of the brain which holds man's higher consciousness. Fear is no longer a factor.

Commentary:

Jake is now aware of the tiniest senses and sounds. He comments about Neytiri, "She's always going on about the flow of energy, the spirits of animals." Grace interjects, "Try to see the forest through her eyes."

Metaphysical Breakdown

Jake describes his new found reality into higher consciousness. He is now able to see the energy that was invisible to him before. It is all about consciousness. Jake is making the transformation from being left brain dominant to right brain dominant in his perception of reality.

Commentary:

Jake is trying to emulate Neytiri. Jake jumps out after she has leaped of a tree. She lands softly and gracefully. He tumbles down hard and a mushroom breaks his fall.

Metaphysical Breakdown

In the ancient world, mushrooms were taken as a hallucinogenic. It was used to activate the Pineal gland artificially. This scene pays homage to the mushroom and its characteristics to activate the Pineal gland. Because it is artificially induced, Jake navigates the fall or trip but it is not as graceful or as effortless as Neytiri's version of the same fall or trip. Neytiri is activated naturally, while Jake must ingest a substance that he cannot produce naturally. This is the difference between people of color and Caucasians. Black people inherently possess these abilities naturally while Caucasians must introduce substances outside of themselves to acquire the same effects.

266

Commentary:

In this scene, Neytiri is seen drinking water from a tall, purple flower. She has to reach up and bring it down to her level. She is very pleased by how the water affects her when she drinks it.

Metaphysical Breakdown

Purple represents the crown or highest chakra. The water she drinks is the consciousness level at the highest chakra. That's why she has to reach up and grab it. She shows pleasure from drinking the water because she sees reality at the highest level of consciousness. Life is blissful at this level of consciousness.

Commentary:

Jake says Neytiri has a deep connection to the forest. "She talks about a network of energy that flows through all living things. She says all energy is only borrowed and one day you have to give it back." Neytiri is then shown holding a seed from the sacred tree and placing it in the grave of an elderly person who has deceased.

Metaphysical Breakdown

This is the mindset of dissecting reality from the point of view of higher consciousness and how she perceives life. We are all one energy that can be neither created nor destroyed. This concept of reality is of the highest level of understanding. The seed from the Sacred Tree represents the lotus flower which is the symbol for resurrection into higher consciousness in ancient Kemet. The holding it in Neytiri's left hand symbolizes the activation of the right brain of higher consciousness. This symbolizes the recognition that life begins after the physical body dies.

Commentary:

Next scene, Jake is killing a deer like animal. He says, "I see you brother. And thank you. Your spirit goes to Eywa. Your body stays behind. To become part of the people." Neytiri responds that Jake is ready.

Metaphysical Breakdown

Jake now views all life as coming from one source. All life is connected. Everything has a spirit that lives forever after the body dies. Jake pays homage to this fact and acknowledges the sacrifice that all living things play a crucial role in all our lives here in the physical realm. This is higher consciousness. Jake is now ready for his final initiation or resurrection into higher consciousness.

DVD Chapter Sixteen: Banshee Rookery (5:06)

Commentary:

Jake is seen with his initiation class, riding his horse on a treacherous trail up the Hallelujah Mountains. The group must climb these dangerous rocks up high in the sky. Once they get to the apex, they must jump to these vines and climb up even steeper and higher rocks. They continue to cross narrow walkways and bridges made of vines and rocks way atop the sky. They are very graceful and deliberate in their ascent. They have no fear and a newfound confidence. Jake has his face painted. There is a "V" shape on his face and a painted spot where his Pineal gland would be.

Metaphysical Breakdown

The physical climbing represents the ascension of the activation of the chakras. Each climb is distinctive to passing a conscious level held in that chakra. The climb is more mental and spiritual, then physical. Jake's consciousness is being raised. This is called, Kundalini energy. This energy starts at the lowest chakra and "climbs" up to the highest crown chakra. The act of Jake "climbing" these physical obstacles represents the mental, physical and spiritual work he has done to raise his consciousness. The "V" shape on his face represents the feminine principle or higher spiritual energy. The letter "V" resembles a cup or container to receive higher consciousness. It is "open" to understanding enlightenment. The mark on his forehead symbolizes the activation of the Pineal gland, which produces Melanin.

Commentary:

There are two other Na'vi that are being initiated with Jake. A male and a female. Jake is now chosen to pick his Ikran first. Jake leaves his weapon behind. Neytiri comments, "Now you must choose your Ikran. This you must feel inside. You will have one chance, Jake." Jake

269

responds, "How will I know if he chooses me." Neytiri answers, "He will try to kill you."

Metaphysical Breakdown

The other two Na'vi that are being initiated with Jake, represent the first Holy Trinity of Ausar, Auset and Heru. They represent the father, the son and the mother. To oppress the woman, the mother was left out of the equation and replaced with the Holy spirit or ghost in Christianity. Jake, like Jesus, represents the son or Heru.

This is the final test into Jake achieving higher consciousness. The Ikran represents higher consciousness. Remember, it has the ability to fly. Birds, in ancient Kemet, represents man's ability to achieve higher consciousness. This mindset was symbolized by the hawk, otherwise, known as the god Heru. Heru represented man's highest consciousness. It is what the character of Jesus in the Bible symbolized. He had to "crucify" his lower self in order to attain his higher self or Christ consciousness. Thus, he was resurrected or born again. Jake's higher consciousness is the Ikran. He must face his lower self and destroy it in order to attain his higher self. His lower self is defined as facing his worst fears and submit to them completely in order to transcend. Man's biggest fear is death. That's why Neytiri tells Jake that the Ikran that belongs to him, will try to kill him. That is how he will know it is for him. The Ikran is also has colors of green, blue and purples. These are the colors of the higher level chakras. The Ikran, being able to fly great heights and see things from higher perspective represents characteristics of higher consciousness.

The original "Trinity" in Kemet. The father, Ausar in the middle, The mother Auset on the right and the son, Heru on the left. Later, Christianity would steal this concept and call it the father, the son and the Holy Ghost. They left out the woman in order to oppress her true identity.

DVD Chapter Seventeen: First Flight (5:25)

Commentary:

Jake subdues his Ikran. He makes his bond. Neytiri immediately tells him to jump off the cliff with his Ikran to "make the bond." After Jake tumbles and tosses he suddenly flies straight. First command he gives to the Ikran is to bank left. When the Ikran expands his wings it looks similar to an "X" pattern.

Metaphysical Breakdown

Higher consciousness can only be attained by facing all our fears. Jake had to take a "leap of faith," in order to break the threshold from left brain to right brain thinking. This point is further made by Jake commanding his Ikran to bank to the left when he is trying to fly. The left side represents the activation of the right hemisphere of the brain. The Ikran is now under control and Jake is flying! Jake has passed his initiation into higher consciousness.

The wingspan of the Ikran resembles the letter "X." As we stated earlier, "X" was the symbol of resurrection in ancient Kemet. It represents the god Ausar, who was the first god to resurrect himself.

Commentary:

Neytiri joins Jake in flight. Jake starts to get cocky and says, "Yeah baby I got this!" He then exclaims, "Oh,shit." As he almost loses control. He swerves to the right to avoid running into a rock. Later, Jake states, "I may be not much of a horse guy, but I was born to do this."

Metaphysical Breakdown

Jake temporarily forgets the mindset he needed to achieve his higher consciousness. Jake lets his ego get in the way. Because of this, Jake almost falls off the Ikran or "falls" from higher consciousness to lower consciousness, when he gets cocky. This is further exemplified by Jake breaking to the right to avoid falling while Neytiri stays to the left. Jake "going right" symbolizes the activation of the left hemisphere of the brain or lower consciousness. Moral of the scene, check your ego at all times. It has the potential to lower all of us at any given time.

Horses are relegated to living their lives on the ground. The ground represents lower consciousness. A bird or the Ikran, represents man's ability to raise his consciousness by having the ability to transcend or fly. All people of color are born with the potential to "fly" or raise our consciousness.

Commentary:

Jake and Neytiri race down a cliff side on their Ikrans. Neytiri is on the left and Jake is on the right side.

Metaphysical Breakdown

Neytiri, being the female, represents higher, spiritual consciousness, on the left side, which activates the right hemisphere of the brain. Jake, being male, represents lower consciousness, on the right side, which activates the left hemisphere of the brain.

DVD Chapter Eighteen: Last Shadow

Commentary:

Jake and Neytiri are flying on their Ikrans. Suddenly, a giant, flying creature attacks them from above. Its colors are red, orange and yellow. They both narrowly escape. Jake now has headband and lenses over his forehead and on top of his eyes. Neytiri explains the history of this giant flying creature. His name is Toruk, which means, "Last Shadow." Since the times of the first songs, Toruk Macto or "Rider of Last Shadow," has only appeared five times. She further states, that he brought the clans together in the time of great sorrow. He was very mighty.

Metaphysical Breakdown

Ancient Kemet was a metaphysical civilization which promoted higher consciousness as the basis of its culture. Many lower level, European invaders tried to ransack Kemet for all its knowledge, resources, wealth and power. Although Kemet's culture promoted higher consciousness, they had to display lower consciousness, in order to fend off these barbarians, who meant them and their children harm. Lower level or animalistic behavior was acceptable only in efforts to protect that which was sacred. They were great warriors and banded together in times of war.

Toruk represents lower level consciousness. This is displayed in its colors of red, orange, and yellow. These colors represent the lower level chakras or consciousness levels in man. This is why this creature never looks up. Looking up represents acknowledging the higher chakras. If this creature never looks up, he is only conscious of himself and his environment through the interpretation of his lower level consciousness, thus there is no reason to "look up."

Toruk Macto represents, the leader of the Na'vi that has achieved higher consciousness, but must display lower level behavior, in order to protect his people's culture and way of life. This behavior was only acceptable in times of war. Having only appeared 5 times in the past, Jake will represent the sixth time. Six is the number of the beast in man or lower level consciousness. Jake will have to exhibit this behavior for the good of the Na'vi people and civilization. Only in the time of great crisis or war did this great warrior spirit or consciousness was allowed to display lower level behavior. This mindset was only utilized to protect the way of life and people of Kemet. That was the only reason to exhibit lower level consciousness. Only the pharaoh, a person of higher consciousness, was able to handle and balance this lower level behavior and not have it consume his heart. This lower level consciousness was only temporary and was terminated after the threat was gone and balance was restored to the people.

Commentary:

The next scene is flashed showing a close up of Jakes right eye. The back ground lighting is Indigo in color.

Metaphysical Breakdown

Jake's right eye symbolizes the activation of the left brain which is lower consciousness. This accentuates the point of Jake preparing for war. The Indigo lighting in the back ground represents the activation of the first eye or sixth chakra. This chakra houses intuition. Jake is recognizing what he must do before the situation arises.

Commentary:

Jake states, "Everything is backwards now. Like out there is the true world and in here is the dream. It's hard to believe it's only been three months. I can barely remember my old life. I don't know who I am anymore.

Metaphysical Breakdown

Jake has completed the transition from being the left brain dominant to being right brain dominant. He sees things from a perspective of higher consciousness. His view of the world has been completely turned upside down. He does not define himself by his lower level consciousness he once did in his past.

275

Three months can be interpreted as 90 days. In numerology, this number comes out to be the number 9. Nine represents man's judgment or test he must pass to achieve higher consciousness. Jake passed his test during that time period. The three, in three months represents Jake's resurrection into higher consciousness. Just as Jesus "rose" on the third day. Jake has been resurrected in higher consciousness.

Commentary:

Col. Quaritch questions Jake's resolve. He tells Jake, "Your last report was two weeks ago."

Metaphysical Breakdown

The number two in numerology represents separation or division. Jake has sided with the Na'vi people and has separated his allegiance from his commanding officer.

Jake is also wearing another shirt with birds on the front. The bird in ancient Kemet, represents higher consciousness.

The Kemetic god Tehuti on the left represents divine wisdom and knowledge.

The Kemetic god Heru on the right representing higher consciousness courage and bravery.

DVD Chapter Nineteen: Son of the Omaticaya (4:36)

Commentary:

Jake says, "The Na'vi say every person is born twice. The second time is when you earn your place among the people forever."

Metaphysical Breakdown

The concept of one's recognition of lower and higher self is what Jake is referring to. We are all born once into lower consciousness, but to be resurrected into our higher selves is the birth of our true selves. Not everybody achieves this level of consciousness. The second "birth" is what few people ever achieve, which is the birth of one's higher self or consciousness.

Commentary:

Jake's body is painted with white paint and a peculiar symbol on his front torso. This is part of the ceremony of being "born again."

Metaphysical Breakdown

In ancient Kemet, the color white represented death. Jake's body being painted white represents the death of his human or lower self and the acceptance of him as one of the Na'vi people.

To further this point Jake has a big phallic symbol painted on his chest. It is also white. This symbol represents the death of his recessive, Caucasian gene pool and the introduction of his Na'vi or Black blood. Remember, the only way for Caucasians to reach higher consciousness, is to acquire Melanin. The only way they can obtain Melanin is through the intermingling into the Melanated gene pool of people of color. This is the act that Jake is doing in this scene. It is the only way to be accepted as "one of the people" having higher consciousness. It is his initiation.

Commentary:

After the initiation, Jake and Neytiri are seen running through the forest or jungle. Jake reaches out and grabs Neytiri's tail as she passes him.

Metaphysical Breakdown

This is another subliminal example of sexism. What Jake is really seen doing is grabbing Neytiri's ass. Of course, one of higher consciousness would never disrespect a woman in this manner. This is the director's "inside joke" with other occult members. The scene was added to the movie to accentuate his sexist views even in a movie about achieving one's higher self.

Commentary:

Neytiri tells Jake, "This is the place for prayers to be heard and sometimes answered. They call these trees Utraya Mokri. 'The Tree of Voices.' The voices of our ancestors." Jake also grabs three strands from the tree and connects his braid to them. He replies, "I can hear them." Neytiri responds, "They live Jake, within Eywa."

Metaphysical Breakdown

Neytiri and Jake are not in a physical location. They are actually in a state of consciousness. This is what happens when a man and a woman of higher consciousness come together to have sexual intercourse with a specific purpose. The place Neytiri is talking about where prayers are heard and answered is the "gateway" or union of the man and woman. In Kemet, sex was used to manifest the ideas of the combined intent of man and woman into the material world. It was the gateway to ideas and thoughts into the physical dimension. This gateway of electro-magnetic energy, tapped into the one source of all creation. If a couple was able to raise their vibration to the highest level, they could astro-project themselves and visit other dimensions. One of these dimensions is where our ancestors dwell and where future children in the spiritual realm reside. The grabbing of the tree strands of the tree to connect to the source represents the perfect

278

trinity one needs to raise their consciousness in the physical dimension. Jake and Neytiri are in the process of opening this gateway that gives them access to their ancestor's genetic memory bank to be used in the physical dimension.

Commentary:

Jake reaches out with his left hand to kiss Neytiri.

Metaphysical Breakdown

The act of sex has already begun. This scene further displays Jake operating in higher consciousness by using his left hand to touch Neytiri. His left hand represents the activation of the right brain or higher consciousness. This union symbolizes the act of sexual intercourse at the highest spiritual consciousness.

Commentary:

As Jake and Neytiri make love, Neytiri is seen on top of Jake. After they make love, the next scene is a close up of Jake's left eye, with the background lighting in Indigo.

Metaphysical Breakdown

In ancient Kemet, the woman or feminine energy always comes from above. The woman held the wealth and the power. The queen would choose the next pharaoh, not the other way around as we are led to believe. The pharaoh had to prove that he was worthy to be king. For the woman to be on top sexually, meant the man had to control his lower self in order for the woman to achieve an orgasm. This was the opening of the gateway. If a man wasn't strong enough or could not master his lower self, he failed his test, i.e. pre-mature ejaculation. If a man proved himself worthy and was able to open the gateway, it was one sign he was worthy to be pharaoh. This is in direct contrast as to how sex is viewed today with the man on top. For this reason the woman is never fully appreciated for who she is and the potential

279

power that lies dormant in her. Consequently, man does not have to raise his consciousness. He becomes complacent in pleasing his woman and never achieves higher consciousness or the opening of the gateway.

The focusing in on Jake's left eye with the color Indigo in the back ground, represents the activation of the right brain and his first eye chakra. All symbols of higher consciousness.

DVD Chapter Twenty: Willow Glade Destruction (6:25)

Commentary:

Next scene Jake and Neytiri are seen sleeping. They are awakened by the sound of bulldozers destroying Willow Glade. The number on the main dozer is 12 and 8.

Metaphysical Breakdown

The bulldozer represents the Caucasian's history and mindset when it comes to dealing with people of color. They have intentionally tried to destroy every Melanated culture they have come in contact with. The number twelve represents completion. The number eight represents eternity. These numbers on the bulldozer signify the white man's goal of destroying the culture of the indigenous and replacing it with his own. He will not rest until the task is completed.

Commentary:

Jake is seen rushing to get back to his sleeping Avatar body. Grace frustrated with his actions exclaims, "Jesus marine!"

Metaphysical Breakdown

Grace is calling Jake, by the name of Jesus. This is in recognition of his Christ or higher consciousness. It is a play on words. Jake is the Christ or the one who has transcended into higher consciousness.

Commentary:

Selfridge responds to the bull dozer operator as he stops because Jake and Neytiri are in his way. He says, "Keep going he'll move. These people have to learn that we don't stop. He pushes the controls with his right finger.

Metaphysical Breakdown

This further exemplifies the white man's ideology and mindset when it comes to darker people around the world. The white man's mentality will never change. People of color need to respond appropriately to this fact and quit thinking that he will one day wake up and see the error of his ways. What you see is what you get. They will make no apologies for who they are and how they operate. He will never have the best interests of people of color. He will always take their kindness and spirituality, as their weakness.

Commentary:

Another scene they show another bull dozer with the number nine on its side.

Metaphysical Breakdown

The number nine in numerology represents judgment. The white man's system is the darker people of the world's judgment. He was put here to test or ability to overcome him by raising our consciousness and seeing the system for what it is. We need to overcome our fears and walk out on faith when it comes to solutions to white supremacy. The system was meant to be overthrown, not to be participated in.

Commentary:

Col. Quaritch lands his helicopter at the campsite where they have the

Links to the Avatars. His helicopter number is 19.

Metaphysical Breakdown

The number 19 has very powerful meanings in the occult and secret societies. I do not have enough knowledge on this number to give you a definitive answer. I leave the research to the reader or future discussions of the book.

Commentary:

Col. Quaritch shuts down the link to Jake's Avatar body. Jake's body falls limp to the ground. Tsu'Tey lifts Jake's head and holds a knife to his neck. He says, "You see. It is a demon in a false body!"

Metaphysical Breakdown

Throughout history, people of color have referred to their Caucasian invaders as demons and devils. People of color cannot understand how somebody who is supposed to be human, can act at such a low level of consciousness. Thus, the Caucasian's human body deceives the indigenous people into believing that these pale foreigners all think and act like other native peoples. Unfortunately, for people of color, time has proven otherwise.

Commentary:

Grace explains that the trees they just destroyed were very sacred to the Omaticaya. Selfridge responds," You know what? You throw a stick in the air around here, it's gonna land on some sacred fern for Christ's sake!"

Metaphysical Breakdown

The Omaticaya view all nature as God, no matter how big or small. There was no separation between God, nature and man. This is a Kemetic ideology. Selfridge's comment "for Christ's sake" exemplifies this ideology. It is a spiritual ideology, not religious.

Commentary:

Grace speaking on the culture and the connection of the Omaticaya and nature says, "What we think we know is that there is some kind of electrochemical communication between the roots of the trees, like the synapses between neurons. And each tree has ten-to-the-fourth connections to the trees around it. And there are ten-to-the-twelfth trees on Pandora. Its more connections than the human brain. Get it? It's a network. It's a network and the Na'vi can access it. They can upload and download data and memories."

Metaphysical Breakdown

This discovery by Grace pays tribute to people of color's holistic view of nature and self. There is no separation. In fact, in Kemet, the word for God and nature was the same word, Ntr. There was no ideology of man being predisposed to conquer and use nature as he wishes. To destroy nature, in Kemetic culture, was to destroy God. Because of this relationship, the people could communicate with nature and decipher the personality traits and characteristics of God. Nature holds the blueprint to higher consciousness. People of color have access to hundreds of thousands of years of information that is held in the DNA of the plants, trees, water, air, fire and soil. Consequently, they also have access to hundreds of thousands of years of information in their DNA as well. This is part of the reason why people of color "call" on the ancestors for wisdom, knowledge, guidance and support. It is at their disposal when called upon. But if Black people and people of color are taught to view themselves and nature through their lower selves, they are cutting off their natural connection to God.

Commentary:

Grace continues, "The wealth of this world isn't in the ground, its all around us. The Na'vi know that and they are fighting to defend it. If you want to share this world with them, you need to understand them."

Metaphysical Breakdown

This represents two conflicting views of reality. One Eurocentric and the other is Afrocentric. People of color have adopted the European's lifestyle and worldview as a means of so-called, "making progress." Unfortunately, time tells otherwise. People of color find themselves in a worst position for adopting this view, instead of fighting for and protecting their own indigenous cultures. For white people, the only way to share this world with them is for you to adopt their way of thinking. Otherwise, they will try to eliminate you and your ideology. Caucasians only know one way to function and that is represented by their lower consciousness or left hemisphere of the brain. Anything contradictory to this lifestyle, they will view as beneath them or will take people of color's higher consciousness or spirituality as a sign of weakness and try to exploit them.

Commentary:

Selfridge responds sarcastically," What the hell have you people been smoking out there. They're just God damn trees!' Grace responds, "You need to wake up Parker." Selfridge says, "No! You need to wake up!

Metaphysical Breakdown

Grace represents people of color's worldview or ideology, which is called Afrocentric or Eastern philosophy. Selfridge, represents the Caucasian's worldview, which is Eurocentric. Afrocentric is represented by the right brain and Eurocentric is represented by the left. Neither the two shall meet as one can only activate one hemisphere of the brain at one time. This is the struggle that people of color do not realize when dealing with Caucasians. There is no compromise with them. People of color will never convince Caucasians or change ever their minds or culture.

Commentary:

Jake referring to the Omaticaya says, "They're not gonna give up their home. They're not gonna make a deal. For what? Lite beer and blue jeans? There's nothing we have that they want."

Metaphysical Breakdown

The indigenous, people of color were always content and satisfied with their culture and way of life before the European came into their world. The Caucasian had to trick the people into believing in his culture and ideology. If they did not accept it voluntarily, he used lethal force. Years later, you have people of color forgetting who they are and where they came from, selling out to a system that can only provide them limited, material things. They have learned to place more value in material things than to preserve and protect the remnants of way of life and a culture that has been forsaken'. This culture was the quest for higher consciousness to be closer to God, not materialism.

Commentary:

Jake speaks while holding up a book about the Na'vi, "When people are sitting on shit that you want, you make them your enemy. Then you're justified in taking it!"

Metaphysical Breakdown

This concept is pretty straight forward. The only thing hidden is the fact that this is how Caucasians were able to rule the world. This strategy can still be seen today, worldwide in Iraq, Iran, Venezuela, Cuba, Afghanistan and the like.

Commentary:

Trudy informs the group that Col. Quaritch is planning an attack on Home Tree. Grace gasps, "My God!"

Metaphysical Breakdown

The "My God" Grace is referring to is the higher consciousness held by the Na'vi people, not a religious deity or arbitrary response.

Commentary:

Selfridge gives Grace and Jake the permission to link to their Avatars. Technician says, "Calibrating 3 and 4. Max adds, "Initiating. Thirty seconds." Selfridge responds, "You got one hour."

Metaphysical Breakdown

Numerology: 3 + 4= 7. Seven represents God's divinity in the physical plane. 30 is three. This represents divine perfection. These numbers are used to describe Jake and Grace's mission to risk their lives to save the Na'vi. One hour equals 60 minutes or the number 6. This represents the beast in man or his lower self. This number was spoken by Selfridge when explaining the consequences to Jake if he doesn't succeed.

DVD Chapter Twenty-One: You Will Never Be One of the People (3:34)

Commentary:

Neytiri speaking to Jake after he told her he betrayed the Omaticaya people. "You will never be one of the people!

Metaphysical Breakdown

Proof the Caucasians do not have the capacity to reach higher consciousness. Sooner or later, their true colors or lower self will be revealed. Thus, indigenous people can never allow them in their culture or way of life. They should always protect and preserve it from them.

DVD Chapter Twenty-Two: Assault on Home Tree (3:19)

Commentary:

On route to bombing Home Tree the pilots communicate with each other. The first pilot says, "Roger that. Stay on heading 030." The second pilot repeats the first command. "Roger, 030."

Metaphysical Breakdown

In numerology, 030 + 030= 6. Six is the number of the beast in man. This lower level consciousness is being displayed as they are going to wage war on the Na'vi people.

Commentary:

The Na'vi leader tells Tsu'Tey, "Take the Ikran, attack from above!"

Metaphysical Breakdown

What the Na'vi are really referring to is to attack from your higher consciousness. When two people fight in lower level consciousness, there are no winners. They both lose, so the only way to succeed in fighting lower level behavior is to attack with higher consciousness. This should be the only strategy people of color should adopt when encountering white people. This is where people of color have the advantage or upper hand when dealing with Caucasians. They should embrace and exploit this fact.

Commentary:

Col. Quaritch orders gas canisters to be shot at Home Tree. The soldier acknowledges and replies, "CS 40's going hot. Firing!"

Metaphysical Breakdown

In numerology CS 40 comes out to be the number 8. In numerology, eight represents eternity or infinity. This is the Caucasians mindset when it comes to pushing his agenda. He refuses to change or back down. He will always have this mentality. He will never change his ways.

Commentary:

Col. Quaritch orders "H.E." missiles to knock out Home Tree's columns. The camera immediately shows Trudy reluctant to fire on the Na'vi.

Metaphysical Breakdown

In numerology H.E. equals the number 13. Thirteen is the number of resurrection. Trudy is now going against orders and listening to her higher consciousness. Trudy is being resurrected into her higher consciousness.

Commentary:

The other pilots respond, "Ones good." Pilot 2 says, "Two's rocks up." And pilot 3 says, "Threes up."

Metaphysical Breakdown

There are three pilots, pilot 1, pilot 2 and pilot 3. In numerology, these numbers add up to the number 6. Six represents man as a beast or his lower self. This is appropriate as these pilots are about to kill innocent men, women and children.

Commentary:

Pilot says over radio, "Charlie Oscar, gunrunner standing by." Trudy is shown in the scene contemplating her decision to be a part of this preemptive strike or massacre. Later Trudy exclaims, "I didn't sign up for this shit!"

Metaphysical Breakdown

Charlie(C) Oscar (O) in numerology represents the number 9. Nine is the symbol of man's judgment. This is Trudy's moment of truth. To stand up for what is right or go along with the flow?

DVD Chapter Twenty-Three: Aftermath (1:58)

Commentary:

In the aftermath, Neytiri finds her father laying on his right side. He has a giant wood splinter piercing the left side of his body. He instructs her to protect the people. He is dying.

Metaphysical Breakdown

The wound in the left side of his body means that he has been damaged spiritually, more than mortally wounded. He gives Neytiri his weapon with his right hand to symbolize to her that she has the permission to activate her left brain or lower consciousness to protect and save the Na'vi sacred culture and way of life.

Commentary:

Jake, "I was a warrior that dreamed he can bring peace. Sooner or later, you have to wake up." Jake is wearing another shirt with birds on the front of it.

Metaphysical Breakdown

Jake "waking up" symbolizes the activation of the left brain. When indigenous people are together, they can relate to one another at a level of higher consciousness. When they are dealing with Caucasians they need to understand that they must operate on a lower level of consciousness to communicate with them. This is what Jake is referring to when he says he must wake up.

Commentary:

Norm punches soldier with left fist to try to keep him from pulling the plug on Jake and Grace.

Metaphysical Breakdown

Norm's left side of his body represents the activation of his higher consciousness or right brain. This act symbolizes Norm is fighting the soldiers with his higher consciousness.

Commentary:

Grace is unplugged. The Na'vi children make a sled to carry her in. The sled is shaped like an "X" on top of it.

Metaphysical Breakdown

The "X" in ancient Kemet, symbolized a person's resurrection. Because Grace was willing to give her own life so that others can live, this was her initiation into higher consciousness. Grace is now reborn.

The Kemetic god, Ausar on the left in white. Notice the "X" on his chest. King Tut, in the middle, is being introduced to Ausar to be resurrected in the afterlife.

DVD Chapter Twenty-Four: Escape From Hell's Gate (4:12)

Commentary:

Trudy pistol whips the guard who is watching Jake, Grace and Norm. Before she does it she tells him to get, "Down, all the way down."

Metaphysical Breakdown

Her statement, "Down, all the way down" refers to her state of consciousness. She must lower herself to save her friends and the Na'vi people. She does this by hitting the guard in the back of the head.

Commentary:

The group is escaping in Trudy's helicopter. They are under fire. Norm is helping Jake get into the helicopter. He extends his right arm and grabs Jake's left forearm. Norm says, Grab my hand! Come on, we're in. Let's go!"

Metaphysical Breakdown

This handshake is known as the "Lion's Paw" in the occult and secret society sects. It is a sign of the initiate being resurrected or "raised" into higher consciousness. This is a symbol of Jake's Christ or higher consciousness. Jake is an example of the Kemetic god, Heru. This is where we get the word "Hero" from today. As you can imagine, Jake is the Hero or Heru of the movie.

This depiction is a secret society "raising" ceremony, where the member is initiated into a higher degree or level of consciousness.

Notice the Lion is grabbing the initiates left arm with his left arm to symbolize the activation of the right hemisphere of the brain which represents higher consciousness.

Commentary:

Col. Quaritch uses up all his ammunition shooting at the copter. He pulls his last gun out as the crew is getting away. He fires six more shots before he gives up. One of these shots hits Grace.

Metaphysical Breakdown

The numerology of the number six, represents, man's lower self or the beast in him. Quaritch is displaying his lower consciousness by trying to murder innocent people.

Commentary:

As the crew escapes Norm yells out, "All Right!" Trudy also asks, "Is everybody all right back there?"

Metaphysical Breakdown

The words "all right" are to be taken literally. Grace is wounded on her right side. This is her mortal side. Grace is mortally wounded in the right side of her body which represents her lower, physical self.

Commentary:

Trudy hooks up the Avatar link to the helicopter. Jake tells her, "Keep going North. Deep into the mountains."

Metaphysical Breakdown

The direction implied by north always means up. North symbolizes higher consciousness. This is where they will be safe and regroup. It is a state of mind, not a geographical location.

Commentary:

Trudy replies, "At least they can't track us up here. Not this far into the Vortex."

Metaphysical Breakdown

People, who operate at a lower level of consciousness like Quaritch and Selfridge, cannot function or communicate at higher level frequencies. So they cannot "track" our crew because they do not have the capacity to reach higher consciousness. This is the only way they can follow them. The letter "V" in Vortex represents feminine energy. Feminine energy is higher, spiritual consciousness. Again this consciousness cannot be attained by people who operate at lower consciousness.

Commentary:

Jake tries to comfort Grace by telling her they are going to get help. She replies, "I'm a scientist, remember? I don't believe in fairy tales.

Metaphysical Breakdown

Western scientists operate predominantly using the left hemisphere of the brain. They only view logic and facts that they can see, hear, touch, feel or taste. They are very analytical and do not take into consideration anything outside of their point of view. Grace, being a scientist, pays homage to this way of thinking. Jake, being of higher consciousness views life as a place where miracles can happen. He operates from the right hemisphere of the brain. He can do what people say is impossible. He is not limited by his left brain rules and paradigms. He has access to infinite possibilities.

Commentary:

The crew lands at the Tree of Souls. While landing, one notices the arch shaped rocks all around its environment.

Metaphysical Breakdown

The arches are a symbol of feminine energy or higher, spiritual consciousness. The letter "M" has two arches. It is the 13th letter in the alphabet. The number of resurrection. The arch represents the female gateway to higher consciousness.

DVD Chapter Twenty-Five: There's Something We Gotta Do (11:22)

Commentary:

Jake is back in his Avatar body. He is covered in ash from all the burning trees.

Metaphysical Breakdown

The covering of the ash on Jake's Avatar body is further proof that Jake is really a Black man operating at his highest level of consciousness.

DVD Chapter Twenty-Six: Toruk Macto (1:50)

Commentary:

Jake flies over Toruk Macto. He explains, "The way I had it figured, Toruk was the baddest cat in the sky. Nothing attacks him. So why would he ever look up?'

Metaphysical Breakdown

As we covered earlier in the book, Toruk represents the behavior a hero or Heru, who achieves higher consciousness, must display in order to protect and save his people. This behavior is only allowed in very rare instances where the people and their culture are in danger. Where there is no other alternative to defend those who cannot defend themselves.

Toruk never looks up because he represents the lower level chakras represented by the colors red, orange and yellow. Lower consciousness never wants to raise itself. Thus it has no reason or interest in looking up.

Jake calling Toruk the baddest "Cat" in the sky, pays homage to the Kemetic goddess, Sekhmet. Sekhmet was the goddess of God's wrath and swift justice. Jake describes Toruk Macto as such to call on God's power to uphold the Na'vi's righteous way of life.

The Kemetic goddess Sekhmet, represented by the female lion. Her main objective or role is to protect God's divine order. If this order becomes unbalanced, Sekhmet will unleash God's wrath on the unjust.

Commentary:

Jake goes to the Tree of Souls as Toruk Macto. The people accept him back. When Tsu'Tey faces Jake, Toruk Macto is seen over Jake's left shoulder, in the background, spreading his wings that resemble the letter "X." Tsu'Tey reaches out with his left hand and touches Jake on the left side of his body. He says, I will fly with you."

Metaphysical Breakdown

Tsu'Tey touches Jake on his left side with his left hand to represent that he will go with him in battle with higher consciousness. The left side of the body representing the activation of the right hemisphere of the brain which operates at higher consciousness. The battle is spiritual, not physical. This is the only way the Na'vi people can win is to fight a spiritual battle where rules and the laws of the physical dimension do not apply.

Toruk Macto being superimposed behind Jake over his left shoulder symbolizes his higher consciousness and role as the savior.

298

DVD Chapter Twenty-Seven: She's Real (1:25)

Commentary:

Jake is shown carrying Grace to the Tree of Souls. She is wearing a mask. The left side of the mask is illuminated by the reflection of the trees around her.

Metaphysical Breakdown

The left side of the face represents the activation of the right hemisphere of the brain. This side represents man's spiritual and higher consciousness. That's why this side is illuminated.

Commentary:

As Grace looks around the Tree of Souls, She replies, "I need to take some samples."

Metaphysical Breakdown

Grace has switched back to her analytical and logical, western scientist mind. This mindset is held in the left hemisphere of the brain. This is Grace's lower consciousness. She is jeopardizing her ability to transcend into higher consciousness.

Commentary:

They lay Grace on the ground next to her Avatar body. The Avatar is laying on its right side. Grace is laid on her left side.

Metaphysical Breakdown

This is an Afrikan initiation ritual that secret societies use as well. The Avatar laying on its right side of her body with her left side facing the sky, represents the suppression of left brain function and the enlightenment of right brain function.

Grace's position represents the opposite of her Avatar. Her left side or right brain is being suppressed or held to the ground, while her right side or left brain is facing the sky. This symbolizes the embracing of lower level consciousness.

Just by the positioning of Grace's human body, the viewer can tell that she doesn't have the capacity to cross over into higher consciousness. The body is an a lower level position of consciousness.

Commentary:

Mo'at explains that for Grace to be saved and have a new life in her Avatar body, "She must pass through the eye of Eywa and return. But Jake Sulley, she is very weak."

Metaphysical Breakdown

Remember, the Avatar represents people of color who operate according to their higher consciousness. Grace, being white, or lacking Melanin, may be "too weak" to make the transition from lower consciousness to higher consciousness. The weakness is her non- melanated, recessive genes that all Caucasians have. Dominant or "strong" genes are held by people of color.

Her "passing through the eye of Eywa" symbolizes the ancient Kemet symbol of the Eye of Ra or Heru. This eye depending on the left or the right represents man's moral standing as well as man's spiritual awareness. These two things, the physical and the spiritual sides of man, will be judged in our pursuit of everlasting life when we transcend. Grace's life and consciousness is now being tested. If she passes, she will make the transition to the Avatar body. If she doesn't, she will die.

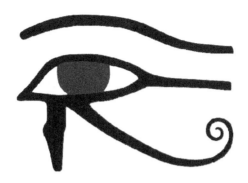

The "Eye of Ra or Heru." The left eye represents man's higher or spiritual nature, whereas the right eye represents man's morality as a physical being.

Commentary:

The connection of the roots from the Tree of Souls to Grace and her Avatar body, when seen from above, resembles a lotus flower.

Metaphysical Breakdown

The lotus flower in Kemet, represented the ideology of resurrection. The flower grew from the mud of the banks of the Nile river. It overcame its environment to bloom a beautiful flower above the water. Man also, has this ability, depending on his free will. Grace is also being tested.

Commentary:

All the Na'vi's hair braids are connected to the ground. They are glowing as they chant and move in unison.

Metaphysical Breakdown

The hair braid represents the Na'vi's DNA structure and its ability to communicate with the environment around it. They have access to all information that nature or God has. Thus they have the power to produce the miracles of life by deciphering its code. It is the Na'vi's concentrated and collective will that is focused on saving Grace's life. This is where the power of melanated people lies. It lies within the access to 100's of thousands of years of knowledge of the universe that they can access through their genetic DNA.

Commentary:

The Tree of Soul's roots are seen attaching themselves to the back of Grace's neck. They are glowing.

Metaphysical Breakdown

This part of the head is where the Cerebral Cortex or brain stem is found. It is also known as the Reptilian Brain. This part of the brain contains man's lower consciousness. It is very primitive and under developed. This brain's function is all about self survival by any means necessary. There is no compassion or connection to anything else but its survival. This is the part of the brain Caucasians operate from. It is a very low level of consciousness.

Commentary:

Grace looks up at Jake. Her mask is illuminating on the left side again, by the reflection of the Tree of Souls. She says that she sees Eywa and that Eywa is real. A tunnel of bright light is seen traveling at a high rate of speed. Grace has died.

Metaphysical Breakdown

The mask represents the activation of the right brain by the illuminating light of the left side of Grace's mask. Because of this, she is able to see Eywa or God. The tunnel Grace sees is the activation of the Pineal gland. She finally believes in a higher power and dies.

Commentary:

Mo'at responds, "Her wounds were too great. There was not enough time."

Metaphysical Breakdown

The wounds Mo'at is referring to, is the wounds in Grace's DNA. Non-melanated people, contain in their DNA recessive genes. These genes can be considered weak or dysfunctional when it comes to biology. Grace did not have enough time to heal her DNA before she died. Healing her DNA can be broken down to providing and carrying Melanin in their blood.

DVD Chapter Twenty-Eight: Recruiting the Clans (5:11)

Commentary:

Jake speaks to the Na'vi after Grace dies. He says, "You tell them Toruk Macto calls to them. And you fly now with me! My brothers! My sisters! And we will show the Sky people, that they cannot take whatever they want! And that this, this is our land! Jake then grabs Ney'tiri by the left hand. Al the Na'vi join in and raise their fists to the sky, as Jake and Neytiri ride of on Toruk.

Metaphysical Breakdown

This is a Black power speech. Malcolm X could not have said it any better. They also give the Black power salute by raising one fist in the air when they cry out. The scene is giving people of color a blueprint into overcoming and conquering their white oppressors. A people must be united as one when fighting a common enemy. They also must raise their consciousness and be self-sacrificing in a cause they deem greater than themselves.

Commentary:

Jake says, "We rode out to the four winds. To the horse clans of the plains."

Metaphysical Breakdown

The horse clans refer to the Native Americans who fought a common enemy along with the Afrikans who were kidnapped and forced into slavery.

Commentary:

Jake says, "Back to the stars! To the Ikran people of the Eastern sea." They show a woman of this tribe painted in red and white, holding her bow in the air, leading the charge.

Metaphysical Breakdown

In Afrikan mythology, our ancestors come from the stars; mainly the Eastern star or what is otherwise known as, Sirius. The East always represents Afrocentric philosophy and culture.

The red and white paint on the woman warrior represents the Kemetic god Heru. He is also represented by these colors. He is the Hero. He is courageous, brave, self-sacrificing and always triumphs. He represents the spirit of the revolution or righting that which is wrong.

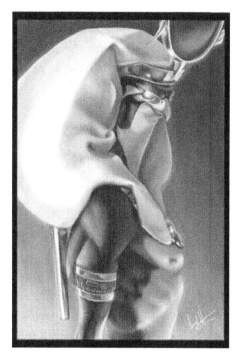

The Kemetic god Heru, shown wearing the colors of red and white. The name Heru is where we get the word "hero" from.

DVD Chapter Twenty-Nine: Preamble to Battle (3:42)

Commentary:

Quartich tells his troops that the Na'vi have grown from a few hundred, to 2,000 in one day. He further states, "In a week's time there could be 20,000 of them. At that point they will overrun our perimeter."

Metaphysical Breakdown

In numerology 2,000 and the number 20,000 represent the number two. The number 2 stands for separation or division. This represents the indigenous people separating from the white establishment and building their own civilization. The white man has always been fearful of this scenario.

Also, the thought of being overrun by the horde gives credence to the white man's psychological fear of the potency in people of color's DNA to destroy him as a race.

Commentary:

Col. Quaritch announces, "Our only security lies in a preemptive attack. We will fight terror, with terror."

Metaphysical Breakdown

This mindset exposes the Caucasian's psychology of fear and a predisposition of feeling like he is living under constant attack. He feels he must lash out first, before he is ultimately exterminated. This is the psychology of white supremacy. The white man feels he is being terrorized by the darker people of the world and is intimidated by their sheer numbers. Because of this, he feels he is justified in lashing out, killing and oppressing them.

Commentary:

Col. Quaritch, "Now the hostiles believe that this mountain stronghold of theirs is protected by their.......their deity. And when we destroy it, we will blast a crater in their racial memory so deep that they won't come within 1,000 klicks of this place ever again. And that too is a fact"

Metaphysical Breakdown

This strategy was used to oppress and annihilate Afrikans and all indigenous people the European has come in contact with. When you destroy a people's concept of God, you destroy the people and their cultural memory. Christianity has been used to destroy people of color's God and cultural memories. When you force the people to give up their God and you replace their God, with the image of their oppressor, you have psychologically cut off that people from their history and culture. Simple concept, you destroy a people's God and you destroy the people's will to fight. You destroy their will and concept of reality, one can enslave them and replace their cultural beliefs with a mindset you have chosen for them. This has been the strategy of white supremacy throughout history.

Commentary:

Next scene, we see one of those mechanical robots called Amp suits, loading an air craft with explosives to be used on the Tree of Souls. The Amp suit has the number 27 on its right shoulder.

Metaphysical Breakdown

In numerology, the number 27 breaks down to the number 9. Nine is the symbol of man's judgment. The robot, delivering a bomb to the Na'vi, will be their test. The Na'vi will be judged on how they handle this attack. A man's character is represented by how he responds to and handles adversity or crisis, not when he is comfortable.

Commentary:

Max informs Jake that they will be dropping the bomb as some sort of "shock and awe" campaign. He says that they will be heading out 0:600, tomorrow.

Metaphysical Breakdown

In numerology, 0:600 breaks down to equal the number 6. Six represents the beast in man or his lower self. Murdering innocent people represents the "beast" in man's behavior.

Commentary:

Jake, "I have over 15 clans out there. That's over 2,000 warriors."

Metaphysical Breakdown

In numerology, adding the numbers 15 + 2,000 = 8. Eight represents infinity or eternity. This symbolism implies that people of color will be fighting Caucasians forever. They will never change their system of white supremacy to include the darker people of the Earth. Thus if people of color want their freedom, they must be willing to fight until the very end.

Commentary:

Norm comments, "If they get to the Tree of Souls, its over. That's their direct line to Eywa, their ancestors. It'll destroy them.

Metaphysical Breakdown

This is further proof of the White man's strategy to attack people of color on a spiritual front. It has worked for him in every encounter with indigenous people. It is their main strategy throughout history. Undermine the culture of the indigenous through the introduction and enforcement of Christianity.

Commentary:

Jake, talking to the Tree of Souls says, "See the world we come from. There's no green there. They killed their mother. And there gonna do the same here."

Metaphysical Breakdown

Jake referring to "no green" is referring to the heart chakra, represented by that color. The heart chakra is the first chakra level of higher consciousness. So no green or having no heart refers to the white man's inability to raise his consciousness.

Jake says, "They killed their mother and there gonna do the same here." Anthropologist all agree that the mother and father of the human race were Afrikan. The Na'vi representing the Afrikan, shows the white man out to destroy their mother.

Commentary:

Neytiri touches Jake on the left shoulder. She informs him, "Our great mother does not take sides Jake. She protects only the balance of life."

Metaphysical Breakdown

The great mother Neytiri is referring to is the ancient Kemetic goddess named Maat. Maat weighs a person's heart against her feather on a scale to see if one has lived a moral standing life, when one has departed. This is the same symbol of the woman with a blindfold holding the scales to represent the justice system in America. Maat does not interfere in affairs. She just keeps the balance of righteousness, propriety, reciprocity, honor, justice and balance of the universe. The old adage of "what goes around, comes around" is a direct principle of this Kemetic universal law. The universe, nature or God will always work to balance and correct itself. Man need not interfere, just trust, know and believe in the law.

Kemetic Goddess, Maat. She symbolizes justice, righteousness, balance, order, honor and reciprocity.

Commentary:

Next scene Jake and Neytiri place both their foreheads together. The next scene you see to helicopter blades, one on top of the other speeding in unison.

Metaphysical Breakdown

Jake and Neytiri are combining their Pineal glands together as one. They are focused on bringing their thoughts together to create miracles in the physical dimension. The helicopter blades represent the feminine and masculine energy becoming and working as one to create an electromagnetic gateway. Notice one blade is on top of the other. It represents the feminine principle spinning in opposite direction of the blade under it representing the masculine principle. This action creates the electro-magnetic gateway from which to manifest thoughts and ideas into the physical dimension.

310

DVD Chapter Thirty: Battle for Pandora (5:39)

Commentary:

Jake tells Tsu'Tey and Neytiri that he wants to punch a hole through the convoy. He instructs them to follow him.

Metaphysical Breakdown

Jake, Tsu'Tey and Neytiri represent the original Holy Trinity of Ausar, Heru, and Auset. They represent the father, the son and the mother. Christianity left out the mother or feminine principle to subject the woman under man's rule. This was the start of sexism. To win the war all facets of the first Holy Trinity must work together as one.

The original, Holy Trinity of Kemet. The father, the god Ausar, in the middle. The mother, Auset on the right and the son Heru on the left.

Commentary:

There are so many numbers and letters tossed about as the battle begins. Also, as many left and right body symbols being displayed. At this point, the reader should be able to come up with his own conclusions when deciphering the hidden messages. I will leave this chapter up to your findings and interpretation.

DVD Chapter Thirty-One: Fall of the Heroes. (:36)

Commentary:

Trudy goes head up against Col. Quaritch's massive ship. She dies in battle for what she views as a noble cause.

Metaphysical Breakdown

Trudy lives out the true meaning of her name. She is a brave soldier and dies for a cause she views greater than herself.

Commentary:

Tsu'Tey jumps on the ship with his left leg forward. He kills several soldiers before he plunges to his death.

Metaphysical Breakdown

Left foot forward exemplifies higher consciousness because it activates the right brain which houses our spirituality. By Tsu'Tey giving his life for a cause greater than himself, guarantees him his resurrection into eternal life. He has completed his initiation in the physical realm in order to transcend in the spiritual realm.

Commentary:

Norm is shot on his left side in battle. He is sent back to his human body.

Metaphysical Breakdown

Norm also passes his physical dimension test. He is shot on his higher consciousness side, the left side of the body. He earns the right to be resurrected into the spiritual realm.

313

DVD Chapter Thirty-Two: Eywa (1:00)

Commentary:

The Na'vi are losing the battle. All seems hopeless as their people, nature and the animals are dying all around them. All seems lost. Out of nowhere, a herd of Thanators come to the rescue and the tables are turned! Neytiri pronounces, "Jake, Eywa has heard you! Eywa has heard you!"

Metaphysical Breakdown

In the physical dimension, it seems like man must be pushed and tested to the point of giving up. It seems like this test is the threshold one must pass in order to manifest their dreams and heart's desires by transcending to higher consciousness. One must be pushed to the breaking point in order for true miracles to happen. This is the universal law our Kemetic ancestors mastered. There are rules and regulations that must be followed for the universe to be decoded in an effort to have its laws work in man's favor. This is one of them. There are no other ways around it. One must pass the test and never lose hope, for miracles to happen.

Commentary:

The giant, mother Viperwolf faces Neytiri. She bows down favoring her left side as a sign of submission to Neytiri. Ney'tiri understands the gesture and rides the giant beast into battle.

Metaphysical Breakdown

Neytiri is operating at higher consciousness. This gives her the ability to communicate with nature or God. The Viperwolf has submitted their spirit to Neytiri shown by the bowing down of the left paw. Neytiri and the Navi people now have access to nature and the animals, as they view themselves as an extension of the one God.

Commentary:

Jake blows up Col. Quaritch's ship. He escapes in his amp suit. His right shoulder is on fire. He jumps out of the plunging aircraft in his Amp suit. When he lands, he is bleeding on the right side of his head. He puts on his glove to the amp suit with his right fist first. Col. Quaritch's amp suit number is 11.

Metaphysical Breakdown

The damage to Col. Quaritch's shoulder and putting on the right glove symbolizes his inability to operate at a higher conscious level. The left side of the body represents one's higher consciousness. Col. Quaritch is injured on his right shoulder. This is where his focus and attention lies. On his lower self. This is how he defines himself and his survival. This is his reality that he chooses for himself.

Eleven in numerology is a master number. Eleven represents the god in you or the devil in you looking itself in the mirror. It's represented by the number one, looking at its reflection. It has dual meanings based on a person's consciousness level. In this case, it represents a lower consciousness. Too much of a good thing can be destroying. Quaritch has been put in a position of power, influence and control. Because he operates at such a low level of consciousness, he abuses these attributes. If he was operating at a higher conscious level, he would not act in such a trite way.

Commentary:

Jake falls from the sky after he blows up Col. Quaritch's aircraft. He blows the aircraft's right engines. His fall is soften by the many leaves, trees, branches and vines of the dense jungle. He lands safely on the ground around these giant purple flowers.

Metaphysical Breakdown

Jake makes the ultimate sacrifice to blow up the aircraft. He did not care about his own well-being. Jake took his leap of faith. For this, his reward is higher consciousness at the crown chakra, represented by the purple flowers he landed in.

Jake blew up the right engine because that is where the power of their enemies lies. It represents the left hemisphere of the brain where lower consciousness dwells.

DVD Chapter Thirty-Three: Quaritch Fight (3:06)

Commentary:

Col. Quaritch looks over his right shoulder to look in his side mirror. He sees Neytiri coming up on him from behind.

Metaphysical Breakdown

Quaritch displays lower level consciousness, represented by looking over his right shoulder which activates the left hemisphere of the brain, that houses lower level consciousness. This activates the beast in him which is motivated by fear for his survival.

Commentary:

Jake tells Quaritch, "Give it up Quaritch. It's over." Quaritch responds, "Nothings over while I am still breathing!"

Metaphysical Breakdown

Quaritch represents the Caucasian's mindset and culture. He is not interested on changing his interpretation of reality. He will die with this mindset and if necessary, take everyone, including the earth with him. They do not know how to change. This is who they are and they make no excuses for it. They will never change their thought process.

Commentary:

Quaritch does battle with Jake.

Metaphysical Breakdown

Quaritch needs technology and artificial means to represent his strongest self, whereas, Jake uses natural or holistic resources to represent his strongest self. Remember, Jake represents man's higher consciousness so he is closer to nature or God. Jake does not need any artificial or so called technology to succeed. Quaritch, on the other hand, must use technology and artificial means to represent himself. He is further from nature or God, thus his disconnect from nature or God limits his resources and consciousness to define his reality.

Commentary:

Quaritch speaking to Jake says. "Hey Sully, how does it feel to betray your own race? You think you're one of them? Time to wake up."

Metaphysical Breakdown

This scene gives more proof that Jake represents a Black man of higher consciousness. He also points out the white man's inability to reach higher consciousness unless he comingles with Melanated people by saying, "It's time to wake up." White people fool themselves and other people of color when they surround themselves around people of color who accept them into the community. They are still white and will always hold this genetic disposition no matter what. They are great imitators but never internalize indigenous cultures. They are masters at mimicking someone who has achieved higher consciousness. They know all the right things to say and do but when it comes down to it, they will always revert back to lower level consciousness.

Commentary:

Neytiri frees her right leg from under the Viperwolf. She uses her left arm to shoot her arrow that kills Col. Quaritch. His Amp suit falls on his right side.

Metaphysical Breakdown

Quaritch killed her Viperwolf. This is what trapped Neytiri. It was this lower level of consciousness that trapped her. She let herself be blinded by her anger for Quaritch. She stooped down to his level of consciousness. This is the strategy of the Caucasian race. The only battles they can fight are fueled by lower level consciousness. That is why Black communities operate at this lower level frequency. They are filled with guns, drugs, violence, toxins, unemployment, low level housing, nutrition and medical care. It is a strategy of white supremacy. Once Neytiri raised her consciousness, observed by firing the bow and arrow with her left hand, she was able to overcome her oppressor. The European cannot fight at a higher consciousness or spiritual battle with people of color. Thus, they must get us to lower ours.

DVD Chapter Thirty-Four: I See You (3:26)

Commentary:

Jake is suffocating because he cannot reach his oxygen mask. Neytiri jumps in the lab and cradles him on her left side with her left knee forward.

Metaphysical Breakdown

Jake and Neytiri's power always lies in their higher consciousness. This is where people of color's strength lies. This is what has been hidden and suppressed in the system of white supremacy. To resurrect the Black man and woman, the only way is to raise their consciousness. If they choose to stay in this lower state, they will forever be manipulated and controlled. People cannot fight the system of white supremacy on their playing field. Raise the frequency and you will raise your chances of being free. It is a spiritual battle, not physical. The body will follow what the mind wills.

Commentary:

Jake says, "The aliens went back to their dying world. Only a few were chosen to stay. The time of great sorrow was ending. Toruk Macto was no longer needed."

Metaphysical Breakdown

The aliens going back to their dying world represent the coming of a new age where lower consciousness will not be able to function. With the coming of the year 2012. It is the Age of Aquarius. Aquarius is represented by the Black woman bearing water. This means the activation of feminine energy will be the key of life. Feminine energy is the higher self or spiritual consciousness. The old way of doing things is going to become obsolete or dead. We are entering the Age of "I Know" or the Age of Knowing. It is a higher state of mind then the Age we are leaving which is the Age of Pisces, the fish. This was the Age of

"I Believe." The Age of blind allegiance, ignorance is bliss, materialism, patriotism, ego and religious dogma. This has been the time of great sorrow for people of color around the planet. The fish is immersed in the water and must obey its ebb and flow, temperature and intent. It is dependent on it to provide it it's life giving sustenance. In this new Age of Aquarius, we become the water! We become the life giving substance that can be activated by our thoughts or intent.

Toruk Macto is no longer needed because peace is among the people. The scales of Maat are now balanced. Toruk Macto or a higher conscious man who must operate at a lower consciousness to protect his civilization, only purpose is to right the unbalanced scales. Once the scales are balanced, lower consciousness is no longer needed. This concept has always been a temporary fix that was not meant to be permanent.

The fact that only a few humans were chosen to stay, represents the white man's strategy to insert himself into history as a means of his future survival. He must constantly inject himself into history in an attempt to hijack the future at a later date. If he is always included amongst people of color, he will always have a chance to not only survive but dominant the world as he is doing today. This scene gives the Caucasian hope for the future.

Commentary:

Jake's last video log is #98. He mentions that it is his birthday and he is never coming back to this place again.

Metaphysical Breakdown

In Numerology, the number 98 is broken down to the number 8. This is the number of eternity or infinity. Jake has vowed to eternally convert to his Avatar body. This represents Jake's higher consciousness as a Black man. Jake is being resurrected one last time. He is totally committed in defining his reality through his higher consciousness.

Commentary:

Just like Grace's scene, Jake is laying on his left side, while his Avatar body is laying on its right side. The seeds from the Sacred Tree are all around him. The camera focuses in on Jake's Avatar's forehead. Jake opens his eyes. The end.

Metaphysical Breakdown

Jake's human body lying on its left side represents Jake's lower self. This position suppresses the body's spiritual side and enhances the body's lower consciousness. The left side of the body represents higher consciousness. So when one lays on this side, it restricts the movement. Whereas, the right side being on top, has unlimited mobility and freedom. Jake's Avatar's body being the opposite position, suppress the lower self and enhances his higher consciousness. This scene is Jake's initiation and commitment to always operate and see reality according to his higher consciousness. Jake is being reborn or resurrected into a state of higher consciousness as a Black man.

The camera focuses on Jake's Pineal gland, which is located in the middle of his forehead. This scene shows the activation of Jake's Melanin, which is produced by the Pineal gland. This is the chemical needed for higher consciousness. Unfortunately, this is also the chemical people of European descent do not have altogether or in very small amounts because of the calcification of their Pineal gland.

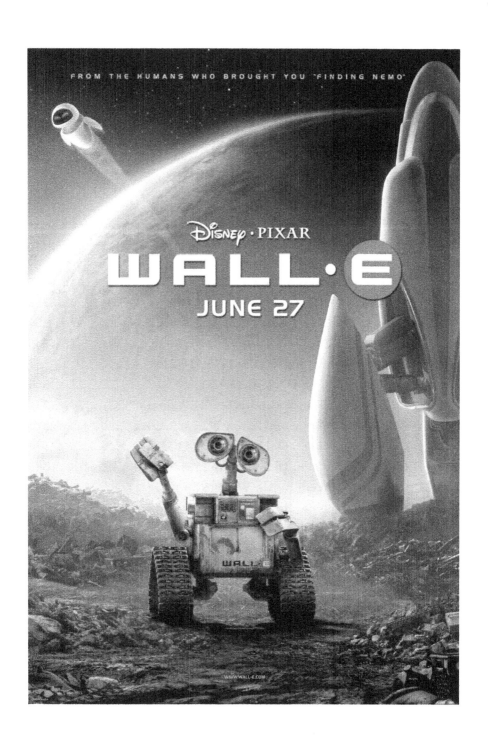

Contents

"CAST" of Characters

WALL-E- Meaning, "ruler of the army." This character represents the Kemetic god Ausar. Ausar was tricked and killed by his brother and cut up into pieces and discarded. The Kemetic goddess, Auset who was Ausar's wife, tirelessly searched and found the pieces to her husband and put him back together. Ausar was the first god to resurrect himself with the help of his wife. Resurrection can be defined as putting to "death" one's lower conscious behavior and thoughts in order to be "reborn" and transcend into one's higher consciousness.

This Afrikan story is the blueprint for resurrecting the Black man here in America and throughout the world. This is what this film is all about. WALL-E, meaning ruler of the army, must take his rightful position as head of his family, community and nation. With the Black woman believing and investing her time and energy in her man and not the system that oppresses her man, the Black community will rise out of its lower state of consciousness and transcend into their true selves. WALL-E represents the consciously dead, Black man who was programmed to work for a system that enslaves him. With the help and faith in him from the Black woman, represented by the robot EVE, and the realization of his true self and not his programming, the Black man will rise from the ashes and build a community that is beneficial for him, his woman and his children.

The Roach- Represents WALL-E's melanin. One of the traits of melanin is that it is indestructible. The roach gets run over, stepped on and shot at, but he never dies. Whenever WALL-E has an epiphany or intuitive thought, the roach is there to lead the way. WALL-E even lets the roach make the decisions when he is confused. All these are character traits of melanin. Melanin represents pigmentation. The roach is dark brown in color. The theme of this character is to always follow your intuition and gut feeling in your surroundings. That is one's melanin acknowledging and deciphering the unseen energy around us that makes up over 90% of our reality in the physical dimension. Melanin is the key to higher consciousness. If one embraces and believes in their melanin, it will embrace you back, by showing you the way to higher consciousness.

EVE- Meaning, "the solution and the life giver." This character represents the feminine principle or the Black woman, in general. She is the Kemetic goddess, Auset. She is the key to resurrecting the Black man. Once the Black woman changes her focus and starts to invest her time and energy into the Black man, then her family, community and nation will be resurrected.

EVE representing the feminine principle is stronger than the masculine principle of energy. Feminine energy is on a higher frequency than masculine energy. Because of this it is closer to God. That is why EVE is far superior in regards to her strength, speed, power and agility. One thing EVE needs to complete her is the "spark" given only from masculine energy. It is WALL-E who represents masculine energy, which awakens EVE to higher consciousness or what can be interpreted as love.

Axiom- Meaning, A principle that is accepted as true without proof. The ship represents the system that the elite, ruling class of secret societies, have implemented to keep the masses enslaved without them even knowing it. They control our perception of reality through the elegant implementation and infusion of lower level consciousness. They have hijacked our ability to embrace our higher selves by nurturing and exploiting our egos, passions, fears, insecurities and immaturity. We have accepted this reality without questioning the validity of our quality of life. We live in the richest country the world has ever known yet we have never been more ignorant, superficial, stressed, dissatisfied, unhealthy, unhappy, barbaric, selfish, lost, immature, hurt and confused.

The Axiom is the ship in the middle of outer space. The outer space represents the fear of the unknown the masses do not want to venture out to because they are controlled by their lower selves. The masses have been conditioned to believe that what they are given and what they experience in the now, is better than any other experience outside of their reality. The masses represent the slave that does not want to leave the plantation for fear of what is out there. We have been conditioned to fear the freedom of the unknown. On the plantation, represented by the Axiom, we are comfortable in our routines and are not willing to give those things up even though they may not have our best interest at heart. We have become the slave that is comfortable being a slave. We do not look within ourselves to discover our own happiness, but feel better letting someone else tells us what makes us happy.

Shelby Forthright- Shelby meaning a place where Willows grow. A shelter. Forthright meaning, **squarely: directly and without evasion; not roundabout; "to face a problem squarely"; "the responsibility lies squarely with them"; "spoken to the point"**

This is the name of the Earth's "Global CEO." The elite have an agenda and they do not pull any punches in its implementation. It is the masses that are asleep and cannot see the writing on the wall. Once a person discovers the hidden or secret agenda of the ruling elite, they still do not change their lifestyle but continue to support and live in the system.

willow tree--a symbol of death, tears, mourning, and reflection. Perhaps this is the origin of the term "weeping willow".

MO- Short for Maurice which **is of** Latin **origin, and the meaning of Maurice is "**dark-skinned, Moorish**". Dark or swarthy.**

This character also represents the properties of melanin. The name means Black. This is the trait of melanin. MO's job is to clean up "foreign contaminate." That is another code word for the chemical of melanin that is abundant in Black people. This is why WALL-E is covered in it. This is what activates WALL-E's higher consciousness. MO plays a vital role in the relationship and dynamics between WALL-E and EVE. MO learns to literally step out of line to define his reality. MO or melanin is the key to WALL-E and EVE's relationship. MO or melanin is what saves the two from destruction.

The Captain- Represents the political leaders of our time. The captain is controlled by AUTO who stays in the background. The captain is the "figure of leadership" that is presented to the masses. The captain really doesn't have any power he is just a figure head. He is the representative of the concept the elite want you to look up to. Throughout the movie, one will see that the captain is relegated to doing remedial jobs. The true power behind the Axiom is AUTO, who represents the elite, ruling class. Just like in real life, the captain has no power, just perceived power. He must obey the commands of the elite ruling class. If the captain does not cooperate with the elite, ruling class represented by AUTO, they will eliminate him through assassination of character or murder. They will then manipulate the masses to choose another leader who they have already handpicked, behind the scenes to take his place. The captain represents the political system the elite ruling class has set up to give the masses the feeling that they really have a voice as to how their country will be run. It is all smoke and mirrors. The Democrats and the Republicans are both controlled by the same entity. One party appeals to the right hemisphere of your brain while the other relates to your left. That is the only difference between the two. In the end, both parties implement the policies that serve the ruling class and further enslave the people.

AUTO- The elite, ruling secret societies that control and manipulate the world's resources, governments, religion, politics, economics and population from behind the shadows.

DVD Chapter One: Out There

Commentary:

During the opening of the movie, one will see the Disney introduction at the beginning of the film. One sees the beautiful colors of deep blues, purples and indigo. The camera pans down to the earth from the heavens.

Metaphysical Breakdown

These colors represent the 5ᵗʰ, 6ᵗʰ and 7ᵗʰ chakras. These are the top three energy centers in man. These colors denote the concepts of higher consciousness. This is why the camera starts from the heavens and descends down to Earth. The camera coming from the sky represents the ascension into higher consciousness.

Commentary:

The viewer will also notice the winding river in the opening scene.

Metaphysical Breakdown

The winding river represents the kundalini energy that one possesses to achieve different levels of consciousness. All energy moves in cycles or waves. The snake represents the acknowledgment of this unseen energy in higher consciousness.

The pictures below show the snake representing the "unseen" kundalini energy that travels up and down a person's spinal column.

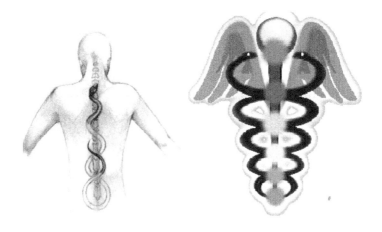

Commentary:

The viewer will also see a train crossing a bridge over the river.

Metaphysical Breakdown

The train represents the system the ruling elite have maintained to keep the masses in a perpetual state of servitude. A train can only travel according to who lays the tracks. The ruling class control the tracks, thus the train cannot go where it wants to go. It is a slave to the tracks. What this does is give the train the illusion that is is making progress or going somewhere. But in reality, it is just going in circles.

Commentary:

Next one sees a white flag with a gold flag pole on top of the Disney castle. The castle has several "steeple-like" structures pointing to the sky.

Metaphysical Breakdown

I was not able to decipher the meaning of the flag at this moment. However, the steeple-like structures on the castle were stolen fom the Kemetic Tekken that represents the Kemetic god

Ausar. Ausar was a symbol of resurrection. The Tekken represented Ausar's penis. The penis maintains the genetic material that Ausar will pass on to his offspring. Thus, Ausar's DNA or genetics will last forever through the legacy of his children. In fact, the word erection comes from the word resurrection.

Commentary:

We see several firework explosions around the top of the castle.

Metaphysical Breakdown

The fireworks exploding represent the masculine principle of energy. It is positive. It is electric. Masculine energy gives out energy. It is needed to ignite or initiate things in to motion or existence.

Commentary:

Next we see the reflection of the castle in the body of water in front of it.

Metaphysical Breakdown

This image represents the Kemetic law of "As above, so below." It represents the concept of the macrocosm is related to the microcosm. No matter how big or small something is, they are all governed by the same rules and laws. Thus, everything is related and is the reflection of everything else.

Commentary:

A firework shoots from the left side of the castle to the right side of the castle to from a semi-circle.

Metaphysical Breakdown

The left side represents one's higher self or spirituality. The right side represents one's lower self defined by the physical dimension. The fireworks represent masculine or electric energy that one needs in order to spark creation into the physical realm. So this part of the logo represents the spark that brings the spiritual realm into the physical dimension. This is the symbolic aspect of creation. This is what Disney does. It gives life to people's dreams in the form of its movies and other productions.

Commentary:

One can see that the opening or main door of the castle is open and the viewer can see straight through to the other side.

Metaphysical Breakdown

The main door represents the gateway from which Disney brings the spiritual dimension into the physical realm. This is why one can see straight through it. It connects both worlds together.

Commentary:

Next scene is the Pixar logo. A white desktop light comes out from the left side of the logo.

Metaphysical Breakdown

Remember, the left side represents the spiritual dimension or higher consciousness. The light represents enlightenment or the ability to see and decipher higher consciousness. The white lamp represents the Caucasians that use this knowledge in order to rule the world, while keeping the darker people of the world asleep or in the dark.

Commentary:

It proceeds to seek out the letter "I" and stomps on it so the viewer cannot see it any more. The light than takes the place and position of the letter "I."

Metaphysical Breakdown

The letter "I" represents independent or individual thought. It is this concept that is a threat to the secret, ruling class that runs the world in the shadows. The power and control of the elite, ruling class comes from their brainwashing and thought manipulation of the masses. If the masses were to one day wake up and start thinking for themselves, these secret societies would have no power. So the ruling class seeks to "stomp out" individuals who display independent thought. This is shown by the light stomping out the letter I" in the logo. The light, representing the ruling class, then proceeds to take the place of the "I" or the individual in the logo.

Commentary:

In the opening scene, the viewer sees several structures shaped like pyramids both skinny and wide in shape, all throughout the city.

Metaphysical Breakdown

This scene pays homage to our Afrikan ancestors who cultivated the highest civilization man has ever known. Their offspring are now waking up all throughout the world to return back to this way of life. All the while, Western or European civilization is on the road of destruction.

Commentary:

Next scene we see an aerial shot of a winding road with WALL-E traveling on it.

Metaphysical Breakdown

The winding road represents the Kundalini energy that permeates throughout one's body. This energy has a lower vibration as well as a higher vibration. It is up to man's own freewill to use this energy as he chooses.

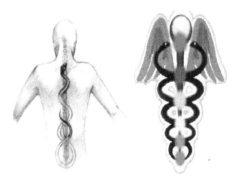

Examples of Kundalini energy represented by the snake. All energy moves in cycles or waves. This is why our Kemetic ancestors used the snake to symbolize this unseen energy or consciousness. The higher the snake reaches up the spinal cord the higher the consciousness one has access to and vice-versa.

Commentary:

As WALL-E travels throughout the city, several red and white buildings stand out in the mundane and bleak environment.

Metaphysical Breakdown

The colors of red and white, symbolize the Kemetic god Heru. Heru is where we get the word Hero from. Heru represents good conquering evil and displaying courage and bravery when faced against insurmountable odds and difficult adversaries.

The Kemetic god Heru, who represents bravery and courage in the fight between good versus evil.

Commentary:

WALL-E is seen gathering trash into his body and converting it into blocks from which he builds pyramid structures. WALL-E is in the shape of a square.

Metaphysical Breakdown

In the occult, the square represents 360 degrees of knowledge and standing on moral ground of righteousness. WALL-E represents this upstanding man that has the knowledge and ethics to achieve and activate his higher consciousness.

Commentary:

WALL-E carries on his back a red and white cooler. The "E" in WALL-E is also red and white.

Metaphysical Breakdown

Again, the colors red and white represent the Kemetic god Heru. WALL-E is the "Hero" in the movie. WALL-E will display courage, bravery and higher consciousness in his quest to bring about righteousness.

Commentary:

The viewer will notice a roach coming out of a tin can. This is WALL-E's companion. The roach leaves the can and makes a left turn.

Metaphysical Breakdown

The roach symbolizes the activation of WALL-E's melanin. The tin can represents the Pineal gland that produces melanin. The left turn by the roach represents the higher consciousness one can achieve by activating their melanin. The left side of the body activates the right hemisphere of the brain, which represents one's higher, spiritual consciousness.

Commentary:

WALL-E also makes a left turn to stack one of is blocks to create another pyramid structure. His companion, the roach is right there with him.

Metaphysical Breakdown

WALL-E, having activated his melanin, is now operating according to his higher consciousness. This is symbolized by WALL-E also making a left turn. The left side of the body activates the right hemisphere of the brain, which represents one's higher, spiritual consciousness.

Commentary:

WALL-E pulls out a hubcap in the shape of a five pointed star.

Metaphysical Breakdown

In the occult, the symbol of the five pointed star represents man at his highest level of spiritual consciousness. This is why WALL-E holds it above his head. WALL-E has mastered his lower self or physical body to achieve higher consciousness. Coincidently, if the five pointed star is inverted or turned upside down, it represents man at his lowest level of consciousness. It symbolizes man as a beast driven by his lower level urges and desires.

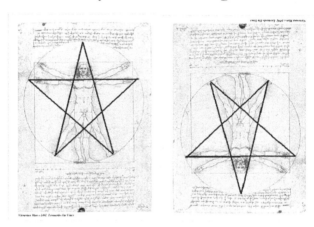

The upright star representing man's higher consciousness and the inverted star on the right, representing man's lower consciousness.

M

Commentary:

WALL-E looks up at the Sun and stares back down at the hubcap as it reflects the Sun. He then proceeds to store it inside of himself.

Metaphysical Breakdown

In the occult, the Sun represents enlightenment of access to higher consciousness. WALL-E literally is seen internalizing higher consciousness and enlightenment by putting the Sun's reflection seen on the hubcap, star into his midsection.

DVD Chapter Two: Walk Home (3:42)

Commentary:

WALL-E rolls by a bank. He runs over several denominations of cash that is lying in the street.

Metaphysical Breakdown

WALL-E is not placing his value or is he defining himself of his environment in the monetary system. WALL-E understands the concepts of money come and go. WALL-E's real worth and wealth comes from within and not some artificial paper with ink and numbers on it. Money is worthless in WALL-E's world. It is scattered throughout the city relegated to trash or litter.

Commentary:

WALL-E sees many signs of businesses run by Buy n Large. WALL-E than passes a sign that shows his robot model with the caption, "Working to Dig You Out!" There are four robots in the background and one in the front.

Metaphysical Breakdown

The business name, "Buy n' Large," symbolizes the Western, Capitalistic society which represents bigger is better. It does not take into consideration any adverse effects to the environment or the quality of human life in general. It is based on a system of greed and consumerism. WALL-E's world is the end result of this Eurocentric ideology. WALL-E, representing the Black man, must now return to his past way of life in order to advance the world into some semblance of order, balance, prosperity and peace.

In numerology, the number five, as in the number of robots in the sign, represents God's grace. God has favor in WALL-e's undertaking to dig the world out from this lower level European culture and society.

338

Commentary:

WALL-E passes by a train station on his way home. He pauses and gets the approval from his roach before he proceeds in the opposite direction of the train.

Metaphysical Breakdown

In the occult, trains and train stations represent the system of white supremacy that subjects the masses under the white man's rule. The people represent the train and the elite, ruling class represent the entity that lays the tracks for the train. The people may think they have control or power over their lives because they seem to be moving from one place to another. This is just an illusion that the secret societies have created for the masses. In reality, the people are literally going around in circles, in accordance to the tracks that have been laid for them to travel on.

WALL-E by getting approval from his roach, who represents the activation of his melanin, is operating according to his higher consciousness. When one listens to their melanin in the form of intuition, imagination and foresight, they will avoid many pitfalls their lower consciousness will put them in. Trust your intuition, it is your higher consciousness trying to communicate with you. Coincidently, WALL-E goes in the opposite direction of the train. This symbolizes WALL-E going against the system in search of his own truth.

Commentary:

In the foreground, as WALL-E is traveling by the train, one can see a sign on the skyscraper in front of him that says, "Synthetic Lifestyle."

Metaphysical Breakdown

This sign represents the world and the reality the elite ruling class has designed for us. We go through our whole lives oblivious to what true life is all about. We have become the slave who doesn't even know that he is a slave because we never ventured outside of a system that did not have our best interests at heart to begin with.

Commentary:

The roach starts to rattle around on WALL-E's shoulders. WALL-E stops and switches his wheel tracks for new ones. This satisfies his roach.

Metaphysical Breakdown

WALL-E is shown paying attention to his roach. He is motivated by keeping his roach, who represents his melanin, a priority in his life. Because of the roach, WALL-E realizes that he must change his wheel tracks by switching his with another robot the exact same model as his. WALL-E is better off after paying attention to his melanin, represented by his roach.

DVD Chapter Three: WALL-E's Truck (5:56)

Commentary:

WALL-E takes out the hubcap he found and places it over his head.

Metaphysical Breakdown

This is another sign that WALL-E is operating according to his higher consciousness. The hubcap has the five pointed star on it. Holding it above his head symbolizes that he has mastered his lower self.

Commentary:

He then takes out a Rubik's Cube and a spork. He doesn't know if the spork belongs with the spoons or the forks so he places it in the middle.

Metaphysical Breakdown

The Rubiks Cube represents higher knowledge. A cube is a square. A square has 4 ninety degree angles. These angles add up to 360 degrees. In Kemet, true understanding represents knowing 360 degrees of knowledge.

The spork represents the Eurocentric ideology and acceptance of homosexuality, but in this case more specifically bisexuality. In the occult, the fork represents the man and the spoon represents the woman. In Kemet, everything in the universe adheres to the same laws form the largest macrocosm to the smallest microcosm. All of nature must play its particular role in order for the cosmos to be balanced and righteous. The European has made exceptions and has added categories for things that go against these universal laws. He has done this because he goes against universal law. So in order for him to find a place within the universal concepts of our ancestors, he must include other abnormalities into the fold in an effort to validate his existence and more importantly, his acceptance.

341

Commentary:

WALL-E takes out a lighter and adds it to a collection of lighters that he has saved.

Metaphysical Breakdown

As we stated in the beginning of the book, the light, fire or electricity represents the masculine principle of energy needed to spark the unseen realm into the physical dimension. WALL-E, representing the Black man, is that spark.

Commentary:

WALL-E focuses his attention back on the T.V. It shows a man and woman holding hands. The T.V. handle is made up of several diamond shape patterns.

Metaphysical Breakdown

The T.V. handle represents the geometric shape of the Freemason symbol. The elite, ruling class, use this secret society as a "Trojan Horse" to hide their covert actions they want to incorporate in their quest for continual domination of the world's resources.

The Free Mason symbol of the compass and the square. These two instruments combined in the symbol form a "diamond shape." The diamond shape is represented in many occult movies.

Commentary:

WALL-E focuses his attention on the couple on the screen holding hands. He pushes his red record button with his left hand. He also mimics the couple by clasping his hands together.

Metaphysical Breakdown

The couple holding hands in the video tape, represent sex or the concept of male and female energy coming together. WALL-E's red button symbolizes the physical engagement of sex. The color red represents man being ruled by his lower or animalistic desires and urges. It also represents man's drive for survival and procreation. Sex is the way man survives. He must procreate. The fact that WALL-E pushes his red button with his left hand symbolizes that WALL-E's main purpose for having sex is not motivated by his lower animalistic desires but his higher consciousness. The left hand activates the right hemisphere of the brain which represents man's higher, spiritual consciousness. So WALL-E's motivation and dream is to have sex with a female in order to have access to their higher consciousness. Once WALL-E is able to achieve this feat, he will be able to bring the spiritual or unseen realm into the physical dimension. The combining of male and female energy in higher consciousness and with intent, can bring the manifestation of miracles into the physical realm.

The Sephedet, otherwise known as the Star of David or the Seal of Solomon, is an ancient, Kemetic symbol of the coming together of male and female energy in an effort to create a

gateway from the spiritual realm into the physical dimension. The upside down triangle represents the feminine principle and the right side up triangle represents the male principle. This is what WALL-E is referring to when he clasps his hand together to show this male and female union.

Commentary:

WALL-E goes outside to clean his cooler. His roach is already out there. He pounds the cooler on the ground six times before he looks up to see the stars. He pushes his blue button in the process.

Metaphysical Breakdown

WALL-E clears his head of sex by going outside to empty his cooler. In numerology, the number six represents man defining himself by his physical body and motivated by his physical desires and urges. By WALL-E looking up to the sky he is raising his kundalini energy to master his lower self and define himself and his reality through his higher consciousness. Of course, his melanin, the roach, is already there to lead the way for him.

The color blue represents communication. In this case it represents WALL-E's ability to communicate with his higher consciousness by putting down lower level thoughts and actions.

Commentary:

WALL-E's red light comes on to signal that a storm is coming and that he is in danger.

Metaphysical Breakdown

The color red represents man being motivated by his own survival. The red light comes on to symbolize that WALL-E's basic survival is in jeopardy.

Commentary:

WALL-E starts to close the door of his home when he notices his roach is distracted by a blinking red light. WALL-E calls out to it and it gets in the home just as the door closes.

Metaphysical Breakdown

The red light symbolizes man's lower thoughts and animalistic desires. The fact that WALL-E's roach, who represents his melanin, is distracted by these animalistic urges, almost causes him to lose his life. Moral of the story. Do not invest your time and energy into lower level thoughts that are ruled by your animalistic desires. This mindset will keep you distracted and keep you from reaching your higher self where true freedom and understanding lies.

Commentary:

WALL-E climbs in to his shelf to go to sleep. ON the left side of the shelf is a basketball that takes the place of a globe.

Metaphysical Breakdown

This is a message for the Black man. Sports have become the whole world for Black men. Whether playing them or being a fan. We need to redirect our energy into our communities and not on a child's game. We need to reevaluate our priorities and invest our time and energy into our women and children to rebuild our communities.

DVD Chapter Four: A Day At Work (9:24)

Commentary:

WALL-E's battery is low. He is solar powered and get his energy from the Sun.

Metaphysical Breakdown

Black people and people of color get in general, get our energy from the Sun through the activation of our Pineal gland that produces our melanin. This is why WALL-E, who represents the Black man, is solar powered. It takes the Sun to stimulate the Pineal gland so it can produce the melanin needed to achieve higher consciousness.

Here we have a picture from the walls of Kemet, depicting the activation of one's Pineal gland by the Sun. Notice the figure has a body of an animal and the head of a man. This represents man's lower, animalistic nature must be mastered in order for one to reach higher consciousness located above the neck.

Commentary:

WALL-E runs over his roach with his right wheel. The roach miraculously bounces back to life.

Metaphysical Breakdown

The roach, representing, WALL-E's melanin is indestructible. The right wheel of WALL-E represents his lower consciousness. Even though we may partake in this behavior, our melanin will always be there to let us know the conscious level of our actions.

Commentary:

WALL-E scolds the roach and directs him to stay on his left side.

Metaphysical Breakdown

By WALL-E scolding the roach and redirecting him to his left side, symbolizes that the Black man must always be aware of his consciousness. If he lowers it, he must also be responsible for raising it as well.

Commentary:

While WALL-E is working, he proceeds to find a woman's bra. He proceeds to put it over his eyes so he cannot see.

Metaphysical Breakdown

The bra represents WALL-E investing his time and energy into lower sexual consciousness of lust that is driven by his sex drive. This behavior "blinds" him into reaching his higher self. The Pineal gland was referred by our ancestors as our "First Eye." It was through the activation of the Pineal gland that one can truly see into higher consciousness.

Commentary:

WALL-E puts a toy dog and duck into his cooler for safe keeping.

Metaphysical Breakdown

The toy dog represents the Kemetic god, Anpu. Anpu represented the activation of one's melanin needed to guide them in the afterlife in order to reach the concept called heaven.

The duck is in the bird family. The bird in Kemet symbolized knowledge, enlightenment and higher consciousness. All is needed for the Black man to transcend into his higher self.

Commentary:

WALL-E proceeds to play with a paddle with a red, rubber ball. The red ball continuously hits him the eyes.

Metaphysical Breakdown

The color red, represents man's lower, animalistic consciousness. WALL-E playing with this lower level toy becomes blinded by it. If the Black man continues to play with lower level distractions motivated by his animalistic urges, he blinds himself to his true, higher self. He will never reach his higher consciousness.

Commentary:

WALL-E finds a diamond ring in a purple box. He discards the ring and keeps the box.

Metaphysical Breakdown

The color purple represents the highest consciousness located at the top of one's head. It symbolizes the mastery of the lower self and the ability to transcend outside of one's physical body. The Black man must redefine what is more important or valuable to him. His higher consciousness of his bling?

Commentary:

WALL-E saves an old left shoe in his cooler.

Metaphysical Breakdown

In Kemet, our ancestors always represent their gods walking out with their left foot forward. The left side of the body activates the right hemisphere of the brain, which contains higher, spiritual consciousness.

"Left foot forward to trample down evil so that the heart can move forward." –Ashra Kwesi

Commentary:

WALL-E saves a trophy in his cooler as well.

Metaphysical Breakdown

In the occult, the cup or gourd represents the feminine principle of energy. It is in this principle, that man's higher spiritual nature dwells. It is in this principle where man will discover and attain his higher consciousness.

Commentary:

WALL-E finds a red fire extinguisher and starts to spray it. He cannot control himself. The extinguisher sprays uncontrollably so WALL-E feels the need to throw it away.

Metaphysical Breakdown

The color red, represents man's lower, animalistic desires. The fire extinguisher represents WALL-E's phallus. WALL-E is being controlled by his lower sexual urges. This causes him to lose control. Moral of this story, do not invest your time and energy into lower, animalistic consciousness for you will find yourself in a state of being out of control and lose touch with your higher self.

Commentary:

WALL-E continues to build his square which is the foundation for building his structure.

Metaphysical Breakdown

The square representing the internalization of 360 degrees of knowledge, represents man's moral standing in his effort to achieve higher consciousness. This is the key for WALL-E, who represents the Black man, to achieve his higher consciousness.

Commentary:

WALL-E cuts open a refrigerator door. He finds a plant inside. He proceeds to replant the plant into the left footed boot he found. The roach shows his approval and leads the way back home.

Metaphysical Breakdown

WALL-E finds life represented by the plant. He immediately nurtures it with his higher consciousness, symbolized by the left boot. His melanin is satisfied by his higher consciousness actions and deeds. WALL-E's day is done as if to hint that this is what his life purpose is really about.

DVD Chapter Five: EVE Arrives (12:08)

Commentary:

WALL-E is attracted to a red light on the ground. He seems almost hypnotized by it.

Metaphysical Breakdown

The color red, symbolizes man's lower or animalistic nature. This scene represents WALL-E's preoccupation with his lower self. He is being distracted from achieving his higher consciousness by focusing his time and energy into his lower level thoughts and actions.

Commentary:

WALL-E becomes reckless in his pursuit of the red light. He puts himself in harm's way by having his undivided attention focused solely on the red light.

Metaphysical Breakdown

WALL-E's recklessness is a direct result in his focus on his lower self represented by the red light.

Commentary:

As WALL-E pursues the light, he seems to go around in circles. This pattern makes the letter "G" in the ground.

Metaphysical Breakdown

The "G" pattern pays homage to the Free Mason secret society that the Illuminati uses to put out its agenda. Free Masons say the "G" stands for God, divine geometry and or the gnosis view of metaphysics early, mystical Christians subscribed to and practiced.

Commentary:

As the red dots emerge, we see that there are 13 dots that make up the circle and one in the middle.

Metaphysical Breakdown

In numerology, the number thirteen represents resurrection. One can define resurrection as the putting to death one's lower level consciousness so that one can be reborn into their higher consciousness. This is what is about to happen to WALL-E as he witnesses the coming of the Black woman represented by EVE, the robot.

Commentary:

The rocket has three thrusters that touch down on the Earth.

Metaphysical Breakdown

In numerology, the number three represents divine perfection. In this scene it represents the potential union of the man and woman to produce a child. The original trinity upheld in Kemet. Christianity later, eliminated the woman and changed it to the father, the son and the holy ghost.

Commentary:

WALL-E being scared, tries to bury himself in the ground.

Metaphysical Breakdown

In the occult, man originated from the ground or the Earth. The woman is the one that came down from the heavens. This scene plays out this ideology.

Commentary:

One of the arms of the ship comes out. Its components resemble a vagina. Suddenly a tubular cylinder comes down from a tube. It has indigo lights. Out comes the activation of a robot named EVE.

Metaphysical Breakdown

This scene represents the Black woman coming from the spiritual realm to be born into the physical dimension. The color Indigo represents the manifestation of the spiritual realm into the physical dimension by way of the activation of the Pineal gland that produces the melanin needed for this transformation.

Commentary:

EVE has a blue light that shoots out where her throat would be. She uses it to search for life.

Metaphysical Breakdown

The blue light and its position on EVE's body represents the fifth chakra. This chakra is known for communication. EVE is communicating with her environment in an effort to find and protect life.

Commentary:

The ship blasts off back in space after dropping off EVE. The ship resembles a phallic symbol.

Metaphysical Breakdown

The ship represents the masculine energy needed to bring EVE into the physical dimension. Male energy being electric, is needed to spark all life into existence.

Commentary:

Once the ship has left, EVE starts to display her characteristics. She is more powerful, faster, sleeker, more efficient, more durable and stronger than WALL-E. WALL-E seems outdated when compared to EVE.

Metaphysical Breakdown

The feminine principle of energy is closer to God because it is a direct link to the spiritual dimension. This being the case, the female or feminine energy does not have to adhere to the laws and physics of the physical realm. So the female can display attributes that appear stronger, faster and more powerful than the male in the physical dimension.

Commentary:

WALL-E accidently makes a noise that startles EVE. She reacts by activating a weapon in her right arm.

Metaphysical Breakdown

The right side of the body activates the left hemisphere of the brain which represents our lower consciousness. This is why a weapon of destruction is attached to EVE's right side and not her left arm. She is partaking in lower, animalistic consciousness by being motivated by her sense of fear and self preservation.

DVD Chapter Six: Confrontation (18:01)

Commentary:

WALL-E's roach is curious about EVE. It approaches the robot. EVE proceeds to blast it but it does not die. EVE embraces the roach by playing with it.

Metaphysical Breakdown

The roach, who represents melanin, is showing its characteristic of being indestructible. Once EVE over comes her lower self, in the form of her fear of the unknown, she embraces her melanin.

Commentary:

WALL-E startles EVE again with a sudden sound. This time WALL-E can't hide. He encloses himself into a box because he fears EVE's power.

Metaphysical Breakdown

This is an example of WALL-E being on his square. When a man is righteous, all he has to do is stand his ground and he shall not be defeated. This is what is being displayed in this scene. WALL-E is ready to be judged.

Commentary:

WALL-E's roach comes from EVE's right hand to WALL-E's left hand. EVE does not destroy him.

Metaphysical Breakdown

EVE is ruled by her lower self that is why she is so analytical, logical and cold. The domination of her right arm signifies her lower level of consciousness. WALL-E on the other hand, is dominated by the use of his left arm. He receives his melanin, represented by the roach, with his higher consciousness. EVE has not recognized this fact or state of existence yet.

355

DVD Chapter Seven: La Vie En Rose
(19:38)

Commentary:

We see both robots riding over fallen leaves. WALL-E is always seen falling, getting buried or running into things.

Metaphysical Breakdown

In the occult, the season we know as autumn or fall represents the time of creation of man. The term fall is alluding to the time when the spiritual being "fell" from the heavens because of the newly acquired material it gathered from the ethers to create a physical body. The denser the spiritual being got, the heavier it became. This is how the creation of man came to pass. It had to be a female, spiritual being, who is represented by magnetic energy. This energy was needed to attract and gather the elements needed to create a physical body. The term autumn relates to the Kemetic god Atum. Atum represents the hidden or unseen energy that permeates all life forces. Atum is the God consciousness that always was and always shall be.

Commentary:

EVE picks up a pinwheel in the shape of a star. It has 12 sides.

Metaphysical Breakdown

In numerology, the number twelve represents completion. EVE representing the Black woman is complete by finding her male principle that is needed to ignite her. This male principle is WALL-E.

DVD Chapter Eight: Courting (21:14)

Commentary:

EVE gets trapped by a giant industrial magnet.

Metaphysical Breakdown

This scene is further proof to the occult ideology of the female being magnetic and the male being electric.

DVD Chapter Nine:
WALL-E's Favorite Things (23:53)

Commentary:

WALL-E seems a storm coming. He grabs EVE by the left hand and leads her to safety at his home.

Metaphysical Breakdown

The left hand of EVE represents her higher consciousness because it activates the right hemisphere of her brain. This side of her brain is responsible for her higher, spiritual consciousness. It is WALL-E's intuition, which is a characteristic of melanin, that saves them from the oncoming storm.

Commentary:

The first thing that EVE does in WALL-E's place is look up at WALL-E's lights. They resemble the stars.

Metaphysical Breakdown

This act displays higher consciousness. It symbolizes that EVE is looking for her higher self. If she was to look down it would mean that she is focused on her lower self. In Kemet, our ancestors placed above their entrance ways the saying, "Know Thyself." One had to look up to see this inscription. It was this gesture that reminded and activated the individual into seeking their higher consciousness.

Commentary:

The majority of WALL-E's lights are purple.

Metaphysical Breakdown

The color purple represents the seventh chakra located above one's head. It symbolizes the mastery of your lower consciousness and closeness or oneness with the Creator. This is the level of consciousness WALL-E is displaying.

358

Commentary:

EVE is startled by WALL-E's talking fish. She raises her weapon as if to destroy it. The fish sings the song called, "Don't worry, be happy."

Metaphysical Breakdown

The fish is a symbol for the religion of Christianity. It comes form the Age of Pisces from which Christianity was born. It represents the Age of, "I Believe." It represents blind faith without questioning. It is this religion that the elite ruling class has used to put out it's secret agenda. That agenda is to have the masses define themselves and their reality through their lower, animalistic consciousness. Christianity took man's higher, spiritual consciousness out of himself and placed it outside of man in a place he could not reach until after he dies. The ruling class have lowered the bar as to what man can become or achieve in the physical dimension. He has also given man a crutch that allows him to accept his faults and shortcomings as normal. This has restricted man's consciousness and has left him vulnerable to the traps and pitfalls of his lower level consciousness. As long as man asks for forgiveness and believes that all he has to do is recite the magic words of his church leaders, he shall reach higher consciousness, otherwise known as heaven, once he crosses over. The elite want the masses to not worry about making themselves better or raising their awareness or consciousness because if they were to wake up, the elite would have no control over them. Thus the saying, "Don't worry, be happy."

EVE knowing what the symbol of the fish represents, naturally wants to destroy it.

Commentary:

WALL-E hands EVE a hand mixer. She does it so fast the mixer shoots up in the sky.

Metaphysical Breakdown

The mixer represents the combining of male and female energy. This creates a vortex of electro-magnetic energy. This is the gateway for bringing the spiritual dimension into the physical realm. Once this vortex is open, the sky is the limit on what the Black man and woman can manifest.

Commentary:

WALL-E hands EVE a sheet of bubble wrap. WALL-E only pops one at a time whereas; EVE goes through the whole sheet in seconds.

Metaphysical Breakdown

EVE representing feminine energy, is closer to spiritual or higher consciousness. Because of this, she is more efficient and stronger than WALL-E who represents the male.

Commentary:

WALL-E hands EVE a light bulb. She grabs it with her left hand. When she touches it, it immediately lights up. When WALL-E holds it, it doesn't do anything.

Metaphysical Breakdown

The left hand of EVE activates the right hemisphere of the brain which represents one's higher consciousness. EVE is showing the power of her higher, spiritual consciousness. Since WALL-E, representing the male gives out positive energy, he is not as strong as his woman counterpart.

Commentary:

WALL-E hands EVE a Rubik's Cube. When he returns she has completed it.

Metaphysical Breakdown

Again, another scene showing EVE, who represents the Black woman, being stronger and more intelligent than her male counterpart.

Commentary:

WALL-E shows EVE a dance step from the video. He has the hubcap over his head. EVE does not have the grace or rhythm that WALL-E has when she tries to dance.

Metaphysical Breakdown

The hubcap over WALL-E's head signifies a ceiling or barrier in regards to his potential to transcend in the spiritual realm. EVE representing the Sacred Feminine, is infinite with no boundaries or limitations.

Commentary:

WALL-E's right eye gets damaged after EVE accidently injures him.

Metaphysical Breakdown

WALL-E has slipped into his lower level consciousness. The injuring of his right eye, which represents his lower consciousness, pays tribute to this fact.

Commentary:

EVE picks up one of WALL-E's lighters. She lights it and holds it between her eyes. She is intrigued by it.

Metaphysical Breakdown

The flame represents the positive or electric energy that men have naturally. EVE, representing the female, needs that spark in order for her to manifest or create. This is why she is so fascinated by it. You also see the reflection of the flame between her eyes. This is the place of the Pineal gland that produces the melanin needed to obtain higher consciousness. This is what she wants and needs in WALL-E.

Commentary:

EVE is suddenly intrigued by the couple on the screen holding hands. It catches her attention for awhile.

Metaphysical Breakdown

Immediately after seeing the spark she views the couple on the screen holding hands. The holding of the hands represent the union of male and female energy or what we call sex. It doesn't just represent the idea of sex, but the idea of sex when two people come together joined by their higher, spiritual consciousness. It opens up the "Gateway" to bring ideas or spiritual concepts into the physical realm of manifestation.

Commentary:

WALL-E shows EVE his plant he saved in a left footed boot. EVE immediately responds by opening up and inserting the plant inside her. A green light where her heart would be starts to pulsate. EVE proceeds to shut down after that.

Metaphysical Breakdown

The left footed boot represents the activation of the right hemisphere of the brain which houses one's higher, spiritual consciousness. This is what WALL-E is offering to her. This is where new life begins. EVE accepts WALL-E's spark of higher consciousness and proceeds to open herself up to nurture his seed. The color green represents the activation of one's heart chakra. It is the first level of higher consciousness. It represents the concept of unconditional love. EVE was programmed to shut down once she discovered unconditional love from a male. This is her sole purpose in life to nurture the spark of higher consciousness given to her by her man.

Commentary:

On the green light of EVE, is a sign of a plant with three leaves on it.

Metaphysical Breakdown

The color green represents unconditional love. In numerology, the number three represents divine perfection. It is the Black man, the Black woman and their seed.

DVD Chapter Ten: Bad Date (29:23)

Commentary:

While WALL-E is protecting EVE from the storm by holding an umbrella over her, he gets struck by lightning.

Metaphysical Breakdown

In the occult, man is defined as electric or having positive energy. The lightening is an example of this masculine energy.

Commentary:

WALL-E tries to jumpstart EVE back to life. When he connects his cables to hers, he gets blown away.

Metaphysical Breakdown

EVE is more powerful than WALL-E is. This is an occult secret that the white man has used to subject the woman under his rule. That secret is that woman are stronger, more powerful and efficient than men when it comes to defining themselves through their higher, spiritual consciousness.

Commentary:

WALL-E and EVE are seen sitting on a bench together. EVE is on WALL-E's left side. WALL-E carves their names on the pole in the middle of a heart.

Metaphysical Breakdown

The *left side of our bodies represent our higher consciousness. That energy is labeled as feminine, magnetic and negative. This is where all women naturally operate from. Women have been conditioned to think like men in an effort to keep them from their higher selves.*

The heart is the first level of higher consciousness. This is where WALL-E places EVE.

Commentary:

WALL-E is seen playing pong on his T.V. The score is 7999. WALL-E scores to make the new score 8000.

Metaphysical Breakdown

In numerology, the number 7,999 breaks down to the number seven. The number seven represents God's divinity in the physical dimension. This relates to EVE returning back to the spiritual world in order to give birth to a child of God. Also, the number 8,000 is broken down to the number eight. This number represents eternity or the concept of infinity. It is this process that all creation must go thru to enter the physical realm. It is what makes the world go round.

DVD Chapter Eleven: Time To Go (31:28)

Commentary:

WALL-E is seen alone lighting the flame to his lighter. Suddenly he looks up in the sky and sees the rocket ship returning to pick up EVE.

Metaphysical Breakdown

It is because of the potential and recognition of WALL-E's spark that causes him to look up. Looking up signifies one's focus and attention into achieving higher consciousness. This is where EVE came from and this is where she shall return.

Commentary:

EVE is being taken up in the ship. WALL-E pursues her. He tells his roach to stay by pointing to his right side.

Metaphysical Breakdown

Since WALL-E is following EVE into the spiritual dimension he does not need to access his physical body. It is irrelevant. This is why he tells his roach to stay behind in the physical realm. He will need him once he returns. The right side of WALL-E is activated by the left hemisphere of the brain which is responsible for lower, physical or animalistic consciousness.

DVD Chapter Twelve: Space Travel (33:32)

Commentary:

The rocket crashes through several satellites as it enters space. One of the satellites is named, "Spy Com." It is in the shape of a beer bottle and its logo looks like a skull and cross bones.

Metaphysical Breakdown

This satellite symbolizes how the consumption of alcohol, although socially accepted, is a drug that keeps people from achieving their higher consciousness.

Commentary:

The ship passes the Sun. WALL-E gets recharged to sustain him on his journey.

Metaphysical Breakdown

Another image that shows WALL-E, who represents the Black man, receiving his power and energy from the Sun. On the other hand, the Sun is toxic to the Caucasian. The Sun is deadly to non-melanated or white people. In fact, the number one cancer that kills Caucasians is the skin cancer called, Melanoma. This type of cancer is almost non-existent in Black people.

Commentary:

WALL-E reaches out to touch the rings of Saturn. He holds on to the ship with his left hand.

Metaphysical Breakdown

The ring represents 360 degrees or a full circle. This was the standard of education in Kemet. In today's Western society, we are satisfied with earning one degree of knowledge. That is because our educational system is based on left brain or lower conscious thought and interpretation of reality. The fact that WALL-E is holding on to the ship with his left hand symbolizes the activation and domination of the right hemisphere of his brain which represents higher, spiritual consciousness.

DVD Chapter Thirteen: Docking (35:25)

Commentary:

Next scene the viewer sees a beautiful deep purple and indigo cloud. Behind it is the ship called the Axiom.

Metaphysical Breakdown

These colors represent the six and seventh chakras. These are the energy centers of higher consciousness. This is the level of consciousness WALL-E has achieved by him willing to sacrifice his life in the pursuit of his woman, EVE. Behind this colorful cloud lies the Axiom. This ship represents man's lower consciousness. Axiom means , a principle that is accepted as true without proof. The masses have been relegated to living their lives as sheep or cattle being led to slaughter.

Commentary:

The ship docks on the Axiom. A small robot named MO, comes out to clean the robots from what he calls, "foreign contaminant."

Metaphysical Breakdown

As we covered in our Character Assassination & Breakdown chapter, the robot MO literally means Black and the foreign contaminant represents melanin.

Commentary:

MO senses that there is 16% foreign contaminant on EVE.

Metaphysical Breakdown

In numerology, the number sixteen breaks down to the number seven. The number seven represents God's divine perfection in the physical dimension. This is what EVE represents. EVE, who represents the Black man, is God's divine perfection in the physical realm.

Commentary:

MO senses 100% foreign contaminant on WALL-E.

Metaphysical Breakdown

In numerology, the number 100 breaks down to the number 10. The number ten represents a person of higher consciousness having access to 360 degrees of knowledge. This quality is known as perfection. This is the level of higher consciousness that WALL-E is operating on. Remember, WALL-E represents the Black man.

Commentary:

WALL-E puts the "foreign contaminant on MO's forehead.

Metaphysical Breakdown

The forehead is the place of the Pineal gland. This is where melanin is produced. WALL-E shows this by putting the "foreign contaminant" on MO's forehead.

Commentary:

EVE is whisked away on a robotic cart number seven. She exits through bay door number A-224.

Metaphysical Breakdown

In numerology, the number seven represents God's divine perfection in the physical realm. This is who EVE represents as a Black woman. The number A-224 in numerology, breaks down to the number nine. The number nine represents man's judgment. EVE entering the Axiom, which represents lower consciousness, will be tested to see if she can maintain her higher consciousness.

Commentary:

MO finds some foreign contaminant outside of the line that he is supposed to stay on. He takes a leap of faith and jumps out of the line. He realizes that he is okay and continues to clean up.

Metaphysical Breakdown

MO has been programmed to always stay in line and do not detour from his given assignment. MO also represents melanin. MO trusts his intuition and steps out of line. This signifies MO going outside of the realm of his programming. Once MO takes this leap of faith, he realizes that his programming has been holding him back. Once he listens to his melanin in the form of his intuition, he has the capacity to achieve higher consciousness.

DVD Chapter Fourteen: Welcome To The Axiom (38:53)

Commentary:

WALL-E tries to follow EVE down the corridor. Traffic is moving too fast for him. WALL-E decides to creep out and emerge onto traffic moving with his left wheel first.

Metaphysical Breakdown

WALL-E overcomes his fears that keep him from his higher consciousness. He walks out on faith by stepping out with his left foot which activates the right hemisphere of the brain which represents higher, spiritual consciousness.

Commentary:

WALL-E runs into several people all wearing red. They are being transported in these futuristic lounge chairs. They are all overweight. They are all mesmerized by these video monitors. They are consumed by this virtual world and are oblivious to the reality around them. Everything is done for them and they can't do anything for themselves.

Metaphysical Breakdown

The color red symbolizes the root chakra. This is man's lowest level of consciousness. Man is driven by his animalistic urges and desires. This is the level of consciousness the elite, ruling class wants the masses to define themselves and their reality by.

The people on this ship do not do anything for themselves. They are controlled and brainwashed by the computers to be ignorant consumers. They are conditioned to rely on the computers to take full control of their lives and not to think or want anything for themselves.

The masses have given up their higher consciousness in exchange for the illusion of security and comfort. Since the people's reality is predicated on fear held in their lower consciousness, the powers that be create the illusion of a threat in order to manipulate the masses into voluntarily giving up their freedoms in exchange for an artificial reality that nurtures their lower consciousness. This brainwashing makes it easier for the ruling, elite class to enslave and oppress the masses.

Commentary:

At the 40:00 mark of the DVD, one will see a Black person on the monitor with their left eye covered by their hair.

Metaphysical Breakdown

In numerology, the number 40 represents man's test or life lesson he must overcome in order to reach higher consciousness. This is a subliminal sign that directly singles out the Black man as the victim of this brainwashing. The covering of the Black man's left eye symbolizes the block or suppression of his higher self by a system that wants to keep him in denial of his higher consciousness. The left eye is activated by the right hemisphere of the brain which represents higher, spiritual consciousness.

Commentary:

WALL-E looks up at the ceiling of the Axiom. There is a clock that reads 12:15 and the temperature is 72 degrees.

Metaphysical Breakdown

In numerology, the number 12:15 breaks down to the number nine. The number nine represents man's judgment or test he must pass in order to transcend into higher consciousness. The number 72 also breaks down to the number nine. This scene is revealing that everyone on the Axiom, which represents the system the elite ruling class uses to oppress the masses, must overcome their lower consciousness in order to reach their higher selves.

Commentary:

There are huge advertising signs all over the ship. A man name John, mistakes WALL-E as a servant. He tries to hand WALL-E his cup with his right hand and falls out of his chair. The man is helpless and cannot get up without assistance.

Metaphysical Breakdown

The man reaching out with his right hand and falling from his right side represents the activation of the left hemisphere of his brain which represents his lower, animalistic consciousness.

Commentary:

WALL-E passes a child care center called, "All Day Care." A robot it brainwashing them as they learn the alphabet. The teacher says, "A is for Axiom your home sweet home. B is for Buy n' Large your very best friend."

Metaphysical Breakdown

The name of the daycare represents the 24 hour constant bombardment of lower level energy that we have been exposed to since birth. We have inherited a world that keeps us from achieving our higher selves. Also, we are programmed to be consumers and not to provide for ourselves.

Commentary:

A computer tells the people to, "Try blue, it's the new red."

Metaphysical Breakdown

The elite, ruling class make all the decisions for the people without them even knowing it. When one can control the choices a group has, that entity controls the predictable behavior of said group when being exposed to that given choice.

Commentary:

WALL-E accidently breaks the monitor of a woman named Mary. Mary seems to wake up from being unconscious. It is like she is seeing the world for the first time.

Metaphysical Breakdown

WALL-E shows Mary a different reality from which to define herself and her environment. This point of view is called her higher consciousness.

Commentary:

WALL-E passes by to pool deck. It is in the shape of a Sun. It has twelve smaller pools that are surrounding one giant pool in the middle. Mary responds by saying, "I didn't know we had a pool?"

Metaphysical Breakdown

In the occult, the symbol of the Sun represents higher consciousness and superior knowledge of how the Universe works. This is what Mary is beginning to discover.

In numerology, the number 12 represents completion. When you add the giant pool in the middle you get the number 13. The number thirteen represents the death of lower consciousness so that higher consciousness can be reborn. This is the beginning of Mary's enlightenment that was sparked by WALL-E.

Commentary:

One of the people asked for shade. The robot puts the umbrella on the left side of the face to shade the person.

Metaphysical Breakdown

The emphasis on shading the left side of the body activates the right hemisphere of the brain which is responsible for higher consciousness. The "shade" also represents the chemical melanin which is needed in order to attain higher consciousness.

DVD Chapter Fifteen: Bridge Lobby (42:58)

Commentary:

WALL-E is confronted by a giant eye guarding an elevator. The eye looks at WALL-E and EVE. It hesitates before it pushes a button with its left mechanical arm that allows them to enter the elevator.

Metaphysical Breakdown

The Eye of Heru is a Kemetic symbol of higher consciousness. The left eye activates the right hemisphere of the brain which is responsible for higher consciousness. This is why the robot pushes the button with its left hand. The elevator represents the access to higher consciousness that the symbol of the Eye of Heru represents.

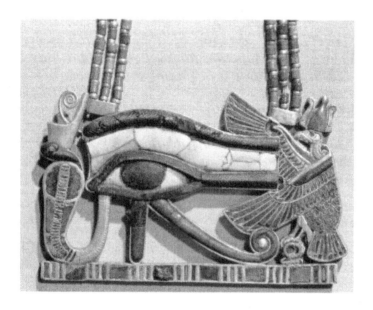

Commentary:

As they are about to leave, WALL-E waves to the giant eye robot with his left hand. The robot's right arm seems to malfunction.

Metaphysical Breakdown

WALL-E confirms this ideology of reaching higher consciousness by waving with his left arm which activates the right hemisphere of the brain responsible for higher consciousness. The robot eye, representing higher consciousness or the Eye of Heru, cannot use his right arm which activates the left hemisphere of the brain which represents lower level consciousness.

DVD Chapter Sixteen: Captain On Deck (43:35)

Commentary:

The elevator stops at a top floor. The viewer sees a ship's wheel with a red light in the middle of it. The wheel has five handles that protrude out from the middle.

Metaphysical Breakdown

The ship's wheel is named AUTO. AUTO represents the elite ruling class or network of secret societies that control the world's population and resources from behind the scenes. Their Free masonry god is named Baphomet. He has the head of a goat and the body of a human. The goat or upside down star is a symbol for this secret society. You will see that AUTO's five handles correspond to the points of the upside down, five-pointed star.

AUTO is located on the top floor which symbolizes the power and control of the Illuminati. No government, religion or economic institution is above their control and manipulation. They simply run the world behind the shadows of so-called world leaders and multi-national corporations.

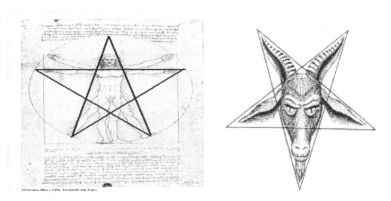

In the occult, the upright star is a symbol of man operating at his highest level of consciousness. The upside down star, resembling the head of a goat, denotes man operating at his lowest, anmalistic level of consciousness.

Commentary:

The Ship's Wheel flashes the number A113 in the middle of its red eye.

Metaphysical Breakdown

In numerology, A113 breaks down to the number six. Six represents the number of the beast in man or his lowest level of consciousness. This is the frequency the Illuminati promotes to keep man from discovering his higher self. It is in this state of consciousness where man is easily controlled and manipulated.

The color red is also a sign of man's lower level or animalistic consciousness maintained in his root chakra.

Commentary:

The Ship's Wheel opens a hole in the floor and descends down to the captain's quarters to wake up the captain.

Metaphysical Breakdown

The Ship's wheel is above the captain's quarters. This scene suggests that all world leaders must secretly answer to the agenda of the elite and secret ruling class sometimes referred to as the Illuminati.

Commentary:

The floor and the doors have the same logo on them.

Metaphysical Breakdown

If one looks closely they will see the symbols on the doors and the floor are very similar to the Free Mason symbol of the compass and the square.

The symbol on the left is the Free mason symbol. The symbol on the right that represents the Axiom or the system from which we live under, is very similar to the Free Mason symbol on the right.

Commentary:

The captain notices the time is 12:30:43pm.

Metaphysical Breakdown

In numerology, these numbers add up to the number thirteen. The number thirteen represents resurrection. Resurrection can be defined as the putting to death of lower level consciousness so that one can be reborn into higher consciousness. This is the path that the Captain is about to embark on.

Commentary:

The captain announces that they have been on the Axiom for 255,642 days.

Metaphysical Breakdown

In numerology, this number breaks down to the number six. The number six represents man's lower or animalistic nature. This is the level of consciousness that the people on the Axiom have been operating on. The Axiom represents the system that keeps the masses from achieving their higher consciousness in an effort to enslave them without them even knowing they are slaves.

Commentary:

The captain turns the clock back to 9:30am. He can control the time and temperature at his discretion. It is also 72 degrees.

Metaphysical Breakdown

In numerology, 9:30 breaks down to the number twelve. The number twelve represents completion. In this scene it is referring to the steps the captain has taken to fully internalize his higher consciousness. This is what will allow him to see the sytem for what it is and rise above it.

In numerology , 72 breaks down to the number nine. The number nine represents man's judgment or test he must pass to overcome his lower self in his effort to achieve higher consciousness. This number signifies the test or judgment the captain must overcome.

Commentary:

The captain says that is their 700th anniversary of their 5 year cruise.

Metaphysical Breakdown

In numerology, these numbers add up to the number twelve. The number twelve signifies completion. The captain has completed his task that puts him in a position to be judged in his test to achieve higher consciousness.

Commentary:

The captain grabs the operation manual labeled, "Operation Recolonize" from WALL-E with his left hand. It is obvious the captain has never read a book before.

Metaphysical Breakdown

By the captain grabbing the manual with his left hand, it signifies that he is operating according to his higher consciousness. The left hand is activated by the right hemisphere of the brain which represents higher, spiritual consciousness. This tells the audience that "recolonizing" is an act of higher consciousness.

Commentary:

The Captain is startled by the discovery of WALL-E. WALL-E shakes the Captain's left hand and leaves a dirt-type substance in his hand. While the captain is holding the manual in his right

Metaphysical Breakdown

Shaking the Captain's left hand signifies that the two are operating according to their higher, spiritual consciousness. The dirt WALL-E leaves in the left hand of the Captain symbolizes the activation of the Captain's melanin which is needed to achieve higher consciousness.

DVD Chapter Seventeen: Define Earth (51:12)

(None.)

DVD Chapter Eighteen: Repair Ward (52:10)

Commentary:

EVE and WALL-E arrive at the Repair Ward. They were sent there for repairs and maintenance because they are believed to have malfunctions. The Repair Ward resembles a jail that houses other robots that seem to have defects.

Metaphysical Breakdown

The Repair Ward represents the criminal and mental health system that is used to keep "free thinkers and doers" at bay and in control. If one does not fit in to the society or what the ruling class has defined as "normal," they are isolated and locked away as criminals. "Free thinkers" and unique individuals are a threat to the system that the ruling class uses to oppress the masses. If you are outside the threshold of the status quo or what people have been programmed to view as "normal," then you are a potential threat to the system that oppresses the masses without their consent.

Commentary:

WALL-E grabs EVE's right arm and blasts the control panel that controls all the cells and robots in the repair ward. All the robots escape with WALL-E and EVE.

Metaphysical Breakdown

WALL-E uses attributes of his lower level consciousness to facilitate the promotion of higher consciousness. Sometimes people of higher consciousness must use attributes of their lower consciousness to put themselves in a position to nurture their higher selves. In other words, sometimes slaves need to rise up and defeat the slave owners as a means of liberating themselves in an effort to pursue their freedom. If one is not willing to give their life in an effort to reach their higher consciousness, it will never be attained. Sacrificing one's life is the test or threshold to acquiring higher consciousness.

384

DVD Chapter Nineteen: Rogue Robots (54:49)

Commentary:

WALL-E runs into the police robots. They all have a white right hand with a red background on the screen. They tell WALL-E to halt.

Metaphysical Breakdown

The police represent the suppression of higher consciousness and the regulators of lower consciousness. In other words, the main objective of the police force is to keep people in line with the system that oppresses them and stamp out individuals or groups that want a different reality outside of it. The right hand of the police represents lower consciousness. It is activated by the left hemisphere of the brain which represents man's lower, animalistic consciousness.

Commentary:

On the wall on the right side of the police robots is the number 96. On the wall on the left side of WALL-E's group is the letter "H."

Metaphysical Breakdown

In numerology, the number 96 breaks down to the number six. The number six represents man's lower or animalistic consciousness. This is the level of consciousness the police department is operating on.   On the other hand WALL-E's group is represented by the letter "H." In numerology, the letter "H" breaks down to the number eight. Eight represents the concept of eternity or infinity. In this scene it represents the innate desire in all men to be free. No matter how long the oppression, man's nature will always yearn to be free.

Commentary:

The police robots take a picture of EVE and WALL-E. They are seen with a red and yellow background. Their picture is posted throughout the ship.

Metaphysical Breakdown

The colors of red and yellow appeal to one's lower consciousness. Red is the color of the root chakra. This color promotes animalistic behavior that is predicated on self-survival. The color yellow appeals to one's desires and passions. So in this scene, when the people see WALL-E and EVE's picture as criminals in red and yellow, they will define them and view them through their lower level or animalistic consciousness. They will automatically see them as dangerous and will come to the conclusion that they must be eliminated.

Commentary:

The message under the picture says, "Rogue Robots."

Metaphysical Breakdown

Rogue- 1. An unprincipled, deceitful, and unreliable person; a scoundrel or rascal. An organism, especially a plant, that shows an undesirable variation from a standard.

Commentary:

While escaping the police robots, WALL-E and EVE make a left turn. On the wall behind them is the number 12.

Metaphysical Breakdown

The left turn symbolizes that WALL-E and EVE are operating according to their higher consciousness. The left side represents higher, spiritual consciousness housed in the left hemisphere of the brain. Anytime some makes a left turn or uses the left side of their body one can assume they are operating according to their higher consciousness.

DVD Chapter Twenty: Escape Pod (56:09)

Commentary:

As EVE and WALL-E exit the elevator doors, we see the numbers L9 and 12 on them.

Metaphysical Breakdown

In numerology, these numbers add up to six. The number six represents man defining himself and his reality as a beast through his lower level consciousness. Going through these doors one can expect this scene to display this type of behavior.

Commentary:

EVE wants to save WALL-E by sending him back to Earth by himself. WALL-E does not want to go unless EVE is with him.

Metaphysical Breakdown

WALL-E is displaying his higher consciousness. He is willing to sacrifice his life to save his woman, represented by EVE. This is a display of what it takes to achieve one's higher, spiritual self.

Commentary:

The gopher robot, puts the plant in the left boot in the escape pod. He is trying to destroy the plant so that the Axiom does not go back to Earth.

Metaphysical Breakdown

This scene shows the suppression of higher consciousness by the elite ruling class. They work night and day to try to eliminate the promotion of higher consciousness. They want the masses to be driven by fear and self-survival. This is how the people are easily manipulated and controlled. In order for the system to prosper this is the mentality that must be sustained.

DVD Chapter Twenty-One: Cruising Speed (58:01)

Commentary:

WALL-E tries to save the plant and is caught in the pod before he can get out. The computer on the pod says it has 20 seconds before self-destruct. Then, the computer counts down from the number ten. The pod is seen exploding. EVE thinks WALL-E has died in the explosion.

Metaphysical Breakdown

In numerology, the number 20 breaks down to the number two. The number two represents division or separation. In this scene it is referring to the separation of WALL-E's higher consciousness from himself. By shooting the left boot into space to be blown up represents the attempted annihilation of WALL-E's higher consciousness. If this was successful, WALL-E would forever be a slave to his lower self, thus easy to manipulate and control.

DVD Chapter Twenty-Two: Spacewalk (58:45)

Commentary:

WALL-E escapes and returns to EVE being propelled by a red fire extinguisher. EVE and WALL-E spiral past on another in a spiral formation. The space around them is deep purple in color as they seem to dance in unison with each other.

Metaphysical Breakdown

Once again, WALL-E achieves his higher consciousness by retrieving the plant in the left boot. The red fire extinguisher represents WALL-E'S phallus symbol. The dance he and EVE are doing in space represents the combining of the male and female energy or the act of sex. The fact that the color purple is prevalent in the space background signifies that their sexual union is being performed according to their higher consciousness. Purple represents the highest chakra energy source located right above one's head. Coincidently, this is why the color purple was attributed to royalty or kings and queens. It is the "crown" chakra. So the kings and queens were relegated to God's representatives for the people here on Earth.

Commentary:

WALL-E shows EVE that he saved the plant. EVE is ecstatic. She swirls him around in jubilee. EVE touches her forehead to WALL-E's. This causes a spark. WALL-E is blissful.

Metaphysical Breakdown

EVE and WALL-E touch foreheads. This action creates an electrical spark. The location of the forehead symbolizes the Pineal gland or what our Kemetic ancestors referred to as the first eye. The Pineal gland produces the chemical melanin, which is needed in order for one to achieve higher consciousness. The spark we see is the activation of the Pineal gland that happens when male energy, known as electric, meets female energy, known as magnetic. This electro-magnetic energy creates a "gateway" that can be used to manifest the spiritual dimension into the physical realm. In Kemet, this science of sex was used to achieve higher consciousness.

Commentary:

Mary and John recognize WALL-E and EVE spiraling in a dance in the middle of space. They accidently touch hands and are reawakened.

Metaphysical Breakdown

Mary and John's touching of the hands represents the awakening of higher consciousness through the activation of their combined electro-magnetic energy. They are replaying the process that WALL-E and EVE are undergoing, but on a more simpler scale.

Commentary:

AUTO puts the Captain to sleep. The captain was excited to learn about Earth.

Metaphysical Breakdown

AUTO representing the secret, elite, ruling class, wants to keep him asleep in his lower level consciousness so that he can be more easily controlled and manipulated. The Captain is finally waking up to this whole new world around him that he is discovering in his higher consciousness.

DVD Chapter Twenty-Three: The Lido Deck (1:02:18)

Commentary:

The captain asks the computer to define dancing? The computer responds, "A series of movements involving two partners where speed and rhythm match harmoniously with music. Just then WALL-E uses up all the fire extinguisher and EVE carries him to the ship.

Metaphysical Breakdown

The "dancing" that the computer defines is really sexual intercourse that is being displayed by WALL-E and EVE in space. WALL-E using up all the fire extinguisher symbolizes the completion of his ejaculation. Notice that EVE has to carry him back to the ship after he shoots off all of his load.

Commentary:

Mary and John are splashing each other in the pool that they just discovered they had. All the other humans are in their chairs going home. The pool is closed but Mary and John disobey the computer's orders.

Metaphysical Breakdown

Mary and John are now becoming "free thinkers" in their new discovery of their higher consciousness. They begin to disobey frivolous rules and laws set up the system that are in place to control them.

Commentary:

EVE witnesses a trash conveyor empty trash in the trash chute. She figures this is the way to deliver the plant to the captain. The number of the conveyor is BQ-03

Metaphysical Breakdown

In numerology, these letters and numbers add up to the number four. The number four represents creation. In this scene it represents the new journey WALL-E and EVE have begun to save the people on Axiom from their lower selves.

DVD Chapter Twenty-Four: It Only Takes A Moment (1:03:25)

Commentary:

The captain is seen playing with a toy Axiom ship landing on the Earth. The captain lands the toy ship in Afrika or more specifically, Kemet.

Metaphysical Breakdown

The Captain is showing the true origin of man reaching his higher, spiritual consciousness. This scene pays homage to the most advanced civilization known to man. It is the foundation of all knowledge on Earth. Coincidently, it was an Afrikan civilization that held humanity to its highest standards!

Commentary:

The captain hooks up a video camera to the left side of EVE's head. The images show Earth's destruction and downfall.

Metaphysical Breakdown

The left hemisphere of the brain is responsible for lower, animalistic consciousness. It is this state of consciousness that destroyed the Earth.

Commentary:

EVE activates her security camera. She witnesses how WALL-E took care of her while she was waiting for the ship to return. She is very touched.

Metaphysical Breakdown

EVE recognizes WALL-E's higher consciousness by witnessing the self-sacrifice and love he showed her when she was incapacitated. Even though she did not reciprocate WALL-E's love for her, he still took care of her unconditionally. This is the behavior of someone who has achieved higher consciousness.

393

DVD Chapter Twenty-Five: Code A113 (1:05:52)

Commentary:

AUTO sees everything in red. On his screen flashes the number A113.

Metaphysical Breakdown

The color red and the number six represented by A113, are both symbols of lower level consciousness. These are the attributes of AUTO, who represents the secret ruling class that controls and manipulates the world's population and its resources. This is the level of consciousness they want the people to define themselves and their reality.

Commentary:

AUTO tries to take the plant from the captain. The captain holds AUTO back with his right hand and holds the plant in his left.

Metaphysical Breakdown

The Captain is displaying lower or animalistic consciousness in his effort to fight off AUTO, who represents the system that enslaves him. This is shown by holding off AUTO with his right arm. The right side of the body is activated by the left hemisphere of the brain which represents man's lower consciousness. Holding the plant in his left hand represents the nurturing of his higher consciousness, which he is trying to protect.

Commentary:

AUTO reveals a secret message from the Earth's global CEO. In regards to going back to Earth he says, "Rather than try to fix this problem it'll just be easier for everyone to remain in space."

Metaphysical Breakdown

This is the mindset that is being forced down our throats by the mainstream media outlets that are controlled by the Illuminati. They have us believing that we must save a doomed and corrupt system because if it fails we will be worse off than we are right now. When one thinks about it, this doesn't make sense. We have been conditioned to be motivated by fear of the unknown. It is in the "unknown" that our true freedom and happiness lies.

Commentary:

The Global CEO continues, "Go to full autopilot, take control of everything and do not return to Earth." This secret directive is labeled, #A113.

Metaphysical Breakdown

This scene shows how the Earth is run and controlled by one unifying entity they call the Global CEO. The Earth is run as a business that benefits the haves at the expense of the have nots. There is a secret and hidden hand behind every global war, economy, religion and politics.

In numerology, the number A113, which refers to the ruling elite's hidden agenda, adds up to the number six. The number six represents man's lower animalistic consciousnsss. This is the state of consciousness of the Illuminati. They are not concerned with poverty, human suffering or quality of life. All they are interested in is staying in power and expanding their wealth at the expense of those less fortunate, who happen to be the darker people of the world.

Commentary:

The captain asks the computer how long ago has it been since they sent that message. The captain responds to AUTO by saying that it was over seven hundred years ago and that life is now sustainable on Earth.

Metaphysical Breakdown

In numerology, the number seven represents God's divine completion in the physical dimension. This is the state of consciousness of the people. They are now ready to embrace their higher consciousness. They are waking up out of their slumber of complacency, immaturity and thoughtless existence.

Commentary:

AUTO tells the captain that is statement was irrelevant. AUTO also states, "On the Axiom you will survive." The captain responds, "I don't want to survive, I want to live!" AUTO replies, "Must follow my directive."

Metaphysical Breakdown

The Captain is referring to man's nature of always wanting to correct and balance itself. It is in this nature that the Captain finds his rejuvenated energy to better his life. The Axiom, which represents the system that breeds and maintains lower level consciousness, is not enough for a person who wants to discover his true self. Life's purpose shifts from wanting to survive to wanting to discover one's self and the potentials of the world they live in.

Commentary:

The captain views the photos of the previous captains of the Axiom. He notices that over the left shoulder of all the captains is AUTO looking over them.

Metaphysical Breakdown

The Captain represents our appointed political, religious and economic leaders. They are handpicked by the elite ruling class and made to deceive the public as if they had a say so in the decision making through a corrupt and farce democratic system.

The fact that AUTO, who represents the Illuminati, is looking over the shoulder of all the Captain's the Axiom ever had, signifies that AUTO is really the one in control of the Axiom, which represents the system of lower level consciousness. The fact that AUTO is over the left shoulder signifies the Illuminati's control and suppression of our leaders higher, spiritual consciousness. The left side of the body is activated by the right hemisphere of the brain, which represents higher, spiritual consciousness.

Commentary:

The captain defies AUTO and orders the Axiom to return to Earth. AUTO disregards the captain's authority and summons Gopher, the small robot, to retrieve the plant in the left boot.

Metaphysical Breakdown

When our appointed leaders go against the wishes of the elite ruling class that appointed them in these leadership positions, they usually respond by character assassination of the individual or ultimately murder in the form of an accident or assassination.

The left boot symbolizes higher consciousness. The retrieving of the left boot from the Captain symbolizes the Captain being forced to operate according to the lower level of consciousness the Illuminati wants to constantly subject the masses to. Anyone who tries to wake up the people from their slumber of lower level consciousness has to be eliminated by the ruling class. This is the biggest threat to their system.

Commentary:

Gopher throws the plant down the trash chute to try to dispose of it before EVE gets it. Unknowingly, it lands on top of WALL-E's head to save the day.

Metaphysical Breakdown

WALL-E, representing the Black man, has the capacity to reach his higher consciousness and the lead the masses out of their invisible prison of lower consciousness. Once the Black man refuses to accept his animalistic mentality and view of his reality, he will be able to lead the people to their higher selves. This is what the system is afraid of. They fear a "Black Messiah."

The plant landing on top of WALL-E's head and situated between his eyes, symbolizes the activation of his Pineal gland which produces the melanin needed to reach higher consciousness.

Commentary:

WALL-E tries to keep the plant from AUTO. AUTO than proceeds to shock WALL-E frying his memory chip.

Metaphysical Breakdown

This scene represents the damage done to the Black man by the white man during the Middle Passage. The Black man was not allowed to keep his culture, religion or language. The white man replaced his worldview and knowledge of self with a dubious culture that would program the Black man to be subservient and docile to the white man. In other words, the white man replaced the God given programming of the Black man with a dysfunctional program that would benefit the white man's agenda. This process was called the "breaking" of the Black man and the making of a slave. This programming and procedure was very similar as to how one would "break" a wild horse so that its owner can ride its back.

Commentary:

AUTO then turns to EVE and shuts down her attachment where her heart would be. EVE tumbles down the trash chute following WALL-E.

Metaphysical Breakdown

To break the Black man during slavery, the white man also had to cause separation from the Black woman in regards to the Black man. Since the Black woman could no longer count on her man to be there to protect and provide for her, she had to separate her feelings and love for him so that she could be strong enough to survive and have some semblance of a family without the dynamics and the participation of the Black man.

This is shown in this scene by AUTO, who represents the elite, ruling class, disconnecting her heart when WALL-E's computer chip is destroyed. EVE becomes numb to the whole situation.

Commentary:

A red light comes on in the captain's quarters. AUTO confines the captain to his quarters. AUTO is in complete control of the Axiom.

Metaphysical Breakdown

The color red, symbolizes lower level or animalistic consciousness. This is the state of consciousness of the Illuminati, represented by AUTO. When the Illuminati do not get their way, they will eliminate the threat and replace them with someone who will do their will. AUTO has always had control of the Axiom. The Captain was just a puppet for the people to follow. The Captain in reality never had any real power.

DVD Chapter Twenty-Six: Garbage Air Lock (1:11:48)

Commentary:

This chapter, we see EVE waking up in the bottom of the trash shoot. Her heart monitor is accidently activated by computer mice. The screen says, "Reboot." It has a circle with three points.

Metaphysical Breakdown

EVE and WALL-E have descended into their lowest level of existence, similar to that of the Black man and woman here in America. EVE's heart chakra is finally activated once again. In this scene the word "reboot" means resurrection.

In numerology the number three represents God's perfection. EVE has now completed the process one needs to undertake in order to be in a position to achieve higher consciousness.

Commentary:

WALL-E and EVE are trapped inside two cubes of compacted trash. They are on their way to being disposed of permanently. The red lights and sirens go off.

Metaphysical Breakdown

The two cubes represent the paradigm or matrix of their individual existence. They both live in two different realities that the other does not understand. Because of their deliberate separation, they cannot understand why they cannot seem to come together as a couple. The color red, symbolizes that the Black man and woman's consciousness is based on their lower level perception of themselves and their environment which makes up their reality.

Commentary:

EVE breaks out of her bondage first. She tries to break out WALL-E before the airlock closes.

Metaphysical Breakdown

The Black woman must break out of her lower consciousness first in order to save the Black man. This was laid out in the Kemetic story os Ausar and Auset, talked about in the beginning of the book. It is the blueprint to the resurrection of the Black man and woman.

Commentary:

MO is seen in the background also being disposed of. He recognizes WALL-E as "foreign contaminant" and rushes to him.

Metaphysical Breakdown

Even though WALL-E is close to dying, he still embraces his melanin as a means to save him when all seems hopeless. MO and the term "foreign contaminant" both refer to WALL-E's melanin.

Commentary:

MO accidently gets caught between the airlock doors. EVE is able to pull WALL-E out of his bondage. She fights to reach MO in her effort to save WALL-E. She finally is able to grab a hold of MO with her right hand. WALL-E is saved!

Metaphysical Breakdown

EVE is showing that she is operating according to her higher consciousness. She has no disregard for her own safety as she tries to save WALL-E. Of course, she has activated her melanin which is needed to achieve higher consciousness. This is displayed by her reaching out to MO, who ultimately saves the both of them.

Commentary:

WALL-E is dying. MO is seen cleaning his left arm in an effort to revive him.

Metaphysical Breakdown

MO, who represents WALL-E's melanin, is concentrating and focused on WALL-E's left side which represents his higher consciousness. It is this mentality that will eventually save and revive WALL-E.

Commentary:

EVE sees the WALL-E's main computer chip is fried. She frantically looks through the trash to find a replacement for it.

Metaphysical Breakdown

EVE realizes that WALL-E's survival is predicated on him finding his original computer chip programming. This means that the Black man must return to his past in order to find his true self. He needs to find out who he was before the white man programmed him to become what he is today. The Black man is not in his right mind. He has been given this program from his enemy and not form his divine creator. The sooner he acknowledges this, the sooner he will find his and his communitie's salvation and freedom.

Commentary:

MO is finished cleaning WALL-E. WALL-E reaches out to shake hands with MO. MO proceeds to clean his right hand. MO repeats his name and WALL-E acknowledges him by repeating it back.

Metaphysical Breakdown

MO, representing WALL-E'S melanin is now located on his right side to symbolize WALL-E's physical return to health. WALL-E acknowledges that it was his melanin that saved him, by repeating MO's name back to him.

Commentary:

EVE tries to insert all the different computer chips she found into WALL-E. None of them are a match.

Metaphysical Breakdown

WALL-E rejects all the different kinds of computer programming chips that do not fit what God intended for him to do naturally. This scene reinforces to the Black man to not accept any other programming his enemy wants to control his behavior with. The Black man must return to God's original programming he made for him in his homeland of Afrika, before he was tampered with by the white man.

Commentary:

WALL-E knows that he is dying. He gives EVE the plant to take to the Axiom as this was the directive she was programmed for. EVE refuses her programmed directive and tells WALL-E that he is her directive now.

Metaphysical Breakdown

EVE refuses to accept the program that was given to her from her oppressor. She has now figured out that her original program was to look out for her Black man, which is WALL-E. Her attention and energy is now focused on uplifting and saving WALL-E.

Commentary:

EVE reaches out to WALL-E with her right hand as WALL-E reaches out with his left hand. They touch hands for a brief moment.

Metaphysical Breakdown

EVE is now focused on giving of herself physically to help save her man. This is displayed by her giving WALL-E her right hand. WALL-E reaches out with his left hand to signify that his higher consciousness is receiving the energy that his woman is physically giving him.

403

Commentary:

WALL-E retrieves the plant and tells EVE that she must go back to Earth to save him. He shows her the lighter as he sparks the flame and then adjusts his left eye.

Metaphysical Breakdown

The lighter represents the spark or masculine energy needed to activate one's melanin. The concentration of the left eye symbolizes WALL-E's higher, spiritual consciousness. It is this level of consciousness that is going to save WALL-E from his lower level of existence.

EVE must return back to nature or God, which is represented by her going back to Earth to save WALL-E.

Commentary:

EVE finally understands. She takes WALL-E in her left arm. WALL-E calls out to MO to come with them. EVE blasts through the ceiling of the garbage dump and all three escape.

Metaphysical Breakdown

By EVE taking WALL-E in her left arm she is symbolizing her higher consciousness is the key for their escape and survival. Left arm is activated by the right hemisphere of the brain which represents higher, spiritual consciousness. Of course, their melanin, represented by MO, must come along with them to ahieve higher consciousness. EVE blasts through the ceiling of the dump to symbolized their resurrecetion from lower consciousness to higher consciousness.

DVD Chapter Twenty-Seven: EVE To The Rescue (1:15:50)

Commentary:

One of the police robots looks into service locker 27F. He tries to apprehend a robot that escaped the repair ward. The robot was found because of a yellow strip of paint that led the police robot to him. EVE comes to the rescue of the robot by locking the police robot into the service locker.

Metaphysical Breakdown

In numerology, the number 27F breaks down to the number six. The number six represents lower or animalistic behavior or thought. This is the mentality of all police forces through the world. This is where they operate from.

The color, yellow represents one's passions and heart's desires. If one knows what you hold close to your heart, one can predict your actions. This is how they find one of the robots that was freed by WALL-E. They followed the yellow line which represented his heart's desires and passions.

Commentary:

EVE and WALL-E run into all the defective robots from the repair ward. They are hanging out in front of Bay 70. They all join suit with EVE and WALL-E.

Metaphysical Breakdown

In numerology, the number seventy breaks down to the number seven. The number seven represents God's completion in the physical dimension. All of the robots who didn't fit into the system of lower consciousness will now use their unique gifts the free themselves.

Commentary:

A blue umbrella from Bay "F" follows the group of robots led by EVE and WALL-E.

Metaphysical Breakdown

The color blue represents communication. The letter "F" represents animalistic or lower level consciousness. In order for our rogue robots to be free they must stand up and fight for their freedom. Animalistic or lower level behavior and consciousness doesn't always need to be interpreted as bad if it is used to raise, protect or maintain one's higher consciousness. This is the level of consciousness our group must communicate by if it wants to be free.

Commentary:

The robots are seen making a left turn on the corner of Bay #2.

Metaphysical Breakdown

In numerology, the number two represents division or separation. Our robots in order to attain their freedom, must separate themselves from their higher consciousness in an effort to fight for their freedom. The making of the left turn signifies their higher, spiritual consciousness they must separate from in order to fight for their freedom.

When one resorts to violence they are operating according to their lower level consciousness. Because our robots have no other choice but to resort to this behavior, they must temporarily divide themselves from their state of higher consciousness to fight for their freedom.

Commentary:

AUTO sends out his entire police force to try to squash the robot rebellion.

Metaphysical Breakdown

AUTO, representing the elite ruling class, must send out his entire police force to squash any resistance from people who want to be free from the lower consciousness the system oppresses them with. These freedom fighters must be vilified and eliminated as soon as possible, as to not stir up the consciousness in the general population.

Commentary:

The captain "hotwires" the computer control panel. He must bypass AUTO's control to get out a message to EVE and WALL-E.

Metaphysical Breakdown

The Captain is now bypassing the controls and the agenda of the Illuminati. He is risking his life in his effort to do the right thing and serve the people. In the Illuminati's eyes, these are grounds for assassination.

Commentary:

EVE and WALL-E are confronted by the robot police. The dysfunctional robots use their uniqueness to subdue the police force.

Metaphysical Breakdown

The same characteristics and attributes today's society look upon as being dysfunctional or abnormal, are the same attributes the people will need to fight for their freedom. The system labels these people as misfits in order to discourage this potential behavior that might be used to set themselves free.

Commentary:

The Captain activates the Axiom to receive the plant. The pool is the main staging area. All the lights now turn to green. We see the people leaving their rooms to go to the pool.

Metaphysical Breakdown

The color green represents the activation of the heart chakra. It is the first level of higher consciousness. This is where the masses must elevate their consciousness in order to beat the system that means to enslave them. One needs to "feel" with their minds and "think" with their hearts. This goes against what the system has taught us in regards to separating our hearts in our decision making. This is where you get the term, "It's just business, nothing personal." In higher consciousness, everything should be personal and take into consideration everyone's fellings that are involved in the process.

DVD Chapter Twenty-Eight: The Captain vs. Auto (1:19:25)

Commentary:

The captain activates the Axiom to receive the plant. The Sun-shaped pool is the main staging area. All the lights now turn to green. We see the people leaving their rooms to go to the pool. One of the room numbers is #77.

Metaphysical Breakdown

The Sun represents the higher consciousness the people need and also the masculine energy or spark to activate the Pineal gland, which produces the melanin needed to attain higher consciousness.

In numerology, the number 77 breaks down to the number five. The number five represents God's grace in the people's undertaking. The Creator is pleased with the people's quest for higher consciousness.

Commentary:

The people all have these head covers which automatically were activated by the Captain. This cover blocks them from eating or drinking anything.

Metaphysical Breakdown

This is a sign that shows how the elite, ruling class uses our food in an effort to keep the masses at a lower level of consciousness. The covers not only block the consumption of food, they supply clean air from which to breathe. We are conditioned to crave and be addicted to food instead of it providing sustenance and nutrition in our effort to achieve higher consciousness.

Commentary:

The babies are gathered in one area by the pool. There is a screen to entertain them that has a Sun, Moon and a star.

Metaphysical Breakdown

These are symbols of higher consciousness located above us in space. Our babies have the potential to reach higher consciousness when they are born. The system works to destroy their potential the moment they come into this world, through their nutrition, education, health and worldview.

Commentary:

AUTO and the Captain continuously fight each other for control over the Axiom.

Metaphysical Breakdown

This is the struggle that our true leaders must undertake if we are serious about achieving our freedom. Everyone that has stood up to this elite, ruling class has been killed or their lives have been destroyed. WE need a fearless leader that is willing to expose the system for what it is and risk their life for the betterment of the people.

DVD Chapter Twenty-Nine: All Feet On Deck (1:20:18)

Commentary:

As the Axiom tilts to one side the people start to slide. Several of the people save each other by grasping each other's hands.

Metaphysical Breakdown

In the occult, there is a handshake called the Lion's Paw. It symbolizes the "raising" of the initiate from a lower degree to a higher degree. In this scene, we see two people grasping hands in an effort to save each other from falling into "lower consciousness." They are saving each other or "raising" each other into higher consciousness.

Commentary:

The captain finally stands up for himself and subdues AUTO. He switches AUTO's switch from auto to manual with his right hand.

Metaphysical Breakdown

The Captain's right hand symbolizes the activation of his lower animalistic consciousness. It is this level of consciousness that must be displayed in his effort to free the people. The Captain gains control of the Axiom or the system the Illuminati has in place to keep the people enslaved to their lower consciousness.

Commentary:

EVE saves WALL-E from being crushed. She calls out for the plant. MO retrieves the plant for her. All the humans realize that they can stand up on their own.

Metaphysical Breakdown

Once this is accomplished, the people start to realize the potential in themselves and start to do things they never thought they could do in a system that suppressed their higher selves.

Commentary:

A Black man is the last one to throw the plant to WALL-E. He throws it with his left hand. WALL-E also puts the plant in the machine with his left hand.

Metaphysical Breakdown

This scene is further evidence that this story is really about the Black man resurrecting himself by overcoming the system that was designed to enslave him without knowing he was a salve. The left hand is activated by the right hemisphere of the brain which represents higher consciousness. The Black man must reclaim his higher consciousness which was stolen from him. He must rediscover his higher, spiritual side in order to free himself from the prison of his lower level consciousness. It is in this lower state of consciousness where he finds himself trapped in a world that uses and abuses him for their own benefit at Black people's expense.

DVD Chapter Thirty: Homecoming (1:24:16)

Commentary:

WALL-E's roach notices the red light on the ground. He gets excited because he anticipates the return of WALL-E.

Metaphysical Breakdown

The roach, representing WALL-E's melanin, is again distracted by the red light which represents the first or root chakra. This chakra defines man and his environment through his animalistic consciousness. WALL-E's melanin relates this consciousness to WALL-E returning to Earth in the physical dimension. WALL-E is about to arrive from outer space which in this case represents the spiritual dimension. This is similar to the Christian doctrine of Christ returning to Earth in the rapture to save humanity.

Commentary:

One of the buildings in the background where the Axiom lands is named Orbital.

Metaphysical Breakdown

A partial description of the quantum state of an electron (or other particle) orbiting the nucleus of an atom. Different orbitals have different shapes and orientations, depending on the energy of the electron, its angular momentum, and its magnetic number. Orbitals have no clear boundaries; the shape of an orbital, as depicted graphically, shows only the regions around the nucleus in which an electron has a relatively high probability of being found. No more than two electrons (each with opposite spin) can coexist in a single orbital because of the Pauli Exclusion Principle.

The electron, which represents feminine or negative energy, revoloves around the proton, which represents masculine or positive energy. It is this basic concept of energy that is played

413

*out throughout the universe that is the key to life. This is the
story of WALL-E and EVE. Their story is a microcosm to the
macrocosm of the universe. They represent the synergy in nature
between the masculine and feminine principles of energy. In
Kemet, to be closer to God meant to become a master of the laws
of how nature operates.*

Commentary:

As the Axiom lands, the captain is seen holding the plant in his left
hand.

Metaphysical Breakdown

*The left hand represents the higher or spiritual consciousness
held in the right hemisphere of the brain in man. This is the
consciousness from which man needs to operate to resurrect
himself from his destructive lower consciousness that destroyed
the Earth. The key for humans to start over is to switch from
being left brain dominant to right brain dominant.*

Commentary:

WALL-E's roach is reunited with WALL-E. They head to WALL-E's
house to replace his computer chip. WALL-E's right eye is damaged.

Metaphysical Breakdown

*WALL-E's right eye represents his lower or animalistic
consciousness. The right eye is activated by the left hemisphere
of his brain. This hemisphere of the brain is responsible for lower
level consciousness. In this case, the injury of WALL-E's right
eye represents his mortality in the physical form. WALL-E will
die unless he finds his appropriate and unique programming
known as his indigenous culture. WALL-E is reunited into his
higher consciousness symbolized by his roach which represents
the activation of his melanin which is needed to attain his higher
consciousness.*

DVD Chapter Thirty-One: Back Together (1:25:47)

Commentary:

The number of this chapter is thirty-one.

Metaphysical Breakdown

In numerology, the number thirteen stands for resurrection. Resurrection can be defined as "putting to death" lower consciousness in order for one's higher consciousness to be born again.

Commentary:

First thing EVE does to revive WALL-E is to prop him up with a red jack. The red jack was hidden behind several gnomes with pointed red hats.

Metaphysical Breakdown

WALL-E is going through the final stages of his initiation into higher consciousness. The color red, symbolizing man as a physical being or his lowest level of existence must be "raised" by the jack in order to achieve his higher, spiritual consciousness. The gnomes or "wizards" represent the initiators that are privy to this knowledge and guard it from the masses.

Commentary:

She then replaces his gears, his right arm and his eyes. EVE finds his computer chip and plugs it in. She then shoots a hole through the roof so that WALL-E can be recharged by the Sun.

Metaphysical Breakdown

Replacing his right arm symbolizes the physical resurrection of WALL-E's body. The computer chip represents WALL-E's, who represents the Black man, culture and worldview that was destroyed during slavery. WALL-E is then exposed to the Sun in order for his Pineal gland to be activated by producing melanin which is needed in order for the Black man to achieve higher, spiritual consciousness.

Commentary:

WALL-E is revived but does not recognize EVE. WALL-E continues to only do the things he was programmed to do. EVE is very sad and frustrated by WALL-E's inability to relate to her.

Metaphysical Breakdown

WALL-E has been disabled even though he has replaced all his parts. WALL-E is still missing the one thing that will revive him into his higher consciousness. The Black man can be given all the things he needs in order to be free, but if his mind is not right he will find a way to give up or ignore all the freedoms that he has access to. You cannot free the body unless you also free the mind.

Commentary:

As WALL-E leaves he accidently runs over his roach with his left wheel without any remorse.

Metaphysical Breakdown

This scene symbolizes WALL-E's inability to recognize his higher consciousness or acknowledge his melanin. He is oblivious to his higher, spiritual consciousness.

Commentary:

EVE stops WALL-E from doing what he is programmed to do. She tries his play button but his memory is erased. She holds and shakes his head but to no avail.

Metaphysical Breakdown

EVE and WALL-E represent the tragedy of the Middle Passage that the Black man and woman endured for over 400 years. The European erased the memory and culture of the Afrikan when they were forced into slavery. They replaced the Arfikan's worldview with a mindset of someone who was brainwashed into thinking they were less than human. This slave mentality is still prevalent today. The Black man and woman with no knowledge of self can never achieve their higher consciousness.

Commentary:

EVE takes WALL-E's left hand and inserts her hand inside his. She intertwines their fingers together.

Metaphysical Breakdown

The left hand activates the right hemisphere of the brain which is responsible for a person's higher consciousness. The intertwining of the fingers represents the two robots are engaging in sexual intercourse. Their union is being done in the mindset of higher consciousness.

Commentary:

EVE bends down to get closer to WALL-E. They foreheads touch which creates a spark.

Metaphysical Breakdown

Because EVE and WALL-E are engaged in sexual intercourse with the mindset of higher consciousness, they have the capability to "spark" their Pineal glands which produce the chemical melanin which is needed to achieve higher consciousness. Having access to this "gateway" is what sets the Black man and woman apart from people who do not have melanin. It is in this gateway where the Black man and woman can manifest the spiritual dimension into the physical realm.

417

Commentary:

WALL-E proceeds to tighten his grip of EVE's hand. His eyes are seen coming into focus. WALL-E finally recognizes EVE.

Metaphysical Breakdown

WALL-E has passed his initiation. He has been resurrected into his higher consciousness. EVE's belief and faith in her man has paid off. Without the Black woman's faith and commitment in resurrecting the Black man, he will never achieve his higher consciousness.

Commentary:

WALL-E then recognizes that they are holding hands. This gets WALL-E very excited!

Metaphysical Breakdown

WALL-E realizes that he is engaging in sexual intercourse with EVE. Because they are participating with the mind set of higher consciousness, they can manifest their thoughts and ideas into the physical dimension.

Commentary:

WALL-E's roach is seen going from EVE's right arm to WALL-E's left arm.

Metaphysical Breakdown

The roach representing WALL-E's melanin is seen going from EVE's lower consciousness and passed on to WALL-E's higher consciousness. This exchange is done through sexual intercourse. EVE, representing the Black woman, allows WALL-E access to her womb in order to open the "gateway." It is in this "gateway" that melanin used to create in the physical dimension.

Commentary:

The dysfunctional robots are seen in the background eavesdropping on the couple. MO chases everyone away so that they can be alone.

WALL-E and Eve are seen touching foreheads again.

Metaphysical Breakdown

MO chases the robots away because he recognizes that EVE and WALL-E are engaged in sexual intercourse. They are seen activating their Pineal glands which produce the melanin needed in order to achieve higher consciousness.

Commentary:

The camera shows the captain teaching the children how to farm. Last person we see is a Black baby watering the plant with a cup and a bent straw coming out of it.

Metaphysical Breakdown

The Black baby has the melanin to resurrect the Earth into higher consciousness. The Earth is represented by the plant. The straw represents the Black man's phallus and the water represents his seed.

Commentary:

SONG PLAYS: *"And that is all. That love's about. And we'll recall when time runs out ---Time is only a moment to be loved a whole life long."*

Metaphysical Breakdown

Love always endures and conquers time.

THE END.

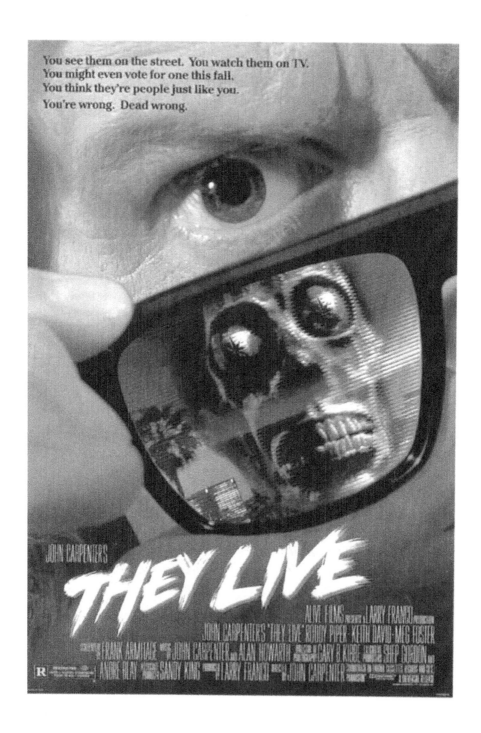

Contents

Main Character Assassinations

Director: John Carpenter (1988)

Nada –Played by Rowdy Roddy Piper of WWE professional wrestling fame. Nada in Spanish means nothing. This is relevant because this character has lost his job, his home and his family. All he has is his will to stand up for what is right and the courage not to compromise his self-worth. Nada also means Hope in Slavic and generosity in Arabic.

Frank- From a Germanic name which referred to a member of the Germanic tribe, the Franks. The Franks settled in the regions now called France and the Netherlands in the 3rd and 4th century. They derived their tribal name from the name of a type of spear that they used. From medieval times, the various forms of this name have been commonly conflated with the various forms of Francis. Frank is the side kick to Nada in their search for freedom. Frank is the muscle or the "spear" that Nada uses to pursue his freedom.

Black Street Preacher- The Black, street preacher is blind but he has knowledge beyond the masses of the common people. He knows about things that one cannot see, hear, touch taste or smell. He represents man with an activated Pineal Gland. The Pineal gland is called the "First Eye." It allows you to see the subliminal and intuitive realms that one cannot see with the common eye. The preacher "sees" the system for what it really is as the masses stumble in the dark, poor, unhappy and enslaved. The preacher has activated his Melanin and has achieved a level of higher consciousness.

Gilbert-Means "bright pledge", derived from the Germanic elements _gisil_ "pledge, hostage" and _beraht_ "bright". Gilbert represents the knowledge of the system that means to oppress and control the masses. He introduces Nada and Frank to the underground movement that is trying to free the people. He is the "bright" light at the end of the tunnel. He has made the "pledge" to sacrifice his life in pursuit of his freedom and he is the "hostage" to a system that means to enslave him.

Holly- Represents "Hollywood." She is the system that uses mind control, subliminal messages, lower level frequencies and manipulation to control the masses. She is the main villain to Nada and Frank even though she seems like she wants to help them fight for their freedom.

DVD Chapter 1: Looking for Work (0:00)

Commentary:

The movie opens with a shot of a wall full of graffiti. On the wall there is a white man spraying something out of a can with his left hand, in the middle of a city. In front of the spray can is a syringe and a circle that seems to spiral.

Metaphysical Blueprint

The large white man in the middle of the city represents the system of white supremacy. The spray can he is spraying represents the promotion of lower consciousness given to the masses to keep them oppressed. The fact that he is holding it in his left hand symbolizes his intention to poison or kill the people's higher consciousness. The left hand is activated by the right hemisphere of the brain. The right brain is responsible for an individual's higher, spiritual consciousness.

The syringe represents the system's use of drugs illegal and legal to keep the people in a state of dependence and lower consciousness. The spiral circle represents the hypnotic state that the people are in that the system promotes.

Commentary:

In the background, there are skyscrapers. On all their windows, there are window panes the resemble crosses. On the tallest skyscraper is a giant cross on top of its roof.

Metaphysical Blueprint

Windows in the occult symbolize entry and exit points for energy or consciousness. Religion, specifically Christianity, has been used to keep people at a lower state of consciousness by brainwashing the masses to look outside of themselves for higher consciousness. In this scene, the crosses placed in the windows, which represent Christianity, block the entry and exit points to the general population's higher consciousness. This is further stated by the largest cross being on top of the largest building in the mural. This cross dominates the whole scene.

Commentary:

Written in white in the far right-hand corner of the wall are the words, "White Boys."

Metaphysical Blueprint

These words resound as to who is responsible for this system of white supremacy.

Commentary:

Our main character, Nada is crossing some train tracks with a back pack on. A red train passes in front of him. Written in white on the train the viewer sees the words, "Shock Wave." There is also a white cross within a circle which is the Santa Fe logo.

Metaphysical Blueprint

Trains in occult movies always represent the current oppressive system that serves the elite, secret societies at the expense of the masses. Trains can only go from point A to point B. Because trains can only travel on the tracks laid out by the train masters, they may seem to be progressing as they move forward but the train is only allowed to go where their masters direct them to. So is the system that these secret societies have implemented today. They are the train masters that lay the tracks and the people are the trains that seem to be in motion or progressing but always wind up back where they started.

In Kemetic mythology, the colors red and white represent the god Heru. Heru is the ancient, Afrikan god that Christianity now calls Jesus Christ. Heru represents the higher consciousness in man called, "god consciousness" or "KRST" consciousness. Heru represents man's higher, spiritual self. Coincidently, Heru is also where we get the word Hero from.

By Nada "crossing" the train tracks with his belongings he symbolizes man going against the system that works to oppress him. Nada is a revolutionary. Nada is activating his higher consciousness by overcoming his fears and walking out on faith to manifest his freedom. According to this scene Nada will be the "Hero" of the film.

Commentary:

Nada is now seen walking the streets of the city. He stops to warm his hands. He rubs his left hand and proceeds to rub up his left arm. In the background across the street, on his left, is a red and white building.

Metaphysical Blueprint

The fact that Nada is concentrating on rubbing his left hand, symbolizes the activation of the right hemisphere of the brain. The right brain is responsible for his higher, spiritual consciousness.

Commentary:

Nada enters a social services building. A man in a wheelchair, who is missing his left leg, rolls right by him.

Metaphysical Blueprint

The man with no leg symbolizes the suppression of higher consciousness by the system of white supremacy. Not having a left leg symbolizes no activation of the right hemisphere of the brain, which contains his higher, spiritual consciousness. The man, who represents the masses, is relegated to living and interpreting his reality according to his lower consciousness housed in the left hemisphere of his brain.

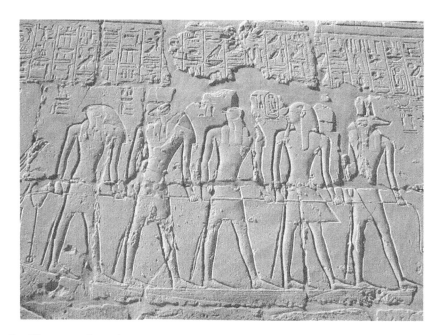

In Kemet, the characters on the temples and walls called Metu Neter, were depicted as walking with their left feet forward. This stance represented the activation of the character's higher, spiritual consciousness by the activation of the right hemisphere of the brain.

Commentary:

Nada is being interviewed by a social worker. He tells her that he is from Denver Colorado, "Worked there for ten years. They lost 14 banks in one week."

Metaphysical Blueprint

Let us breakdown the numerology. The number 10, the number 14 and the number 7 taken from the words, "one week." These numbers add up to the number 31. The number 31 can be interpreted as the number 13 by reversing the numbers. The number thirteen is the number of resurrection in Biblical numerology. It represents the killing of one's lower consciousness and the rebirth into his higher consciousness. This is a clue that our lead character, Nada, will go through this transformation in the movie.

426

Commentary:

Nada is seen walking down a sidewalk with his back pack. Behind him on the left side of the scene is a sign that reads "No right turn." A red and white truck pulls up to the light behind him.

Metaphysical Blueprint

Any movement from the right side of the body in the occult, symbolizes the activation of the left hemisphere of the brain, which symbolizes man's lower, animalistic consciousness. For Nada to transcend into his higher consciousness he must not make a "right turn."

The Kemetic, Afrikan god Heru symbolizes man's suppression of his lower, animalistic consciousness and his transformation into his higher, spiritual consciousness. He is represented by the colors red and white.

Commentary:

Nada runs into a blind Black man preaching to a crowd on the street. He says, "They use their tongue to deceive. The venom of snakes is under their lips. Their mouths are full of bitterness and curses and in their paths, nothing but ruin and misery. And the fear of God is not before their eyes!

Metaphysical Blueprint

The fact that the man is blind, symbolizes the activation of what is called the "first eye" otherwise known as the Pineal gland. Our eyes only see and interpret the physical realm. The physical realm is the lowest state of existence. The Pineal gland can interpret and decipher higher spiritual consciousness not recognized by our eyes. For one to communicate in the higher, spiritual realms, one must activate their Pineal glands, otherwise known by our Afrikan ancestors as the "First Eye."

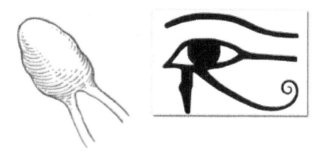

The picture on the left is an image of the pineal gland found in the center of one's brain. Its name comes from the gland resembling a Pine cone.

http://divinecosmos.com/index.php/videos/access-your-higher-self

The picture on the right is called the "Eye of Heru." It is symbolized by the left eye and represents the activation of the Pineal gland, otherwise known as the "first eye.".

The fact that the blind preacher is Black symbolizes the activation of his Melanin, which is needed to achieve higher consciousness. The chemical Melanin is produced by the activation of one's Pineal gland. People of Afrikan descent possess the most Melanin in their DNA. Thus, in the occult, they represent the standard for true universal law, understanding and higher spiritual consciousness in man.

The Black preacher's speech is talking about the elite, secret societies, who run the world behind the scenes. He refers to venom of snakes under their lips. In the occult, snakes represent the knowledge of unseen frequencies that can be used to control and manipulate human behavior. All energy moves in waves just like a snake moves.

In ancient mythology, specifically from Kemet, the snake represented the unseen, or enlightenment of the spiritual or unseen world. The snake moves just like invisible Inner G, in waves or spirals. When you see a snake slither in the sand, you can distinctively see the wave patterns he leaves behind. In the pictures above of King Tutankhamen and the Hindu goddess Shiva, show the cobra on their foreheads, symbolizing the activation of their Pineal glands.

The preacher talks about their tongues and mouths full of bitterness and curses. Words are nothing more than vibrations or frequencies. Words can be uplifting or they can destroy. These elite, secret society uses lower level vibrations and frequencies to destroy and suppress the masses in order to enslave them without them knowing they are slaves. These "unconsciousness slaves" will now view themselves and their environment according to their lower, animalistic consciousness.

FREQUENCIES OF HUMAN EMOTIONS

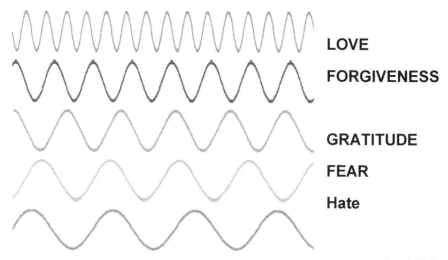

LOVE

FORGIVENESS

GRATITUDE

FEAR

Hate

Invisible frequencies can be used to manipulate human emotions and behavior. The image above shows the unseen vibrations and their perspective characteristics or influence they have on humans.

Commentary:

"They have taken the hearts and minds of our leaders. They have recruited the rich and the powerful, and they have blinded us to the truth! And our human spirit is corrupted."

Metaphysical Blueprint

In order for anyone to be in a position of power, wealth or influence, they must first be initiated into a secret society. No one can be in a position to receive, wealth, power or influence unless they have taken the oath to serve the elite secret societies that run the world. These initiate's allegiance will always be to the secret society and never to the masses that look up to them and think their leaders have their best interests in their hearts.

Commentary:

"Why do we worship greed? Because outside the limit of our sight, feeding off us, perched on top of us from birth to death......Are our owners. They have us. They control us. They are our masters. Wake up! They're all about you, all around you!"

Metaphysical Blueprint

This part of the speech is another example of the masses being forced to embrace their lower, animalistic consciousness by the ruling class, without them even knowing it. He have become so complacent in this system that we don't realize we are being manipulated and controlled by a powerful group of people that benefit from our lower, dysfunctional behavior.

Commentary:

The preacher's pages of his Bible are red and white.

Metaphysical Blueprint

The colors of red and white symbolize the Afrikan, Kemetic god Heru. He symbolizes the suppression of one's lower, animalistic consciousness and the rebirth in higher, spiritual consciousness. The Black, blind preacher is an example of this trait. That is why he has found out what the system represents and is not afraid to take action and expose it.

Commentary:

Next scene they show T.V.'s displayed in a store window. On the T.V. screens are scenes of Mount Rushmore, Native Americans, a rodeo scene and people playing basketball.

Metaphysical Blueprint

Mount Rushmore represents the "founding fathers" who established this secret system of white supremacy to serve wealthy, white men.

Native Americans represent the people they murdered, raped and pillaged to retain this stolen land.

The rodeo scene represents the breaking or domestication of a race of people in order to serve under another race of people.

The basketball scene represents the favorite game people of Afrikan descent dominate. It gives a clue as to who the race of people the white man destroyed mentally, spiritually and physically in order to enslave him for his own purposes and selfish gains.

Commentary:

The T.V. channel is number 54. There is a Black man standing in front of the T.V.'s. He seems to be in a hypnotic state. He is oblivious to his surroundings.

Metaphysical Blueprint

In numerology the number 54 breaks down to the number nine. The number nine symbolizes man's judgment or test he must pass in order to achieve higher consciousness. A Black man is seen being brainwashed by the frequencies the television is giving off. This scene sheds light on the fact that the underlining theme of this movie is really about the Black man overcoming his lower, animalistic consciousness and transcending into his higher, spiritual consciousness. All Hollywood movies at their source are about the historical resurrection of the Black man.

Commentary:

Next scene we see a lady in a red dress on T.V. She says." I stop being myself, and I'm a star of a series....... all I have to do is be famous. People watch me, and they love me. And I never, never grow old and I never die."

The red dress represents the root chakra which houses the lowest, animalistic consciousness in man. This can be defined as operating according to satisfying one's ego. It represents man's innate instinct of self-survival by any means necessary. Hollywood brainwashes people into suppressing their higher self and embracing a definition outside of themselves that the system can control and manipulate.

DVD Chapter 2: Hard Times (5:57)

Commentary:

Nada is seen looking for work at a construction site. He meets a Black man wearing a purple tank top named Frank.

Metaphysical Blueprint

The color purple represents a person's highest consciousness located in the seventh chakra. It is the crown chakra located right above the head. It represents a person who has mastered their lower self and has achieved higher, spiritual consciousness. This ancient science comes from Afrika. It was deciphered and mastered by the Black man. This Black character represents this scientific concept in the movie.

Commentary:

Working behind Frank, is a man wearing a red hard hat and a white tank top.

Metaphysical Blueprint

The colors red and white represent the Kemetic, Afrikan god named Heru. He symbolizes man's higher self by overcoming their lower consciousness. This adds to the color purple symbol worn by the Black man and points to his true identity.

Commentary:

Frank offers Nada shelter and food. Nada declines but insists on following Frank to his place of residence.

Metaphysical Blueprint

This scene shows the relationship between people of Eurpean descent and their dealings with people of Afrikan descent. The Caucasian maintains an ego and a feeling of superiority that keeps him from letting a Black man lead him. The Caucasian always feels that he is more intelligent and refuses to believe that a Black man will ever know more than he does. This is why Nada is reluctant to believe or follow Frank.

Commentary:

Frank tells Nada that he hasn't seen his wife and kids in six months.

Metaphysical Blueprint

In numerology, the number six represents the lower self or animalistic level in man. Because Frank is just trying to survive, this is an attribute of Frank being forced to operate according to his lower self. When you are struggling to maintain the basic necessities of life such as, food, shelter and clothing, you cannot achieve higher consciousness. This is part of the strategy of white supremacy reinforced by the secret, ruling class of elites.

Commentary:

Nada tells Frank that he ought to have a little more patience in life. Frank responds, "Yeah, well I'm fresh out."

Metaphysical Blueprint

Nada being white, still believes in the system of white supremacy because he benefits from it. Frank has no allegiance to a system that was designed to oppress him.

Commentary:

Frank says, "They put you at the starting line and the name of the game is, "Make it Through Life." Only everyone's out for themselves and lookin' to do you in at the same time. Okay man here we are. Here we are. Now you do what you can, but remember, I'm gonna do my best to blow your ass away."

Metaphysical Blueprint

To participate and succeed in this system, one has to embrace their lower consciousness of self-survival and a "me against the world" attitude. Frank does not want to participate in it anymore because it does not make sense to a person who has discovered their higher consciousness.

Commentary:

Nada replies," I believe in America. I follow the rules."

Metaphysical Blueprint

Nada, because he is white, believes in the system of white supremacy because he has benefited from it.

DVD Chapter 3: Subliminal Signal (11:37)

Commentary:

The T.V. signal is hacked. The T.V. is on channel three. The man on the T.V. says, "Our impulses are being redirected. We are living in an artificially induced state of consciousness that resembles sleep. The poor and the underclass are growing. Racial justice and human rights are non-existent. They have created a repressed society, and we are their unwitting accomplices. Their intention to rule rests with the annihilation of consciousness. We have been lulled into a trance. They have made us indifferent to ourselves and to others. We are focused on only on our own gain."

Metaphysical Blueprint

In numerology, the number three represents divine perfection. Being able to see the hackers' signal represents the completion into achieving higher consciousness. The simple fact that one can see the hacker's broadcast reinforces the idea that they have achieved divine perfection.

The hacker's statement reinforces the idea of a secret plan or system that has been implementated to keep the masses at a lower level of consciousness in order for them to be manipulated and controlled by an elite, ruling class or organization. This system is called white supremacy.

Commentary:

Man on T.V. continues, "Please understand. They are safe as long as they are not discovered. That is their primary method of survival. Keep us asleep. Keep us selfish. Keep us sedated."

Metaphysical Blueprint

This scene is further evidence of an esoteric system that has been unleashed on the masses to keep them in a lower state of consciousness in order to manipulate and control them.

Commentary:

The people watching the T.V. broadcast all develop severe headaches.

Metaphysical Blueprint

The headaches stem from the lack of activity of the people's higher consciousness. The people are not used to operating at a higher state of consciousness so this causes them pain and discomfort in their heads. The people are waking up. This is evidenced by them being able to decipher the hacker's broadcast.

Commentary:

Next scene the viewer sees two, giant rock like pillars falling on two houses.

Metaphysical Blueprint

I believe this scene is a precursor to the tragedy of the twin towers falling on 9-11- 2001. Although this movie was released in 1988, I believe the 9-11 attacks were planned out by this elite, secret society many years before to exploit the people's reaction to such a tragedy. This was planned in order to usher in new laws and new fears to further carry out their hidden agenda.

Commentary:

Nada witnesses the blind, Black preacher going into a church across the street. The church has green windows as well as green trim painted on the outside. The church is named "African Episcipal Free Church."

Metaphysical Blueprint

The color green, represents the heart chakra. It is the first level of higher consciousness. It is in this church where the people are aware of the oppressive system. This church, which represents the heart, is the headquarters for the movement that wants to destroy the system that operates in a lower state of consciousness.

The church's name signifies what the masses need to embrace in order to free themselves from the chains of lower level consciousness. The ancient Kemetic science was born out of Afrika. Its concepts are the keys to freedom.

DVD Chapter 4: They Live, We Sleep (14:37)

Commentary:

The church's roof is painted red and its walls are white.

Metaphysical Blueprint

The colors red and white represent the ancient Kemetic, Afrikan god Heru. Heru represents man overcoming his lower, animalistic consciousness and transcending into his higher self. It is in the confines of the church that the freedom fighters call their headquarters.

The Kemetic god Heru. Depicted with a falcon head and the red and white crown on his head. It is where we get the word "Hero" from.

Commentary:

The hacker on T.V. appears again. He says, "They are dismantling the sleeping middle class. More and more people are becoming poor. We are cattle. We are being bred for slavery."

Metaphysical Blueprint

The elite, secret societies that run and control the world view the masses as cattle or sheep. The people are there to serve their benefit only. There is no ot humane attachment or regard to the suffering and misery of billons of people throughout the world so that a handful of ruling families can live in excess and gluttony.

One of their main objectives or strategies is to destroy the middle class. Without a middle class there would be no distinction between the "haves" and the "have nots." The ruling class needs the illusion of a middle class so that people will actually think that all individuals no matter what their backgrounds are, can have the American dream. The so-called middle class acts like a buffer between the rich and the poor.

Commentary:

While watching the T.V. signal, a girl tells her father that she is getting a headache. The father responds that he is also getting a headache. Channel 54 appears on the T.V. screen.

Metaphysical Blueprint

Because the masses live in a state of lower level consciousness, when they raise their consciousness they become uncomfortable and agitated mentally. This is displayed by the daughter and father developing headaches. They are waking up to their higher consciousness by using parts of their brain that were otherwise asleep.

In numerology, the number 54 breaks down to the number nine. The number nine represents man's judgment when he is put into an awkward or compromising position. The number nine in this scene refers to man's obligation to embrace the truth once it is revealed to him. If man refuses to acknowledge the truth and do the right thing, he will be stuck in lower level consciousness until he passes the test.

Commentary:

Nada sneaks into the church. The walls of the room are green. He sees, "They Live, We Sleep" painted on the wall.

Metaphysical Blueprint

The color green represents the heart chakra. It is the first level to higher consciousness. One should think with their heart and feel with their minds. Man will be judged by what he holds in his heart. In this scene, freedom and destroying a system that enslaves people is in the hearts of the underground freedom fighters.

Commentary:

There is a tape recording of a choir singing. The church is not real.

Metaphysical Blueprint

The church is just a front for our freedom fighters. True Christians are led astray and are brainwashed to go against the teachings of he character Jesus Christ. Jesus Christ was a revolutionary. Who went up against a system that enslaved the people. He later gave his life fighting for a cause greater than himself. Today the church has been coerced not to preach this revolutionary message of the Bible.

Commentary:

Gilbert tells his colleagues, "Manufacturing Hoffman lenses till we're blue in the face?"

Metaphysical Blueprint

The name Hoffman is derived from the German word "hof" meaning settlement or farm and "man." The name may originally meant someone who owned their own land opposed to working someone elses land.....<u>http://www.houseofnames.com/hoffman-family-crest</u>

This name they chose for the lenses that allow people to see the system for what it is is very significant. It suggests that true ownership is the basis for freedom. In this system in America true ownership of self, land, property or commerce is just an illusion. Ownership is not allowed in this system, just the appearance of ownership.

Commentary:

The Black, blind preacher confronts Nada. He says, "This world may have blinded me, but the Lord has let me see."

Metaphysical Blueprint

In order for man to achieve higher consciousness by opening up his Pineal gland, otherwise known as the "first eye," he must overcome his lower, physical self. This allows him to truly "see" in the higher, spiritual dimension. This is shown by the Black man relying on his intuition and his clairvoyance to see and not his physical eyes.

Commentary:

Gilbert speaks to people in the camp about the end of the world cults. He says, "You want to know the truth? This kind of shit happens at the end of every century. It does it's just people afraid to face the future. That's all it is."

Metaphysical Blueprint

With every season, year, century and great year, there is a change of consciousness. Like the changing of the seasons, there is a time and place that is conducive for change according to the time. Since the masses are taught to listen, trust and obey their secret masters, they are not conscious of the subtle changes and the ebb and flow of the universe. Their behavior is controlled by fear instilled on them from their masters. The people are moved to act according to their fear and not the natural order of things. Thus, the people embrace their fear when a different consciousness is naturally introduced. The people are conditioned to dislike and avoid change.

DVD Chapter 5: Police Brutality (22:15)

Commentary

The homeless camp is called, "Justiceville." The police demolish it.

:Metaphysical Blueprint

The place of residence our freedom fighters call home is a place where they share all their resources and they all contribute whatever they can. No one is considered more valuable than the other. This is how humans are supposed to live. This camp is the definition of justice and higher consciousness.

Commentary:

The Black, blind preacher is being beaten by the police. He quotes a Bible scripture, "My rod and my staff will comfort me......." The preacher yells out, "Jesus! Jesus!" There is a red light that dominates the scene.

Metaphysical Blueprint

The Biblical reference to the staff and rod goes back to the ancient Kemetic civilization in Afrika. There is a pose where the pharoahs hold a "crook and flail" close to their chest in the formation of an "X." The formation of the "X" is a sign of resurrection.

As we alluded to earlier in the book, the character of Jesus in the Bible was taken after the Afrikan, Kemetic god Heru. Heru represented the higher, spiritual, consciousness in man. The word "hero" comes from the name "Heru."

Kemetic God Heru the KRST vs. Christianity's Jesus

Event	Heru (Horus) circa 3200 BCE (before christian era)	Jesus of Nazareth circa 1 ACE (after christian era)
Conception:	By a virgin.	By a virgin
Father:	Only begotten son of Ausar	Only begotten son of God (in the form of the Holy Spirit)
Mother:	Heru had 2 motherz: Aset (Isis) who gave birth and Nephthys, who nursed him	Jesus had 2 motherz: Mary (aka Miriam) the Virgin who gave birth and Mary the wife of Cleophas raised him

446

Foster father:	Seb, (Jo-Seph)	Joseph
Foster father's ancestry:	Of royal descent	Of royal descent
Birth location:	In a cave	In a cave or stable
Annunciation:	By an angel to Aset	By an angel to Mary
Birth heralded by:	The star Sirius, the morning star	An unidentified "*star in the East*"
Birth date:	Ancient people of Kemet (Egyptianz) paraded a manger and child representing Heru through the streets at the time of the winter solstice (typically Dec. 21)	Celebrated on Dec. 25. The date was chosen to occur on the same date as the birth of Mithra, Dionysus and the Sol Invictus (unconquerable Sun), etc
Birth announcement:	By angelz	By angelz
Birth witnesses:	Shepherdz	Shepherdz
Later witnesses to birth:	Three solar deities	Three wise men
Death threat during infancy:	Seth tried to have Heru murdered	Herod tried to have Jesus murdered
Handling the threat:	The God *That* tells Heru's mother "*Come, thou goddess Isis, hide thyself with thy child.*"	An angel tells Jesus' father to: "*Arise and take the young child and his mother and flee into Egypt.*"

Rite of passage ritual:	Heru came of age with a special ritual, when his eye was restored	Taken by parents to the temple for what is today called a bar mitzvah ritual
Age at the ritual:	12	12
Break in life history:	No data between ages of 12 & 30	No data between ages of 12 & 30
Baptism location:	In the river Eridanus	In the river Jordan
Age at baptism:	30	30
Baptized by:	Anup the Baptiser	John the Baptist
Subsequent fate of the baptiser:	Beheaded	Beheaded
Temptation:	Taken from the desert of Amenta up a high mountain by his arch-rival Sut. Sut (a.k.a. Set) was a precursor for the Hebrew Satan	Taken from the desert in Palestine up a high mountain by his arch-rival Satan
Result of temptation:	Heru resists temptation	Jesus resists temptation
Close followers:	Twelve disciples. There is some doubt about this matter as well	Twelve disciples

Activities:	Walked on water, cast out demons, healed the sick, restored sight to the blind. He "stilled the sea by his power."	Walked on water, cast out demons, healed the sick, restored sight to the blind. He ordered the sea with a "Peace, be still" command
Raising of the dead:	Heru raised Ausar, his dead father, from the grave	Jesus raised Lazarus from the grave
Location where the resurrection miracle occurred:	Anu, an Egyptian city where the rites of the death, burial and resurrection of Heru were enacted annually	Hebrews added their prefix for house ('beth') to "Anu" to produce "Beth-Anu" or the "House of Anu." Since "u" and "y" were interchangeable in antiquity, "Bethanu" became "Bethany," the location mentioned in John 11
Origin of Lazarus' name in the Gospel of John:		

-taken from the website www.daghettotymes.com

The right light in the background represents the root chakra. It symbolizes the beast or animal in man. This behavior is exemplified by to police's brutality executed on innocent people.

449

Commentary:

Nada finds refuge inside an abandoned building where a Black junkie resides. There is also another white family taking refuge in the Black man's residence. The Black man tells them, "Come on in and join the party." He also asks, "Did somebody start World War III?"

Metaphysical Blueprint

Homeless people and drug abusers are the first people to reject this system and try to find other means to change their reality. Both of these types of people refuse to accept the system or the reality that has been forced on them. When the system falls with the ushering in of higher consciousness, the last shall be first and the first shall be last. This is demonstrated by the white family finding refuge in the abandoned building that a Black drug abuser calls home.

Commentary:

Nada is seen walking down an alley with a box he found inside the church. Behind him in the background is a "One Way" sign pointing to the left.

Metaphysical Blueprint

The "One Way" sign pointing to the left, symbolizes the activation of the right hemisphere of the brain which contains man's higher spiritual consciousness. The right brain is activated by the left side of the body. That is why the "One Way" sign is pointing in the direction to the left. It si the path to higher, spiritual consciousness.

Commentary:

Nada put on the sunglasses found inside the box. He is now able to see and hear secret, subliminal messages used to brainwash and keep the masses asleep without them detecting it.

Metaphysical Blueprint

The sunglasses represent the activation of one's Pineal gland. The black color of the sunglasses represents the chemical Melanin produced by the Pineal gland or the "first eye" which is needed in order to achieve higher consciousness. Black sunglasses are also used in the Matrix trilogy movies to represent the same concept. One must activate their Pineal gland in order to see reality for what it really is.

DVD Chapter 6: Hidden World (29:11)

Commentary:

Nada opens the box from the church. He kneels down on his right knee and has his left knee off the ground.

Metaphysical Blueprint

The position of the left knee up and the right knee on the ground symbolizes Nada's transformation into higher, spiritual consciousness. The left knee being up symbloizes the activation of the right hemisphere of the brain which contains his higher self. The right knee being down or on the ground, suppresses the left hemisphere of the brain which is responsible for his lower self. Nada is about to see the world according to his higher consciousness.

Commentary:

Nada starts to walk down the sidewalk. Just before he is about to put on the sunglasses held in his left hand, a lady with a red and white bag walks by him on his left side.

Metaphysical Blueprint

Nada holds the sunglasses in his left hand to symbolize the activation of his higher consciousness held in the right hemisphere of his brain.

The colors red and black symbolize the Afrikan, Kemetic god Heru. Heru represents the supression of man's lower self and the activation of his higher self. This is the initiation into higher consciousness by Nada.

Commentary:

Nada puts on the sunglasses found inside the box. He is now able to see and hear secret, subliminal messages used to brainwash and keep the masses asleep without them detecting it.

Metaphysical Blueprint

Nada's Pineal gland is activated and is producing Melanin. He sees and interprets his reality according to his higher consciousness.

Commentary:

While looking at all the billboards and signs subliminal messages, there is a traffic sign behind Nada's left shoulder that says "Left Turn Only."

Metaphysical Blueprint

Another sign symbolizing the activation of the right hemisphere of the brain which contains Nada's higher consciousness. Moving to the left or using the left side of one's body, activates the right hemisphere of the brain.

Commentary:

As Nada approaches a magazine stand, a man in a Civil War, Conferderate hat walks right in front of him.

Metaphysical Blueprint

This man is another subtle sign of the true identity of Nada. Nada is an example of the Afrikan, Kemetic science in action. Nada is a Black man that is trying to be resurrected into his higher self. The Civil War represents the era of the lowest state of consciousness that the Black man has ever fallen to in the history of the world.

Commentary:

As Nada stops at a magazine rack to look at all the magazines, behind his left side are three books titled; "Edgar Cayce ESP," "Two of a Kind the Hillside Strangler" and "The Bermuda Triangle."

Metaphysical Blueprint

Edgar Cayce is considered the greatest prophet in American history. He is an example of activating one's clairvoyance, imagination and intuition at the highest level. All these traits are properties of the activation of the right hemisphere of the brain, which is responsible for one's higher, spiritual consciousness. This is where Nada views his reality.

The book about the Hillside Strangler represents the duality of man. Man has the freewill of embracing his higher self or lower self. Bianchi, one of the murderers, attempted to set up an insanity defense, claiming he had a personality disorder, and a separate personality from himself committed the murders. This is an example of the duality of man and the constant struggle between the lower and higher self.

The book on the Bermuda Triangle symbolizes the unseen, universal forces that effect ourselves and our environment. The ruling, elite class uses these unseen forces to manipulate and control man's behavior without them knowing it.

Commentary:

Nada can also see these hideous alien creatures that walk around disguised as humans.

Metaphysical Blueprint

These creatures represent the ruling elite that run the world in the shadows. They have no allegiance to anything but the power of their secret organizations that is passed down from generation to generation. They subject the common people to needless pain, suffering, disease, poverty, starvation, illiteracy and hopelessness. They have no conscience or morals and values. They are heartless and ruthless because of their greed and gluttony. They are the hideous beasts or aliens that are portrayed in the movie. One could not be human and think and act the way these people do

Commentary:

Also on the magazine rack, on the right side of Nada, is a GOLF magazine. On its cover it says, "LET TV TEACH YOU."

Metaphysical Blueprint

T.V. programs brainwash the audience into adopting and embracing lower level consciousness. The T.V. is the number one weapon of the elite ruling class. Its unsuspecting targets are the general population, particularly the youth.

Commentary:

The subliminal messages he can read are as follows: Obey, No Independent Thought, Conform, Sleep, Marry & Reproduce, Consume, Submit, Watch T.V., Buy, Work 8 Hours, Sleep 8 Hours, Play 8 Hours, Surrender, Follow, No Ideas, Honor Apathy, Doubt Humanity, No Imagination, Do Not Question Authority. On paper money held by the Black proprietor it says, "This Is Your God."

Metaphysical Blueprint

These are all tools and ideologies to keep the masses asleep in their lower state of consciousness.

Commentary:

Nada can also detect sounds from secret, hidden satellites that repeat, "Sleep. Sleep. Sleep."

Metaphysical Blueprint

Since Nada has activated his higher consciousness, he can detect unseen universal forces that can affect his behavior without him even knowing it.

Commentary:

Nada walks into a grocery store. Inside he sees a politician on T.V. There is a banner behind him that reads, "OBEY." The politician is giving a speech. He says, "The old cynicism is gone. We have faith on our leaders. We're optimistic as to what becomes of it all. It really boils down to our ability to accept. We don't need pessimism. There are no limits. Our ideals. A vision. We don't just want to survive."

Metaphysical Blueprint

All politicians are puppets to the secret societies they have allegiance to. Whether a politician is Democrat or Republican, they all serve secret societies at the expense of the common people. Do not be fooled! It's time to wake up!

DVD Chapter 7: One That Can See (38:01)

Commentary:

The cops push Nada into an alley to arrest him. There is a sign in the background, behind the police that says, "No left Turn."

Metaphysical Blueprint

This sign points to the prohibition of higher consciousness amongst the people, by the ruling class. The right hemisphere of the brain which contains a person's higher consciousness is activated by the left side of the body. This is why Nada is being arrested. He has activated his higher consciousness. He has made the "left turn."

Commentary:

An alien in the bank escapes Nada by using a portal that is opened by the activation of his wrist watch.

Metaphysical Blueprint

The aliens escape by dropping into a hole. This image shows their conscious level. To escape detection, they fall further into a lower state of consciousness. This is exemplified by dropping through the hole sinking even further down in lower consciousness.

DVD Chapter 8: Hostage Situation (43:12)

Commentary:

Nada takes a hostage to help him escape. Her name is Holly Thompson.

Metaphysical Blueprint

The name Holly represents Hollywood. The last name Thompson means twin. Every person is born of a higher self and lower self. Man has the freewill to define himself from which ever level he chooses. Hollywood knows this science and uses it to coerce man into embracing his lower consciousness. From this lower level, the secret societies can easily manipulate and control the masses according to their will. Holly Thompson is not a good person.

Commentary:

Nada comments after taking off the sunglasses, "It's like a drug. Wearing these glasses makes you high, but oh you come down hard."

Metaphysical Blueprint

Nada is referring coming down from a higher state of consciousness to a lower state when he takes off his glasses.

DVD Chapter 9: See For Yourself (47:22)

Commentary:

Nada finds himself in hiding. He finds a alley to sleep in. He crosses his hands over his chest in the shape of an "X." His left hand is closer to his heart.

Metaphysical Blueprint

In ancient Kemet, the symbol of the "X" represented resurrection. In this scene, Nada is going through the initiation of putting to death his lower consciousness so that his higher consciousness can be reborn.

Commentary:

In the alley, the viewer can make out at least six pyramid shape shadows.

Metaphysical Blueprint

In numerology, the number six represents the lowest consciousness in man. In this scene it represents the death of Nada's lower self.

The pyramids represent the Afrikan land of Kemet where this knowledge and science originated from.

DVD Chapter 10: Leave Me Alone (52:19)

Commentary:

Nada is seen walking back to the city. He must cross a bridge to get back.

Metaphysical Blueprint

A bridge in the occult, represents the passing or the initiation into a higher degree or level. Nada has been initiated into higher consciousness.

Commentary:

Frank is now seen wearing a purple sweatshirt.

Metaphysical Blueprint

Frank representing the Black man, wears purple to symbolize his potential to achieve the highest consciousness in man. Purple represents the crown chakra. This concentration of energy is located right above a person's head. It symbolizes the highest conscious level in man once he is able to master his lower, physical self. People of Afrikan desent carry the most Melanin in their DNA. The chemical Melanin is mandatory for an individual to achieve higher, spiritual consciousness.

Commentary:

Nada calls out to Frank. In the background is a red container with white graffiti that says, "XV 3's."

Metaphysical Blueprint

The colors of red and white represent the Afrikan, Kemetic god Heru. Heru is a symbol of higher consciousness that man has the ability to transcend to.

460

In numerology, the letters "X" and "V" and the number 3 break down to the number 94. Ninety-four is broken down to the number thirteen. The number thirteen represents the concept of resurrection. It signifies the death of the lower self and the rebirth of the higher self in man. This is the level where Nada is now operating at.

Commentary:

Nada leaves Frank. He walks by a store window displaying T.V.'s. They all have is wanted picture on their screens. A price tag to one of the T.V.'s is $339.00.

Metaphysical Blueprint

In numerology, the number 339 breaks down to the number 6. The number six represents man's lowest, animalistic consciousness. This is the level the ruling class wants the masses to define and interpret Nada through the television. Nada is demonized through the media to ostracize and neutralize his influence on the people.

Commentary:

Nada goes back to retrieve the box of sunglasses he stashed away in the garbage. A Black garbage man is seen getting back into his garbage truck after he has collected the garbage. The number of the truck is 295.

Metaphysical Blueprint

In numerology, the number 295 breaks down to the number seven. Seven represents divine completion. Nada has came from the garbage or lower level of consciousness

DVD Chapter 11: Let Me Show You (55:19)

Commentary:

This next scene is one of the all-time best fight scenes in Hollywood film history. Frank refuses to put on the sunglasses until Nada beats him to a pulp and forces him to.

Metaphysical Blueprint

Because of the slave history of Black people, they have been conditioned and brainwashed into operating at the lowest level of consciousness. Black people were taught to hate themselves and to always be dependent on white people to give them the answers to their problems. Black people were conditioned to define themselves by the worst in them or their lower, animalistic consciousness. They were never allowed to internalize or even believe that they were even capable of higher consciousness. Because of this, Black people have a very difficult time in believing in the best in themselves or each other. It is much harder for Black people to reach higher, spiritual consciousness because of the continuous conspiracy to keep them at this lower, animalistic state. The ruling class benefits from Black people's insecurities, low self-esteem, animalistic behavior and fears. As long as they remain asleep, they are more easier to rob, exploit, enslave, steal, manipulate,abuse, slaughter and kill.

In this scene, this is why Frank, who represents the Black race, refuses to operate at his higher consciousness, by refusing to put on the sunglasses. He has been conditioned not to see the best in himself or his environment.

DVD Chapter 12: What Are We Gonna Do? (1:00:57)

Commentary:

Frank is finally forced by Nada to put on the sunglasses. Frank can now see all the subliminal messages around them. Nada tells him, "You aint the first son of a bitch to wake up outta there dream."

Metaphysical Blueprint

Finally, Frank transcends into higher consciousness, represented by putting on the sunglasses. The sunglasses represent the activation of the "first eye" or the Pineal gland that produces a chemical called Melanin, which is needed in order to transcend into higher consciousness.

Commentary:

Two aliens spot them in the alley. They say, "I don't know. Maybe they can see. Alley—Fifth and Spring."

Metaphysical Blueprint

In numerology, the number five represents God's grace or God's satisfaction in your undertaking. This is a symbol of Nada's and Frank's transformation into higher, spiritual consciousness.

The word, spring represents the concept of water. In the occult, one needs water in order to bring new life or consciousness into existence. A prime example of this concept is the baptismal or christening ritual.

Commentary:

As Frank and Nada are walking to the hotel, Frank rubs his left arm. It seems to be sore from their fight.

Metaphysical Blueprint

Frank rubbing his left arm symbolizes the activation of the right hemisphere of his brain, which is responsible for his higher, spiritual consciousness. The left side of the body activates the right hemisphere of the brain.

Commentary:

This next scene is very intriguing. As our two combatants enter a hotel, the viewer can see on the left side a T.V. showing some type of UFO footage. As Nada passes by, he points to his left shirt pocket suggesting some sort of secret hand sign or gesture. Just as he points to the pocket, on the T.V. the viewer can see some sort of comet or meteor flashing across the scene.

While this is going on, Frank walks up to a man that he is passing. Frank seems very surprised and startled by the man's presence.

Metaphysical Blueprint

I believe there is a lot going on in this scene. From UFO footage, to aliens living among us, to secret hand gestures that expose the truth. If somebody has any insight to any of these images and symbols please contact me so that I can share with them with our fellow code crackers. Thank you. I can be reached by E-mail: notsocommonscents@email.com

Commentary:

As the two approach the hotel front desk, the viewer will notice a calendar on the left side of the two. It is full of red "X's" marked in white boxes.

Metaphysical Blueprint

The symbol of the "X" in ancient Kemet represented the concept of resurrection. The process of killing one's lower self in order to be reborn into their higher, spiritual consciousness.

The Kemetic god, Ausar on the far right. He was the god of resurrection, symbolized by the "X" on his torso.

The colors of red and white, represent the Kemetic god Heru, who symbolizes man activated according to his higher consciousness.

Commentary:

Their room number is 202. The room across from them is #242.

Metaphysical Blueprint

In numerology, these numbers breakdown to the number 12. The number twelve represents completion. In this scene it represents the completion of Nada and Frank's transformation into higher consciousness.

Commentary:

There is a quick flash showing a street scene. A sign flashes 9:41 and then displays 70 degrees.

Metaphysical Blueprint

In numerology, these numbers add up to the number two. The number two represents division or separation. In this scene it represents Nada and Frank's separation from their lower self and the introduction into their higher consciousness.

Commentary:

Frank and Nada start to have a conversation. Frank tells Nada, "Maybe they love it. Seeing us hate each other. Watching us kill each other off, feeding on our own cold, fuckin hearts."

Metaphysical Blueprint

This is another admission into the underlying workings of the system implementated by the ruling elite on the unsuspecting masses to keep them oppressed.

DVD Chapter 13: A Wake Up Call (1:06:26)

Commentary:

Gilbert tracks Nada and Frank down at the hotel room. He tells them there is a meeting at 11:00. He tells them, "The world needs a wakeup call. We are going to phone it in."

Metaphysical Blueprint

In numerology, the number eleven represents man looking himself in the mirror. This happens in one's moment of truth. It is represented as a defining moment in one's life to reflect what a man is made out of. It is the test of a man's intestinal fortitude. This meeting or "wake up call," is Nada and Frank's defining moment.

Commentary:

Frank and Nada enter the room to go to the secret meeting. There is graffiti on the green wall on the left side. It says "93C." It is in the shape of and upside down triangle.

Metaphysical Blueprint

In numerology, these numbers and letter add up to the number six. The number six represent the beast in man. This is a precursor to violence and murder being portrayed in this scene.

The color green represents the heart chakra. All freedom fighters must display character, self-sacrfice and courage in their hearts to stand for what is right and just.

In the occult, the upside down triangle represents the feminine principle or higher, spiritual consciousness. This is what must be internalized in order to overturn corruption and injustice.

Commentary:

Frank and Nada take off their sunglasses. They rub the bridge of their noses after they take them off. They seem to be discombobulated.

Metaphysical Blueprint

Their sunglasses represent the activation of their Pineal gland which produces the chemical Melanin which is needed to transcend into higher consciousness. The Pineal gland is located on the forehead between the eyes. This is why our heroes keep rubbing this area of their forehead when they take off their sunglasses.

Commentary:

The viewer can hear the television in the background. "There is a signal broadcast from our television sets every day. Even when the television is turned off."

Metaphysical Blueprint

This is another clue of fiction portraying real life. All of our electronics and computer systems have an effect on our consciousness. From cell phones, GPS systems, microwaves, flat screen T.V.'s to computers and video games, all can be used to suppress one's higher consciousness

Commentary:

"All we really are is livestock.

Metaphysical Blueprint

This is how the secret, elite ruling class view the masses. They call the common people, "sheeple." We are viewed as sheep to them being led to slaughter. All they have to do is control the one sheep that leads the flock and the rest of the sheep will follow with blind allegiance.

Commentary:

A Black man has figured out that the aliens wrist watches are used as escape mechanisms. He gives the watch to Frank, another Black man, to fix it.

Metaphysical Blueprint

This scene represents an esoteric concept of higher spiritual consciousness, science and law coming from the ancient, Afrikan civilization called Kemet. This knowledge was orginated and perfected by the Black man. That is why this scene shows two Black men figuring out the science of the aliens technology. These aliens, who represent the secret societies that rule the world in the shadows, now use this Afrikan knowledge and science to oppress and enslave the common people.

DVD Chapter 14: Locate the Transmitter (1:12:09)

[NO SIGNS OR SYMBOLS.]

DVD Chapter 15: Back Stage (1:17:57)

Commentary:

A man is giving a speech in a banquet room in the underground alien base. He says, "Our projections show by the year 2025, not only America, but the entire planet, will be under the protection and dominion of this power alliance. The gains have been substantial, both for ourselves and for you, the human power elite. You have given us entrée to the resources that we need in our ongoing quest for multidimensional expansion. And in return, the per capita income of each one of you here tonight has grown in this year alone by an average of 39%!"

Metaphysical Blueprint

This speech given by the secret, ruling elite gives further evidence to the system that makes the common people of the world the slaves to the power structure. In order for them to keep their power and wealth, they must make sure the masses never wake up to the fact that they are being used for the benefit of a and full of families that rule the world in secrecy.

In numerology the number 39 breaks down to the number 12. The number twelve represents the concept of completion. In this scene, it represents the completion of the ruling classes' implementation of a system that oppresses the people without them being aware of the enslavement.

Commentary:

Gilbert, from the homeless camp, volunteers to give Nada and Frank a tour. Just before he leaves, he gives a waiter his champagne glass. On the waiter's jacket, there is a logo that resembles the Freemasonry symbol.

Metaphysical Blueprint

Look closely at this scene when the waiter passes by after receiving the champagne glass from Gilbert. The logo on his

471

jacket is very familiar to the Freemasonry logo below. This secret society actually has another secret society in its organization that is not known by the uninitiated Freemasons. This secret society is called the Illuminati. They are protected within the confines of the secret Freemason organization. They are one of the organizations that rule the world in secrecy. This scene exposes who is behind these secret organizations.

DVD Chapter 16: Technical Difficulties (1:21:33)

Commentary :

Gilbert shows Nada and Frank where the aliens pump out the signal all around the world to keep the masses asleep. The room is green. He then leads them to a blue room with all blue walls there are two armed guards stationed inside.

Metaphysical Blueprint

The color green represents the heart or the heart chakra. Hollywood calls the place where studio guests wait before they go on the air, the green room. Hollywood needs to capture the people's heart in order to control and manipulate their behavior. The color green in this scene represents that concept.

The color blue represents communication. In this scene, the color blue represents the hidden signal the ruling elite uses to brainwash the masses without them knowing it. Blue represents the lower level vibration or frequency that keeps the people asleep.

Commentary:

Gilbert tells Nada and Frank while he is being held at gunpoint, "There aint no countries anymore. Aint no good guys. They're runnin the whole show. They own everything! The whole god dam planet! They can do whatever they want!"

Metaphysical Blueprint

These secret societies have tricked the people into thinking that they have a choice or say so in their life. The ruling class crosses all boundaries throughout the world. The people believe there is diversity throughout the world but it is just an illusion. Coke or Pepsi, Republican or Democrat, Democracy or Communism, Paper or Plastic, McDonalds or Burger King, Pro life or Pro Choice? They are all the same. Nothing ever changes, just the illusion of progress or improvement.

473

Commentary:

The newscasters ask, "Is this the 2 minute break or the 30 second break? I think it's the 30 second break, but I didn't know they dropped the 12."

Metaphysical Blueprint

In numerology, these numbers add up to the number two. The number two represents division or separation. In this scene, it represents the separation of the alien's signal from its control of the masses. This is a clue that Frank and Nada will be successful in destroying the alien's signal.

Commentary:

As Nada and Frank begin to shoot their way to the roof, there is a red and white "No Smoking" sign seen in between them.

Metaphysical Blueprint

As we alluded to earlier, the colors red and white stand for the ancient, Afrikan god Heru. Heru is where we get the word "Hero" from. Frank and Nada are displaying courage, bravery and self-sacrifice. All these traits are characteristics of the Kemetic god, Heru.

Commentary:

Nada asks a woman at her desk how to get to the roof. She tells him, "Turn left at the end of the hall." She points in the direction he must take with her left hand.

Metaphysical Blueprint

The left hand represents the activation of the right hemisphere of the brain which contains a person's higher, spiritual consciousness. This is the level our hero's need to activate in order to achieve higher consciousness.

474

Commentary:

A person in charge of security says over his radio, "Security 9-5- Zero. Lock down the elevators. They're on the move."

Metaphysical Blueprint

In numerology, these numbers and letter add up to the number 40. The number forty represents the test or journey Frank and Nada have embarked on. If they pass the test, by shutting off the signal, they will achieve higher consciousness.

Commentary:

Another security officer says, "I hear them on the 19th floor above me." Another officer replies, "We gotcha. We're on the 21st. We will be there waitin for them."

Metaphysical Blueprint

In numerology, these numbers add up to the number 40. This scene reinforces my earlier concept stating that Nada and Frank are actively participating in their quest for higher consciousness. In order to achieve higher consciousness, everyone must pass the test. Also, in these statement we can assume that Frank and Nada are on the 20th floor. In numerology, this number represents the number two which stands for separation or division. Frank and Nada are breaking away from the system that means to enslave them.

DVD Chapter 17: You Can't Win (1:27:15)

Commentary:

Holly shoots Frank on the right side of his head.

Metaphysical Blueprint

The right side of Frank's head houses the right hemisphere of his brain. This right side represents Frank's higher self or spiritual consciousness. Holly kills him by shooting his right brain. This is a significant scene as to how the system of white supremacy keeps the Black population in a state of lower consciousness. The ruling elite work night and day to make sure the Black man never recognizes and embraces his higher consciousness. The Black man is the walking dead because the system has declared war on his quest to embrace his higher self.

Commentary:

The helicopter gives Nada a countdown of ten before they open fire. When the officer reaches the number six, Nada kills Holly and then destroys the signal.

Metaphysical Blueprint

In numerology, the number six represents man's lower self or the beast in man. Nada is displaying his animalistic consciousness by killing Holly at the count of six.